GETTING

ENTREPRENEURIAL!

CREATING AND GROWING YOUR OWN BUSINESS IN THE 21ST CENTURY

LARRY C. FARRELL

WILEY

John Wiley & Sons, Inc.

Published by John Wiley & Sons, Inc., Hoboken, New Jersey.
Published simultaneously in Canada.

For general information on our other products and services please contact our Customer
Care Department within the United States at (800) 762-2974, outside the United
States at (317) 572-3993 or fax (317) 572-4002.

Wiley also publishes its books in a variety of electronic formats. Some content that
appears in print may not be available in electronic books. For more information about
Wiley products, visit our web site at www.Wiley.com.

ISBN 0-471-44414-6

Printed in the United States of America.

10 9 8 7 6 5 4 3 2 1

CONTENTS

ACKNOWLEDGMENTS

Getting Entrepreneurial! is my third book over the past 10 years. One thing I have learned about writing books is that it can be a lonely job. At the same time, rather paradoxically, succeeding at this lonely endeavor requires a large network of active supporters and allies.

For me, the first level of support has always come from my family. My wife, Julie, gracefully endures long periods of virtually living alone. Our extended family, including two very young grandsons this time around, obligingly tiptoes around my writing office trying their best to not disturb the family author!

Another level of essential supporters and allies is made up of the great entrepreneurs I interviewed and researched for the book. Without their willingness to share their personal stories, for no personal gain I might add, I would not be able to write these books. In this regard, I must also thank several of my business affiliates around the world who helped arrange some of the amazing interviews in this book.

Next, of course, are the publishing pros who make it all possible. Once again I am indebted to my literary agent, Bob Diforio, who first inspired me to write and has been there for all three of my books. I must also thank Airié Stuart, my Executive Editor at John Wiley & Sons; Emily Conway, her Editorial Assistant; and the rest of the great team at Wiley who have worked with me over the past year to get this book ready to be published.

And finally, I want to acknowledge, in advance, all the readers of the book. They are all members of that elite crowd that I've labeled the entrepreneurial "dreamers, doers, and the dazzling few." This book has been written for them—the future entrepreneurs of the world—and I wish each and every one of them great success and prosperity as they pursue their dream of Getting Entrepreneurial!

PREFACE

Fending for Yourself in a Downsized and Uncertain World

Between the 9/11 terrorists who wiped out 250,000 jobs of innocent workers in a single morning, and the growing betrayal of employee trust by stock-option-rich executives at U.S. companies (think Enron et al.), God help the average worker in corporate America. This one-two punch has left managers, supervisors, and working class Americans in their most vulnerable economic state since the Great Depression.

It's enough to make a dyed-in-the-wool believer in free enterprise wish that government, or labor unions, or someone, would do more to protect loyal, hard-working employees of big business. But fortunately there is a much better way to secure your family's prosperity. It's the option of depending on yourself—by obtaining the best weapon you'll ever have to survive and prosper in a downsized and uncertain world. Of course, using that weapon requires having enough confidence and knowledge about entrepreneurship to make it a viable alternative. It's called *getting entrepreneurial* and this book will show you exactly how to do it.

Certainly, on the morning of September 11, 2001, the last thing on my mind was writing another book. My latest book, *The Entrepreneurial Age*, had been published just six months earlier. That book had taken the better part of a year to write and I was still working with our affiliates to incorporate the book's content into our worldwide training business. But, by the end of that horrific day, the world had indeed changed.

The more I read and thought about good people being economically squeezed between terrorists and tycoons, the more I wanted to find a good, simple way to provide them with some practical and timely help. I knew we had the knowledge to do it. After all, my firm has more experience researching and teaching entrepreneurship than any university or company in the world. And I believed we could give people enough confidence and skills, in a book with application exercises, to start them on their way. So I began to write, and asked Bob Diforio, my long term literary agent, if he would look for a really great publisher for the project. He enthusiastically agreed. Airié Stuart, Executive Editor at John Wiley & Sons also enthusiastically agreed. And *Getting Entrepreneurial!* is the result.

I truly hope the message and practical advice in the book will give you a giant boost in confidence and knowledge—so that you know when economic uncertainty strikes, you can absolutely, positively, depend on yourself! And if that possibility excites and inspires you enough to want to read on, you've already passed the first important lesson of getting entrepreneurial!

INTRODUCTION

As I said, everybody here has the ability to do absolutely anything I do and much beyond. Some of you will, and some of you won't. For the ones who won't, it will be because you get in your own way, not because the world doesn't allow you.
                            —Warren Buffett, Founder, Berkshire Hathaway

APPLICATION 1
You're an Entrepreneur! What Next?

We've posed this question to tens of thousands of managers around the world. It's the opening of every lecture and seminar we give from San Francisco to South Africa to Singapore. There are no right or wrong answers at this stage. The purpose for thinking through the question now is to get the entrepreneurial juices flowing in your veins. Over the 15 years of using this exercise, it has become clear that people absolutely love thinking about this question. They really get into it, and you can almost feel the entrepreneurial temperature rising in the room. There are some very interesting, even amazing, things to say about the answers we typically receive, whether they be from Brazilians, Germans, Chinese, or Americans. But we'll hold that for later, and hope that your entrepreneurial juices will indeed start flowing after pondering what you would actually do on your first day as an entrepreneur. Jot your ideas down on the following Application worksheet—and come back to them when you've finished the book. You may be surprised.

APPLICATION 1-A
You're an Entrepreneur! What Next?

Imagine you've just started your own business. It's the first day in your new role as an entrepreneur. You want to be successful and grow. You sure don't want to go bankrupt. You've mortgaged your family house to raise the money to get started. Everything you have is on the line, including the welfare of your children.

You have an idea of a product and market that excites you. You think it has potential. But with your limited financial resources, you have to get started fast. What will you concentrate on? How should you spend your time? What will your priorities be as an entrepreneur?

My Entrepreneurial Priorities

1.

2.

3.

4.

The New Entrepreneurs—They Are Us!

Look around you. Seventy out of the next one hundred people you see are thinking about becoming an entrepreneur. Fifteen of the hundred will actually give it a go in the next 12 months. At least five will be successful on their first try. All of them, the dreamers, the do'ers and the dazzling few, are part of the greatest explosion of entrepreneurship the world has ever seen. They all believe the best weapon for surviving the economic uncertainties of the 21st Century will be themselves—their labor, their knowledge, and their own entrepreneurial spirit. Of course, they're right. Entrepreneurship is the best model ever devised for creating prosperity. And of course you're right. Getting entrepreneurial is exactly what you need to do to secure your family's future.

In modern industrial history, there have actually been two earlier waves of important entrepreneurial activity. The first coincided with the rise of the industrial age in the 1860s to 1880s. It produced a few captains of industry and more than a few robber barons. The second, fueled by the promise of unlimited capital, occurred between 1910 and 1929, and was cut short by the Great Depression. In fact, these early eras produced relatively few entrepreneurs, compared to the size of the workforce. Even more striking, the entrepreneurial activity that did occur was severely limited in geographic scope. The United States and northwestern Europe accounted for an overwhelming share of the entrepreneurs.

While these two earlier entrepreneurial eras produced some famous companies, and an impressive array of new technologies and products, nothing in our history has prepared us for what is occurring today. The current entrepreneurial revolution is simply unprecedented in size and scope. With over 2.5 million start-ups a year (1.3 million in the United States alone), the numbers are staggering. Even more dramatic is the truly global reach of this revolution. India, Brazil, and China are as chock full of entrepreneurial fervor as the United States. Even Japan has joined the trend, proving once again there's nothing like a good recession with a lot of American-style downsizing to get the entrepreneurial juices flowing. And money is no problem for the rising entrepreneur class. With $25 billion available from 300 venture capital firms and 250,000 private investors (as in Silicon Valley angels), and government Enterprise Funds springing up in every country, there's more start-up capital around than entrepreneurs of the past could have imagined in their wildest dreams. The fact is, the average cost of a business start-up in America is only around $14,000, and the two biggest sources of entrepreneurial funding are available to anyone: personal savings and credit cards. And take my word for it— the list of great companies started for less than $10,000 is very, very long.

All this leads to the most unique characteristic of our 21st Century entrepreneurial revolution: Ordinary people are the main players. This is not a revolution being played out by or for the rich and powerful. It is a new page in economic history that welcomes the participation of all, from welfare-to-work graduates starting daycare centers, to university scientists founding biotech firms, to anyone reading this book who will take the time and trouble to create a product or service that someone, somewhere, will need and pay for.

Of course, the questions we asked back in Application 1 may still be on your mind: What exactly would I do? If I quit my job, or God forbid get fired, or just want to do something when I retire, what would it be? And how would I go about it? What should I really concentrate on, day in and day out, to ensure success? Well, we've got the answers for you in this book—the proven lessons from the masters of entrepreneurial enterprise. Learning these lessons may not turn you into the next Warren Buffett, but they are the guaranteed first steps toward making sure you don't "get in your own way."

Great Myths and Simple Truths

When I started Microsoft, I was so excited that I didn't think of it as being all that risky. . . . The thing that was scary to me was when I started hiring my friends, and they expected to be paid.
                                        —Bill Gates, Co-Founder, Microsoft

In spite of the occasional, high profile odd-ball—Ross Perot comes to mind—the fact is entrepreneurs are not much different from you and me. The really good news is that no one, no matter their station in life, is disqualified from playing this game. Evidence the fact that a whopping 15 percent of Americans now work at least part-time from home in a self-employed capacity. The reality is millions of new businesses each year are fueling economies all around the world. The people behind these start-ups come from every walk of life. All the statistics show they're a pretty average lot. Most never planned to be an entrepreneur. It happens because of circumstance. It's usually a circumstance of crisis, like being dirt poor, or full of frustration, or getting fired—the number one reason that people go into business for themselves. Yes, these are ordinary people who simply find themselves in extraordinary situations.

This is important to keep in mind while both business and popular media bombard us with entrepreneurial myths. It's absolutely essential to keep in mind if you're thinking about becoming an entrepreneur yourself. Here are some of the more damaging myths about those people who create and build businesses.

Myth Number 1

Entrepreneurs are born, not made. It's in their genes. This is the most common myth of entrepreneurship.

The Truth.   If you really believe it's genetic, you never visited Communist East Germany. Listen to Claus Schröder, the founder of a container shipping business in Hamburg, describe what 45 years of goose-stepping communism gets you. Claus says Germany's big gift from the end of the cold war was getting 25 million East Germans who wouldn't know a hard day's work if it were injected into their socialist veins. His parents were originally from the east and in the early 1990s he eagerly expanded his business to the former communist region. Motivated by both family sentiment and business possibilities, his decision turned into a nightmare. "It's just unbelievable. I can't believe they're Germans. They have no concept of work. If the container ship isn't sitting at the dock when they arrive in the morning, they just go home for the day. The ship docks 30 minutes later for unloading and there it sits until tomorrow. Nobody thinks, nobody acts, nobody cares. I'm afraid the whole generation is lost. Maybe their children and grandchildren will be different!" Entrepreneurs are born, not made? Baloney! In western Germany, you had hard working, self-motivated people who transformed their land from total ruin to the world's third richest economy. In eastern Germany, you had lazy, uninspired louts, looking for a government handout—and they all came from the same grandparents! The difference has nothing to do with genes. It has everything to do with their political, social, and economic environment. It really all boils down to one word we'll talk a lot about in this book—*consequences*.

Myth Number 2

They all invented something in a garage when they were 15, wear strange clothes to work, and speak in techno-babble. We may have the same grandparents, but they are kind of weird and just different from you and me. I call this the nerd theory of entrepreneurship.

The Truth.   The mundane facts are, the average entrepreneur is 35 to 45 years old, has 10 years plus experience in a large company, has an average education and IQ, and contrary to popular myth, has a surprisingly normal psychological profile. They dress, talk, and look a lot like you and me—a fairly average bunch.

Myth Number 3

The overriding goal is to be a millionaire. They do it for the money pure and simple.

The Truth.   Every shred of research denies this myth. Relatively few entrepreneurs, in fact, ever earn the kind of bucks paid to CEOs these days. The entrepreneur's real obsession is to pursue his own, personal sense of mission. Money is the necessary fuel to do this. Venture capitalists, shrewd evaluators of the entrepreneurial quotient in people, can spot the get-rich-quick types in a minute and avoid them like the plague.

Myth Number 4

Entrepreneurs are unscrupulous characters, ready to take legal shortcuts, and are generally on the prowl for suckers to con. Reading between the lines, this myth really says that big, well-known corporations and their executives are more trustworthy than entrepreneurs.

The Truth.   This nasty myth gets harder to believe every time another white-collared corporate executive marches off to jail. And compared to some well known CEOs, raking in their $10 million a year salary even as their employees and shareholders are bleeding, entrepreneurs don't seem so greedy after all. Starting with Michael Ovitz's $92 million paycheck for 14 months as President of Disney, Dennis Kozlowski's million dollar birthday party in Monaco for his wife all paid for by Tyco International, and the billion dollar financial games played by Messers Lay, Skilling, and Fastow at Enron, the Hondas, Bransons, and Waltons of the world look more and more like saintly protectors of old-fashioned virtue. The unhappy fact is that low ethics and illegal tactics seem pretty well distributed throughout the population.

Myth Number 5

They're high risk takers. Real dart throwers.

The Truth.   The preface to this book says, "Entrepreneurship is the best weapon you'll ever have to survive and prosper in a downsized and uncertain world." That sentiment comes on good authority. Every entrepreneur I've ever met believes the greatest risk today is to leave your future in the hands of a series of corporate bosses, all of whom have their own agendas to push. Betting on the corporate lottery for the next 30 years is a risk entrepreneurs aren't willing to take. So the risk of leaving a corporate job and starting out on your own has become, as they say, rather relative. And once they get started, a lot of entrepreneurs turn downright conservative. They're still innovators but that doesn't make them fools. Remember, it's their money they're risking. The reality is big company executives regularly take greater risks with shareholders' money than entrepreneurs are willing to take with their own.

Myth Number 6

Getting an MBA is the way to go. Business schools will teach you how to be an entrepreneur.

The Truth.   Save your $50,000 and go learn something useful that can help you create a product the world needs—just as 99.9 percent of the world's entrepreneurs have done. This myth is just the latest big lie propogated by the business education establishment to prop up enrollments. Back in the 1980s, the MBA factories saw that button-down IBM style management was out and entrepreneurial chaos á la Apple Computer was in. So they stuck in a course on entrepreneurship between financial management and long range planning, and called themselves the new breeding ground for the next Steve Jobs. Of course they forgot how Steve Jobs himself complained about the MBA style managers he hired at Apple, "They knew how to *manage* but they couldn't *do* anything." The moral? Until you learn how to *do* something, don't even think about becoming an entrepreneur.

The Magic of Entrepreneurship
Versus the Science of Management

When we started hiring professional managers at Apple, I learned something very interesting. The managers knew how to manage but they couldn't "do" anything!
                    —Steve Jobs, Founder, Apple Computer,
                        NeXT, Pixar

The most fundamental thing we've learned in 18 years of researching and teaching entrepreneurship is that growing a business and managing a business are separate universes. Entrepreneurs are great at growing businesses. Managers are great at managing businesses. Managing is actually the easy part. Creating and growing a business demands that you do more than manage. In Steve Jobs' words, you have to be able to actually *do* something.

I promise you, reading up on the latest management theories, learning how to write a perfect business plan, or spending $50,000 to get a Harvard MBA won't get you through the first 15 minutes in your new venture. To create and grow any business, you've got to have high purpose, absolute focus on customer and product, lots of action, and a ton of self-inspiration. These are the things you're going to learn about in this book. We call it *getting entrepreneurial.*

The Life Cycle of All Companies

Bigger is better turned out to be another 20th Century myth, and Larry Farrell has just explained why.
                                    —Peter Drucker

A couple of years ago I was addressing a *BusinessWeek* CEO conference. I delivered my standard pitch that big business management theory was mostly nonsense and would never be a match for old-fashioned entrepreneurship—with Peter Drucker, the "father of modern management," sitting in the first row staring at me. It was a bit intimidating to say the least. Drucker was to follow me to the podium and he was not known for his subtlety. So I was preparing myself for public humiliation and probably early retirement as a *BusinessWeek* speaker after he got through with me. However, to my everlasting gratitude, Dr. Drucker's opening comment was: "Bigger is better turned out to be another 20th Century myth, and Larry Farrell has just explained why." Many people at the conference, including the *BusinessWeek* brass, would later shake my hand, give that knowing nod, and congratulate me for getting it right according to the great Drucker.

He later explained to me in private that it had become increasingly clear to him that size and mass, at some critical point, begin to make companies less competitive, not more. He called them oversized and overmanaged. He noted that in almost all industries, the best company, certainly the most profitable one, is rarely the biggest. He even confided that he no longer accepted consulting requests from giant companies, "You can give them the best advice in the world, and they just can't implement it. It's so frustrating, I've stopped trying to tell them anything."

When Drucker made his much appreciated and affirming comment that bigger is not better, he was specifically referring to my description of the underpinnings of my own research. That is, of course, that all companies, like people, and countries, and everything else on the planet, exist in a life cycle. And over time, as companies grow from small to big, they will pass through the different phases of that life cycle (shown in the diagram).

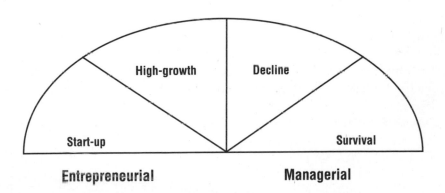

The Life Cycle of All Organizations

High-growth   Decline

Start-up   Survival

Entrepreneurial   **Managerial**

It's important for you, as an up and coming entrepreneur, to be aware of the life cycle. It's very predictable, but there are ways to perpetuate the high-growth phase and avoid the dreaded downside of the cycle. Your movement through the cycle can be very fast, and it can obviously be a huge advantage to know what's coming.

It's a pretty simple concept actually. Creation is followed by growth. Growth peaks and decline sets in, leading ultimately to death. And, of course, there's always the possibility of *untimely death* along the way. The best confirmation of the life cycle is the startling statistic that of the hundred biggest American companies in the year 1900, only 16 are still in business. I'll never forget the Japanese executive who exclaimed, after seeing that particular slide in a speech I gave in Tokyo, "Now I see the problem with lifetime employment. People live longer than their companies."

Here's how it works. All companies begin with an abundance of the entrepreneurial spirit, inspiring workers as well as owners. Basic entrepreneurial practices fuel the start-up and drive the company well into a phase of high growth. During the start-up and high growth eras, everyone is fixated on a few fundamental notions such as getting customers because it's the only way to get paid.

The resultant high growth gets you size. And the passage of time gets you new leaders. The new leaders are almost always professional managers. These subtle shifts in size and leadership produce a new set of objectives. Presto! Planning, streamlining, and controlling the enterprise become the new order. Managing this and that become more important than making this and selling that. The highest paid jobs become managing other managers. Meetings, reports, and bureaucracy erupt on every front. And slowly but surely, lost in the shuffle are the simple, basic entrepreneurial thrusts that got you going in the first place. If you can't turn the company around at this critical juncture, and get it back into high growth, you're headed for survival and death, just like the 84 percent of big American companies last century.

The dominant style of companies on the right-hand side of the cycle—the larger and more mature organizations—is *managerial*. The key management practices are well known: planning, organizing, controlling, and so on. These companies are typically past their prime and on the downside of the cycle. Even so, it is the study of these companies, by the business schools and management consultants that serve them, that has produced most of the management theories and fads over the past 50 years. Consequently, there are thousands of books, videos, courses, and seminars on how to manage.

Conversely, the growth phases on the left-hand side of the cycle are highly entrepreneurial. The important question for all would-be entrepreneurs is, What are the key practices on the entrepreneurial, high-growth side of the cycle? Interestingly, the actual business practices of entrepreneurs during the start-up and high-growth phases of the life cycle have been of little interest to the Harvards and McKinseys of the world. And this is precisely where this book parts company with all the blue-chip management experts. It seems pretty obvious and simple that it's a lot more valuable for aspiring entrepreneurs to learn how to create and maintain a high-growth enterprise than it is to learn how to manage a declining bureaucracy. But simple lessons are often hard to learn. With 20/20 hindsight, we can see that common sense says, if we really want to get at the basics of high-growth enterprise, we should search out the masters who have actually done this. So the lessons of entrepreneurial enterprise don't come from the world's best-managed bureaucracies. And they certainly don't come from business schools and consultants. They have to come from world-class entrepreneurs: Asian giants like Matsushita, Honda and Morita, great European founders such as Lever, Daimler, and Branson, and legendary American enterprisers such as Watson, Disney, Walton, and Jobs. The lessons also come from a million, not-so-famous entrepreneurs. The silent majority who account for 95 percent of the growth in every economy. Regardless of culture or public profile, entrepreneurs are ordinary people who do extraordinary things. They are people who create opportunity and wealth out of thin air. Their mission in life is not to manage, or consult, or teach at a business school. Their mission is to make things and sell them. They create jobs. They build businesses. It's *their* business practices that are the true engines of prosperity. When you think about it, why would you look anywhere else?

Fortunately, you're looking in the right place, right now, to learn those entrepreneurial practices. They are what this book is all about. As a sneak preview and to set the stage, here are the bare-bones descriptions of the fundamental practices of the world's great entrepreneurs.

The Four Practices of the World's Great Entrepreneurs

Lessons from the Masters

> *The conduct of successful business merely consists in doing things in a very simple way, doing them regularly and never neglecting to do them.*
> —William Hesketh Lever, Founder,
> Lever Brothers (Unilever)

What are those *things* we must do simply, regularly, and never forget to do? You won't find them on the managerial side of the cycle. They're not the things that business schools teach or management consultants preach. If you want to find the bedrock fundamentals of enterprise, those simple things practiced obsessively, you've got to look at the entrepreneurial phase of business. Here you will find the lessons of the world's greatest entrepreneurs, from past masters such as Lever, Matsushita, and Disney, to more recent icons like Morita, Jobs, and Perot.

Sense of Mission

> *Our duty as industrialists is to produce goods for the public, and to enrich and make happier all those who use them. A decrease in profit or a loss of revenue is proof that we have not fulfilled our obligations to society.*
> —Konosuke Matsushita, Founder,
> Matsushita Electric

High-minded? You bet. The fact is entrepreneurs believe they are doing something important in the world. They believe they're creating value for customers, employees and, of course, themselves. We call it having a *sense of mission* about their work. Such high purpose however, gets quickly translated into two very practical questions: *What* is our strategy and *How* will we achieve it? The *what* essentially refers to what products for what customers. And the *how* refers to those few operational factors you focus on and become great at. We call them your values. When your values directly support your product/market strategy, hang on! It's the most powerful way ever invented to energize a group of individuals to achieve a common purpose. That's why having a powerful sense of mission is the first entrepreneurial practice.

Customer/Product Vision

> *The computer is the most remarkable tool we've ever built . . . but the most important thing is to get them in the hands of as many people as possible.*
> —Steve Jobs, Founder, Apple Computer, NeXT, Pixar

Steve Jobs wasn't talking about how to manage, or the latest accounting technique, or even how to grow Apple Computer. He was, and still is, obsessed with the two most fundamental ideas in enterprise—customer and product. He said the only thing more important than making computers was having satisfied customers actually use them. The critically important lesson of Jobs and other great entrepreneurs is that, at heart, they are craftsmen. They have a single, integrated vision of customers and products. They don't functionalize them. They are expert at both and they are absolutely passionate about both. The trick for you, then, is to become passionately expert on your own products and customers. After all, they are the two most important words in business.

High-Speed Innovation

> *Anybody can be innovative if his life depends on it.*
> —Akio Morita, Founder, Sony

High-speed innovation is the entrepreneur's secret weapon—and the really great thing about it is, it's virtually free. In today's world, you cannot find a better and cheaper way to give your start-up an enormous competitve advantage. So what exactly is it and where does it come from? There are two golden rules for high-speed innovation: First, you and your people must see innovation as an absolute necessity in the business, and second, there must be a high sense of urgency to take action and implement new ideas. We call it *the necessity to invent* and *the freedom to act*. Encouraging creativity, speeding up action, and keeping all forms of bureaucracy at bay will give you the kind of fast moving, innovative company you'll need to beat the competition.

Self-Inspired Behavior

I'm looking for people who love to win. If I run out of those, I want people who hate to lose.

—Ross Perot, Founder, EDS,
Perot Systems

Self-inspired behavior is the sharpest difference between entrepreneurs and bureaucrats. Great entrepreneurial leaders, like Lever, Honda, Gates, and Perot, display two key behaviors at work. First, they love what they do—they're highly committed to their work. And second, they always try to get better at what they do—their performance is high. These two ideas, high commitment and high performance, are the backbone of an entrepreneurial approach to work. But why are entrepreneurs so self-inspired? Very simple. They face the consequences, positive or negative, of their performance every day. Those consequences come directly from their customers and they are timely, accurate, and extremely powerful. This never happens in a bureaucracy. To start your own business, *you* have to be self-inspired. Then, to grow your enterprise, you have to learn to inspire others. This is why mastering the final entrepreneurial practice, *self-inspired behavior*, is the underpinning of all entrepreneurial success.

Summary of the Entrepreneurial Basics

The inclination of my life has been to do things and make things which will give pleasure to people in new and amazing ways. By doing that I please and satisfy myself.

—Walt Disney, Founder,
The Walt Disney Company

Walt Disney said it best. When asked to summarize his life's work he described the four fundamental practices of entrepreneurs perfectly: "Inclination" as mission, "making things, and giving pleasure to people" is all about customer/product vision, "new and exciting ways" is a perfect description of innovation, and finally, "by doing that I please myself" says I am self-inspired by my work. These are the simple things you need to do regularly, and never neglect to do. If you're serious about getting entrepreneurial, it's time to learn these very old lessons, very fast. It's time to forget all the corporate nonsense and management gobbledygook—and start getting entrepreneurial with the simple basics of enterprise.

Start-Up: *The* Moment of Truth

This leads us back to the big question posed earlier in Application 1. What do you actually do when you start your own business? What will your priorities be on your first day as an entrepreneur? Here's a glimpse into how it usually works.

About 15 minutes into the first morning of your new little business, it hits you like a ton of bricks. Who's going to pay your salary for the week? You certainly don't have a payroll department to cut a check. In fact, you don't even have the cash to cover a check. The sweat begins to break out on your forehead. Then, the moment of truth flashes before you: The only way you're going to get paid this week, and every week for the rest of your life, is to make something or do something that someone in the world will pay you cold, hard cash for. You need a product and a customer this week or your kids won't eat. Welcome to the world of true believers who know exactly why a clear *customer/product vision* is the most fundamental of all entrepreneurial practices.

Next, as you contemplate creating the product and finding a customer, two more insights hit home. First, you realize you have to do this very fast. So you start working at high speed—not because it's your natural bent, but because you have to get this done before you run out of cash. The second insight is, the very best chance you will have of getting someone to buy your product is to make sure they see that it's different and better than other products they could buy. So you know you'll have to be a bit creative and innovative to come up with something that is better, or cheaper, or faster, or easier to use, or something to give you the competitve edge. You've now learned, early in the game, why high-speed innovation is so important to entrepreneurs.

Jump forward a few weeks or even months. You've been able to create and produce a product or a service. And you've also been able to find, sell, and service a few customers. Now your thoughts turn to growing a bit. It's clear that you alone can handle the current product and customer load, but you can't do much more. There just aren't enough hours in the week. You're going to have to take on a partner or an employee to help you grow. So you search around for relatives, friends, or former colleagues who are willing to take a chance and sign on with your fledgling business. After you hire one of them, get him trained, pay him a couple of times, a brand new thought begins to sink in. If this first employee brings in a few additional customers over the next six months, the company will grow and everyone will be happy. If, on the other hand, this first employee doesn't bring in any customers for six months, you're probably facing bankruptcy. Half your workforce isn't *doing* anything. You see this as a matter of survival. But your employee sees it as a point to cover in his first year performance review. Eureka! You've just tripped over the single greatest difference between entrepreneurial and standard employee behavior: Facing the real-life consequences, positive or negative, of your performance. It's what fuels the next fundamental practice of entrepreneurship, which we call *self-inspired behavior*.

Somehow you survive all these challenges and complete your first year as an entrepreneur with a nice little business and a bright future. You've become rightfully proud of what you, and your small team, have accomplished. You think that what you're doing is important and it has the potential to create a lot of value. You even allow yourself to think you may be creating a bit of a legacy for future generations—or at least leaving a few footprints in the sand. You are now deep into that overarching entrepreneurial practice we've labelled *sense of mission*. An entrepreneurial sense of mission usually doesn't form until you begin to believe you're going to survive the start-up phase. You'll know you're getting it when, for the first time, you take a few quiet moments to contemplate what marvelous and profound things the company could achieve over the next several years. In other words, when you actually begin to sense the future mission of your creation.

So yes, despite all the myths, the truth is the new entrepreneurs *are* us: our co-workers, our friends, and even our families. And the things they, and you, will have to do as new entrepreneurs are not so strange or complicated after all. In fact, creating and building a company is sounding more and more like—well—a lot of common sense.

The rest of the book takes an in-depth look at that common sense, distilled into the four fundamental practices of successful entrepreneurs. And be sure to do the Application exercises in each chapter. By the time you finish reading *Getting Entrepreneurial!*, you will have your own personal plan for actually getting entrepreneurial! The rest will be up to you and your own common sense.

CHAPTER

1

Sense of Mission

Leaving Footprints in the Sand

Tremendously important to me was the feeling that we were doing something that had a significance far beyond building a company or what the financial rewards could be. I was convinced we were doing something that had tremendous importance in the world.
—Benjamin B. Tregoe, Ph.D.,
Co-Founder, Kepner-Tregoe

Have you ever noticed how much entrepreneurs love to talk about their company or their product? My experience has been (and I should know after interviewing hundreds of them) if you ask an entrepreneur "how are you?" you get several hours of what a great product they invented or company they started. In fact, it's gotten so bad that when I'm on a long flight and I think the person sitting next to me may be an entrepreneur, I put on the headset and try to avoid all conversation. A couple of years ago I took a flight from San Francisco to Singapore. It takes about 20 hours, so you have to be careful who you sit next to. On this particular flight, my seatmate was a friendly looking fellow from Seattle. I know Seattle is full of entrepreneurs, but this guy looked more like an athlete than a business type, so I took a chance and asked those fatal words: "How are you?" What a mistake! Sure enough, he was an entrepreneur—and I got 20 hours of how his fantastic product was going to change the world. And what was this earth-shattering product? Well, hang on to your seat. He and his little company had come up with a machine that made perfect sand for golf courses. And since Asians love golf, he was sure they would fall all over themselves to get their hands on his wonderful machine—thus his travels across the Pacific. Of course I don't play golf or even watch it on TV, but I heard more about sand and sandtraps than I thought anyone could possibly know. Boring? You bet! But the point is, the young entrepreneur from Seattle really believed he had created something of importance and value for the world. Value for his customers, for his employees back in Seattle, and undoubtedly for himself.

This is the built-in advantage of all entrepreneurs: They really believe they're doing something important, creating a lot of value, and in some small way at least, leaving a footprint in the sand. They're on a mission—and that sense of mission gives them incredible energy, desire, and pride. When is the last time you met government or corporate bureaucrats with a true sense of mission about their work? Or one who talked your ear off for hours on what a fabulously important thing he was doing for the world? Not lately? That's the point. We call it having a sense of mission and it's the first, fundamental practice of entrepreneurship.

The *What* and the *How* of the Mission

If you ask an entrepreneur "what's your sense of mission?" they may look at you like you're crazy—or at least suspect you're a management consultant. Entrepreneurs aren't typically up on such fancy sounding phrases. But what they are up on, and can articulate with unbelievable clarity, is what they're doing and how they go about doing it. When you think about it, to succeed at any mission, whether it be a business mission, a military mission, a political mission, or whatever, you absolutely have to be clear about these two things: *what* the mission is, and *how* you're going to accomplish it. We've labeled these two critical aspects of sense of mission: the strategy (the what) of the business, and the culture (the how) of the business. If the words *strategy* and *culture* sound a bit grandiose to describe your first time entrepreneurial start-up, just call them your business plan and your business values. Whatever we call them, being very good at both—setting a smart strategy and creating a strong, supportive culture—is a characteristic all great entrepreneurs share. It is also absolutely necessary to the creation of a successful, high-growth enterprise.

One of the most articulate entrepreneurs that I've ever come across on this point is a man named Ben Tregoe* in Princeton, New Jersey. Tregoe, a Harvard Ph.D., left the Rand Corporation (the famous think tank) and founded a company to do one thing: to teach business people around the world how to improve their analytical decision-making skills. In 1958 that was a radical idea. Nobody even thought about how to do that. Forty years later, the firm he co-founded, Kepner-Tregoe, Inc., has taught some 5 million people around the world, in over 20 languages, exactly how to do that. Ben Tregoe is truly a man with a mission.

Just listen to him. You can feel it in his words: "We had this strong sense that we were on to something here that was terribly important. Something that could help improve the quality of the world. We had this feeling, and it sounds very presumptuous to say, but we felt that we could really improve the rationality of the world and it was terribly important to get this out to companies everywhere. We believed we could help improve the communication between organizations and between people. This sense of purpose, this sense of mission, is tremendously important. I mean, I know if we had started the business and just said, 'it looks like we can make some money doing this so let's try it and so on,' we never could have gotten this thing up and running. It was too damn difficult."

Tregoe's sense of mission, however, isn't based on hyperbole or theoretical pie-in-the-sky: "When you talk about the strategy of a company, when you talk about the direction that any company is going, it all boils down to your values, your beliefs, and your basic purpose, and then to a real understanding of the product and market. I mean all this stuff about strategy and so on, if it doesn't get down to product/market and your product/market priorities, you really don't have anything. The way you describe any organization, a company or a non-profit, is basically what products and services does it offer and to whom does it offer them."

Tregoe also knows what it takes to stay true to your sense of mission

---

*Our description of the entrepreneurial approach to strategy is influenced by and in part modified from the original work of my friend and former boss, Dr. Benjamin B. Tregoe. We have applied his description of strategy to the entrepreneurial approach for one reason only—it so clearly illustrates why entrepreneurs do what they do.

over time: "A statement of purpose, the beliefs or values of a company, the product/market statement or strategy statement of a company is essential. But it's only useful if it's guiding what the organization does. If it's guiding the decision making on a day-to-day basis. And the only way it's going to guide the behavior of a company on a day-to-day basis, is if it's filed up here in the heads of the people in the business. And that means it's got to be pretty specific and pretty simple."

The bottom line is, entrepreneurs are highly focused on both what they are doing (the strategy or plan) and how they go about doing it (the culture or values). Whether you're General Motors or a one person start-up, the challenge is to be great at both. It's not good enough to have a smart business plan, but a weak, disconnected set of operating values. Conversely, strong values will never overcome a stupid plan. And, of course, you won't be around long if you know neither what to do nor how to do it.

Sense of Mission

	−	+
+	stupid plan strong values	smart plan strong values	**+**
−	stupid plan weak values	smart plan weak values	**−**
	−	+

How (business values)

What (business plans)

New entrepreneurs quickly learn that while both the *what* and the *how* are essential, the plan of the business comes first. You have to know what you're doing before you can determine how to do it. This relationship between your company plan and your company values is often lost as the organization grows big and all manner of management practices are adopted. The reality is, until you set the *what* of the business—what markets, what products, and so on, you have no idea what kind of operating values and priorities you need. Indeed the only purpose of developing a set of company values is to get absolutely focused and operationally superb on those few things that will ensure that you achieve your business plan. And the operating factors that are essential for company A, may not be important at all for company B. For example, if you're starting a commuter airline, safety had better be at the top of your values list. There's no faster way to bankrupt an airline than having a few headline grabbing crashes. On the other hand, if your entrepreneurial start-up is in the software business, where product life cycles are less than six months, product innovation and speed are the values you will probably need to focus on.

One of the great mistakes young companies make is to read about and then try to copy the culture and values of some big company they admire. The values of Daimler-Benz or Sony or Wal-Mart may have worked wonders for them, but that doesn't mean the same values will make your company plans come true. To keep on track with this fundamentally important point, simply go back to the basic purpose and relationship of the *what* and *how*: First determine what you are going to do—and then get very good at those few things that are crucial to doing it.

What—The Entrepreneur as Strategist

> *Our duty as industrialists is to produce goods for the public, and to enrich and make happier all those who use them.*
> —Konosuke Matsushita, Founder,
> Matsushita Electric

Old fashioned strategy takes old fashioned focus. Focus on the *what* of the enterprise. And to entrepreneurs, that can only mean: What customers and what products will they pursue? These are the two questions they have to get right. After all, customers and products are not functions of the business, they *are* the business. Being wrong on either of these questions is certain bankruptcy. Business strategy is all about being right on products and markets. Strategic thinking, however it is done, takes on specific meaning and awesome importance. Being close to customers and products is not an occasional activity designed to wave the flag or impress workers. Rather, it's the most valuable weapon the strategist has in making the most critical decisions in business. This is the lesson of the great Japanese entrepreneur, Konosuke Matsushita.

Matsushita was a young salesman in Osaka. In 1918, he invested his life savings of 100 yen (about $50) in imported electric sockets from Great Britain. He was excited and very focused on getting the first batch sold and ordering more. He was certain this type of product would sell very well in the new, miracle age of electricity. He was wrong. None of the shops he called on were interested in stocking his electric socket. In fact, things got so bad he went bankrupt. So the great Matsushita's first entrepreneurial venture was a bust. And in Japan, at that time, failing in business was about as shameful an act one could commit. Then he did something that few salesmen ever do—and changed his life forever.

He went back to all the shopkeepers who wouldn't buy his product, and for the first time, asked them, "Is there anything I could do to change this socket so that you would want to buy a few for your shop?" Many of the shopkeepers gave him suggestions like make it bigger, make it smaller, change the color, do this, or do that. He took all of their suggestions and began tinkering with his sockets at home. He even fashioned a few prototypes of his own from scratch. He went back to the market with the customized versions and tried again. And again. And again. He was repeating his routine of asking the potential customers how he could change the product so they would buy it. It was this process of back and forth customer–product strategizing that produced Konosuke Matsushita's marvelous invention: the world's first electric double-socket. With it he began winning customers and the fledgling Matsushita Electric played a small, but critical, role in expanding the electrical appliance industry in Japan. Now, a single, electric line to a house could run two appliances—an electric fan and a radio, or a cooker, and so on. This persistence gave birth to the world's largest producer of electric and electronic products. It also was a lesson in corporate strategy that the founder of Matsushita Electric never forgot.

By his own later account, Matsushita was unsuccessful at first because he was thinking too much about selling and not enough about what customers really wanted. So what was his successful strategic process? Simply this: Ask the customers what they want, and then do that rare and unexpected thing, give it to them! When you're looking for simple, practical steps to follow, the no-frills customer–product strategy of Matsushita would be hard to beat.

In 1932, some 14 years after start-up, Konosuke Matsushita again did something that most salesmen (and great entrepreneurs) never do. He started thinking about and putting on paper the principles of enterprise as he had lived them. It took him five years to get it down in writing. The result was a very thin, 23 page booklet titled, *Matsushita Management Philosophy*. This booklet contains as much wisdom about enterprise as some entire business school libraries. It provides a philosophical and strategic framework for any company which, not surprisingly, all boils down to making products that markets actually need. The booklet should be required reading for every MBA program in the world.

For 85 years, the *what* of the business at Matsushita has been driven by knowing very specifically, *what customers* want *what products*. Doing this better and more consistently than their competitiors has always been the ultimate competitive advantage of Matsushita Electric, and its famous brands like Panasonic and National. In so doing, Konosuke Matsushita raised customer–product strategy from black magic to near certainty, and it all comes from those unsold electric sockets back in 1918. If you want to instill that same competitive advantage in your start-up business, read on.

Creating Entrepreneurial Business Plans

There is no more overhyped and overused activity of business than strategy and planning. For some never explained reason, this rather passive aspect of enterprise has generated more books, techniques, diagrams, and consultant engagements than anything else. And almost without exception, would-be entrepreneurs at business schools are advised that the most important step in starting up a company is to write a great business plan. Three hundred pages with lots of charts and financial projections are strongly recommended. Of course, no one bothers to remind the eager-beaver MBA students or, for that matter, the millions of cubicle-bound bureaucrats dreaming about striking out on their own, that no great enterpriser from William Lever to Bill Gates ever started a business this way.

Fortunately, there is a simpler way to do a business plan. It's the old-fashioned, entrepreneurial way. First, ask yourself, what do you really like to do, and what are you really good at doing? Make as complete an inventory as possible. Then examine what needs are going unmet or are being poorly met in markets you are familiar with, for which you could possibly produce a superior product or service. And finally, for each possible product/market idea you've come up with, rate your likely competitive position against the very best providers you know of for that particular product or service. Within these questions you will find the product/market business(es) that carry the highest chance of success for you as an entrepreneur.

Does this sound too simple? Would you feel better with something more sophisticated? Do you want to conduct a full market study, bring in focus groups, and produce reams of financial projections? Of course you can do all that and more, if you've got all the time in the world and a bucket full of money. Just put this book down and get ready to spend the next year of your life doing research and writing a business plan. But remember—that's not the way great entrepreneurs have ever done it since the beginning of time. If you want to try their way first, read on.

The following are the questions you need to ask. Your initial answers may not guarantee your entrepreneurial success. But you can be sure that you have asked yourself the right questions. The rock-bottom questions that every entrepreneur in the world must ultimately answer are:

✔ **What Do I Have a Passion For?**   What do I really like to do?

✔ **What Product or Services Could I Provide?**   What am I really good at doing?

✔ **What Customers/Markets Might I Pursue?**   What is the market need for products or services based on the things I like to do or am good at doing? What unmet needs do I see in the market that require products or services I might like to do or might be good at doing?

✔ **What Competitive Position Would I Have?**   For each possibility, what would my competitive position be, compared to the best providers of similar products and services to the market?

✔ **What Capabilities and Cash Must I Have?**   Can I really make the product or service? Can I really sell it? Can I service it? And can I pay for it?

These are tough questions intended to keep your feet on the ground. That's right, the questions are all about products and markets. There may be other things to examine, but I will guarantee you this: These questions have to be answered. Disregard them at your peril. If you can't answer them, do yourself—and your family—a huge favor and don't quit your day job just yet!

As Ben Tregoe says: "If it (the plan) doesn't get down to product/market and your product/market priorities, you really don't have anything." To the entrepreneur, the *what* of the enterprise always revolves around what customers and what products will be pursued. Strategy and planning have to be all about picking the right products and markets. The more you get into it, the more an entrepreneurial plan looks like a blueprint for survival. It sure doesn't look like strategic planning à la The Harvard Business School. The entrepreneurial approach may not be so elegant or sophisticated, but it has one redeeming quality—it works wonders for getting new businesses up and running.

So, how exactly do you do this? It's pretty simple really. Whether your planning process is formal or informal, covers 6 months or 10 years, and uses discounted cash flows or numbers on a napkin—you have to know what customers and what products to target. The first thing you need to know is, of course, how do you actually come up with market and product ideas? And, then, how do you choose among them? What criteria should guide your choices? Are there any rules to follow in picking customers/markets and products/services? You are now face-to-face with the number one question in enterprise. As Tregoe so simply put it: "What products and services will you offer and to whom will you offer them?" You can read a ton of research and hire a hundred consultants to help you figure this out, but at the end of the day, there are just five things you absolutely, positively, have to keep in mind.

✔ **It's a Matter of Survival.** The goal is survival, not an affirmative nod from a corporate planning committee. If you fail, you probably won't get to try it again next year. You'll be history!

✔ **Don't Make It a Big, Complicated Project.** Doing the plan is not the objective. Growing the business is. Planning is not a high-profile department on the organization chart, or a week in Bermuda with the consultants. So keep it simple, do it fast, and then get back to the real work.

✔ **Stay Focused on Customers.** Think of every market you know anything about, either as a customer or just as an observor. What needs do you see that are going unmet, or are not being met satisfactorily? Carefully thinking this through can be a rich source of business ideas for entrepreneurs. Once you're up and running, remember that your best business partners are your customers. They know more and cost less than market researchers and consultants. Design your strategy *with* them, not *at* them.

✔ **Stay Focused on Products.**   What do you like to do? What are you good at doing? Answering these two questions happens to be the most common way successful entrepreneurs identify the kind of businesses they start. So if you don't want to miss the greatest source of entrepreneurial ideas you'll ever have, stay focused on possible products and services. And, while it's true that entrepreneurs love their product, never forget that what keeps them in business is making sure their customers love their product.

✔ **Know the Criteria That Count.**   There are only two make-or-break criteria in choosing markets and products. They are *market need* and *competitive position*. Great entrepreneurs are obsessed with discovering the needs of the markets they enter—and identifying every possible way they can raise the competitive position of the products they offer. These are the two criteria that always count most!

Picking Market/Product Winners

In choosing the products and markets for your start-up venture, you have to know the answers to these simple questions: How good is my market? and How good is my product? The market you may pursue can range from great in every way to downright lousy. And the competitive position of your product can be anywhere from the best in the world to absolutely awful. To keep it simple, we'll just use *big* and *small* to rate market need, and *high* and *low* for competitive position.

The best story to illustrate the power of these two criteria actually occurred, believe it or not, on one of those dreaded, long flights sitting next to an entrepreneur. It was the Stockholm to New York run, and the Swedish scientist in the next seat was already giving me his life story: "So I now live in Florida . . . I used to be an R&D director for Squibb Pharmaceutical . . . I worked at their headquarters in Lawrenceville, New Jerscy. . . . After years of seeing Squibb reject so many good products because the market need was not big enough for them, I left to start my own small medical products business. . . ." Whoa! This was getting interesting. I turned ever so slightly toward him, airplane etiquette for "Okay, you've got my attention, so please make it good." He not only made it good, he provided a terrific entrepreneurial application of the market need/competitive position idea.

As he told it, everyone in the industry knows there are hundreds of small, unmet needs in the medical and pharmaceutical markets. Giant companies, like his former employer, can't afford to even think about them. A "tiny" $25 million market doesn't get a second look, according to my seatmate. His first product, diapers for elderly people, was a no-brainer. There was a small but real need in the market, and no one was producing diapers specially for aging adults. He leased time at one of the numerous medical research facilities available today, perfected his design, contracted for production and distribution, and had his first successful product. He agreed that it fits squarely in the upper left-hand corner of the Market Need/Competitive Position matrix: Small market need/High competitive position.

This led to a full discussion of his broad perspective on inventing products for different types of markets, first as a small cog in a giant wheel and now as the big wheel in his own business. As he described the rich array of market and product possibilities in the industry, he verbally categorized each one. So we can, courtesy of my Swedish seatmate, complete the explanation of the Market Need/Competitive Position matrix with examples from the world of medicine.

The "Leprosy Business"

For starters, as our Swedish entrepreneur explained, there are a lot of limited medical needs in the world for which there are no products, or only inferior products. Take leprosy for example. It's a horrible disease with a relatively small number of cases—and no cure. And why is there no cure? Because it's a small market, found mostly in poor countries, and the Mercks and Glaxos of the world aren't working on it. But suppose you and your team have a breakthrough and discover the cure. You would have a classic example of a small market need/high competitive position product. The "leprosy business" category is a common place for entrepreneurs. They can do extremely well in these niche type businesses. (There's probably a lesson here for consumers, too. If you're going to get a bad disease, hope and pray it's something popular—so maybe there'll be a cure.)

The "Headache Business"

How about the flip-side of the "leprosy business?" Think of the biggest display section of every drugstore in America. That's right, it's the painkiller section. It seems that all 280 million Americans are suffering from headaches, the flu, and allergies. There are dozens of brands and hundreds of variations. They all make the same claims and have similar sounding ingredients, allowing, of course, for the big medical innovation of non-aspirin aspirin. In fact, I recently noticed that the ingredients are exactly the same for two separate products from the same company. Check it out: Extra Strength Excedrin and Migraine Excedrin are identical, right down to the 65 milligrams of caffeine in each. Why all this marketing madness? Because the market is so damn big. We call it the "headache business" and it perfectly fits the big market need/low competitive position quadrant of the matrix. Entrepreneurs can prosper here also, if they're ready to compete on price at the low end of the market.

The "Polio Business"

The place no entrepreneur wants to be in is the small market need/low competitive position quadrant. There are plenty of recognizable medical needs here—mostly diseases that have been virtually wiped out years ago like polio and scarlet fever. These are markets that are dead or dying, and even if they weren't, the old product patents have expired and everyone could be in the market tomorrow with a me-too, low cost cure. The "polio business" arena is no place for fast-moving, entrepreneurial start-ups. There's little money to be made here by entrepreneurs, pure and simple. Interestingly, some old, big companies, not necessarily pharmaceuticals, do seem to keep plugging away in this quadrant. Maybe you've even worked for a few who just never get around to killing off their losers. Instead of hanging on with commodity products in dying markets, they should kill these businesses and move on to something with a future.

The "Heart Disease Business"

And finally we come to the place where most big companies and entrepreneurs dream about—the big market need/high competitive position quadrant. Think about this. The number one killer in the world, for both men and women is still heart disease. There have been advances in treating all manner of heart problems, but there's still no cure in sight. What if—and here comes the dream—you and your band of entrepreneur/scientists come up with the absolutely perfect, rejection-free, artificial heart? You could give a lifetime guarantee for your perfect heart to your customers. That's a better deal than they get when they're born! So your "heart disease business," would rank right up there with the wheel, electricity, cars, computers, and penicillin, as one of history's true blockbuster products. Can entrepreneurs be successful here? Absolutely. Success is virtually guaranteed—with one caveat. You may become too successful. Getting too successful here will ultimately guarantee hordes of envious competitors, and open the door to government busybodies, all of whom will do almost anything to take you down several pegs. Ask AT&T, IBM, and Microsoft how it works once you're deemed a monopoly. So go for it by all means—and get ready to take the heat of intense competition and the heavy hand of government regulation.

The illustration shows how the four medical examples would be positioned using the criteria of market need and competitive position.

Picking Winners

	Small Market Need	**Big** Market Need
High Competitive Position	"Leprosy Business" Small market need High competitive position	"Heart Disease Business" Big market need High competitive position
Low Competitive Position	"Polio Business" Small market need Low competitive position	"Headache Business" Big market need Low competitive position

Competitive Position

Market Need

Beyond helping you pick market/product winners and getting your entrepreneurial venture off the ground, the two criteria—market need and competitive position—will continue to be important as you grow. They will always indicate what kind of actions you need to take to improve each of your market/product businesses. For example, if you're in the small market need/high competitive position quadrant, you need to find more customers for your great product. So focusing on marketing, distribution, exporting, and so on, would be essential to growing your business. Conversely, if you're in the big market need/low competitive position quadrant, you need to raise the competitiveness of your product. Improving items like product innovation, quality, costs, and delivery time would all be key to generating more growth. The bottom line: These criteria will help you grow your business—which is, after all, what entrepreneurs are supposed to do.

Now you have the inside scoop on how entrepreneurs define and deliver the *what* of their mission. Now it's time to start doing the same for your own venture. You don't have to come up with mega bucks for market research. And you don't need to take six months off to write a detailed business plan. But to do it the entrepreneurial way, you do have to pick some solid market/product winners. Application 2 will get you started doing just that.

APPLICATION 2
Creating Entrepreneurial Business Plans

What do you love to do and what are you good at doing? What needs do you see day after day that are going unmet, or are being met by a company that does a lousy job, or does it too slowly, or too expensively? Within these questions you will find the market/product business(es) that will carry the highest chance of success for you as an entrepreneur. Completing this four-part application won't guarantee your entrepreneurial success, but it will ensure that you have asked the right questions, and that you are focusing on the bedrock fundamentals of enterprise.

- What do I really like to do?
- What am I really good at doing?
- What unmet needs do I see in the market that require products or services that I might like to do or be good at doing?
- What is the size and value of the market need for each product or service I've identified?
- What would my competitive position be, compared to other providers of similar products and services?
- What actions must I take to get started?

There may be other things you will want to examine, and you'll surely want to confirm the answers you come up with today. But I promise you: Answering the questions in Application 2 is the starting point for every successful entrepreneur. So have fun picking your own market/product winners!

APPLICATION 2-A
Picking Market/Product Winners

From the list of things you really like to do and those things you are really good at doing, identify your own possible market/product winners. The third category of market needs suggests you also consider "market-driven" market/product winners, with a caveat: Even if your market/product idea is inspired by a need you see in the market, the entrepreneurial requirement to like what you do and be good at doing it is not diminished. Obviously, starting a business with products you don't like and are no good at is a recipe for disaster, no matter how big a need may exist in the market.

Next, translate your answers from the first column into a potential business activity in the second column. "I like computers" could become "computer repair" or, "I'm good at gardening" could become "landscaping service." Note that some of your interests and skills may require creative thinking to redefine them as a business. A few might not work at all. Just set those aside and move on.

What Do I Really Like to Do?   **Market/Product Winners**

-
-
-

What Am I Really Good at Doing?   **Market/Product Winners**

-
-
-

What Market Need Do I See?   **Market/Product Winners**

-
-
-

APPLICATION 2-B
Picking Market/Product Winners

List your market/product winners (potential businesses) from 2-A. For each of your market/product winners, rate both the market need and your likely competitive position, using a scale of 10 to 1 (10 being the highest and 1 as the lowest). Use your best estimates and your common sense to answer these questions. Be as objective as possible. The generic questions for each rating are:

Market Need.   How big is the market in number of customers and in sales volume? Is it growing, declining, or staying the same? How critical is this need to the market? Is it a necessity, a luxury, or a passing fad?

Competitive Position.   How much better, cheaper, and faster could you provide this product/service compared to how it's currently being offered by others?

Market/Product Winners From Application 2-A	**Ratings (10 High/1 Low)**	
	Market Need*	Competitive Position*
•		
•		
•		
•		
•		

*Note any critical information that you will need to verify later.

APPLICATION 2-C
Picking Market/Product Winners

Plot the ratings of your market/product winners from 2-B on the matrix. For example, a "9 market need/9 competitive position" rating would be very near the upper right-hand corner. A "3/7" would be near the center of the upper left-hand quadrant, and so on. This matrix will give you a visual overview of the combined market need and competitive position for each of your possible market/product ideas.

1. **Small Market/High Competitive Position.** Good possibility of success in this Rolls Royce-type business. Work to find more markets for your excellent product.

2. **Big Market/High Competitive Position.** High possibility of success, but once successful, you will likely attract a high level of competition. Be prepared for strong competitors.

3. **Big Market/Low Competitive Position.** Good possibility of success, but you may have to compete on price at the low end of the market. Work to raise your competitive position.

4. **Small Market/Low Competitive Position.** Poor chance of success. Avoid this business like the plague.

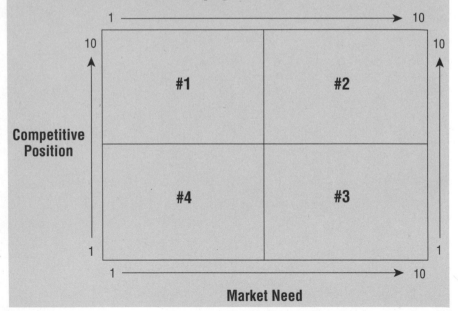

APPLICATION 2-D
It's Start-Up Time!

Application 2-C identified your market/product winners with the best possibilities of success. Based on that, what are the most important actions you should take over the next 90 to 180 days to get started? Your actions should be focused on the fundamentals required to get any business up and running. Although described earlier in this chapter, they are restated here as action questions.

1. What actions will I take to identify and sell the potential customers/markets?   **When**

-

-

2. What actions will I take to design and make the first version or prototype of the product/service to be available for testing by a customer?   **When**

-

-

3. What actions will I take to determine and set up the operating capabilities required to make, sell, and service the products and customers?   **When**

-

-

4. What actions will I take to identify the sources of cash (including customers) and secure the cash to cover the start-up phase of the business?   **When**

-

-

How—The Entrepreneur as Creator of Culture

The beliefs that mold great organizations frequently grow out of the character, the experiences, and the convictions of a single person. More than most companies, IBM is the reflection of one individual— my father, T. J. Watson.

—Thomas J. Watson, Jr.,
Past Chairman, IBM

The "how" dimension can be loosely translated as corporate culture: "How are we going to go about our business?" In companies, as in society at large, cultures are defined by the values or beliefs of the people. To entrepreneurs, the reason for creating and maintaining business values is to make sure the company is focused on those operating factors that are most critical to the accomplishment of the business plan.

Entrepreneurs, by definition, set the values of their companies and reinforce them through their daily behavior. Their actions in fact determine what's important to do and not to do. How employees should behave, how quality is treated, and what level of respect is given to customers, are all determined by the personal example of the founder. An entrepreneurial culture is based on two no-nonsense criteria: what behavior will give us competitive advantage and what behavior am I personally committed to—without compromise? The answers to these questions reveal the values that set the culture of the enterprise. To the entrepreneur, the culture must directly and powerfully support the customer/product strategy. To be guided by values that are unconnected to the business plan simply wouldn't occur to an entrepreneur. It certainly never occurred to T. J. Watson.

IBM still ranks ninth in sales and sixth in profits on the *Fortune 500* list, but it's fair to say they're past their peak, some 15 years into the downside of their life cycle. In an odd sort of way, saying the current IBM is past its peak is actually a tribute to the awesome power and reputation that Big Blue carried for most of the twentieth century. In fact, with the benefit of perspective, you can make a strong case that IBM has been the greatest and most profitable corporation in the entire history of business. If you have to pick a single factor at the core of IBM's long run at greatness, it was that they were the best in the world at doing those few critical things that were absolutely essential to the achievement of their business strategy. Tom Watson, Jr. called it the "power of IBM's beliefs."

His father, Thomas J. Watson, Sr., founded IBM in 1914 and immediately went about instilling all IBM'ers with his now famous set of beliefs: customer service, respect for the individual, and superior effort in all tasks. History shows these beliefs, or as we call them—the values, served IBM well for 75 years. Where did they come from? Did Mr. Watson take a vote among his employees or hire consultants to tell him what the IBM values should be? No, they came from Watson himself, as he figured out what IBM had to focus on to achieve its strategy.

T. J. Watson was an eternally optimistic salesman, and he didn't see IBM's strategy as a product leader and innovator. In fact, in the early days, IBM's products were fairly humdrum: butcher scales, meat slicers, coffee grinders, time clocks, and a primitive assortment of punched card tabulating machines. Watson saw IBM's competitive advantage in providing outstanding customer service, whatever the product. This value was verbalized as a flat-out, uncompromising promise to the world: "IBM will give the best customer service of any company, in any industry, anywhere in the world."

Watson set out on a lifetime mission to make that promise come true. For years, IBM corporate advertising simply declared: "IBM Means Service." IBM salesmen were trained like no sales force ever before. They spent as long as 18 months in IBM schools before seeing their first customer. It was drilled into them from day one that it was more important to not lose current customers than it was to sell new ones—putting more emphasis on servicing than selling even for the sales force! Early on, the company began recruiting sales trainees from college campuses, an unheard of practice at the time. And Watson invented the idea of "customer engineers" being assigned to all sales teams—to ensure that customers had face-to-face contact with IBM's highest level of technical expertise. IBM schools were opened to customer personnel, further fostering interaction and good relations between IBM'ers and the people who paid their salaries. IBM sales and service teams were legendary for working weekends and round-the-clock to get client systems up and running on schedule or back in service after repairs. In a brilliant master-stroke to strengthen respect for customers, IBM publicly declared that 95 percent of all IBM product ideas came from customers. And perhaps most powerful of all, everyone in IBM knew the absolutely, guaranteed way to get fired was to be rude to customers. These and countless other means were used to instill the "customer service belief" in IBM—as the primary competitive advantage of the company.

Next, Watson strongly believed that giving the best customer service in the world required having the best employees in the world. Watson's belief was transformed into the second IBM value: "IBM will respect the dignity of every employee." This straightforward value has probably created more IBM folklore than any other single facet of the company's history. In today's downsized and uncertain world, some of the early IBM "people stuff" may sound quaint, but the principles behind the policies are important. Take the famous IBM dress code for example: white shirt, dark blue tie, and close cropped haircuts for men. Women employees had to tow the company line with white blouses and blue scarves. The reason for creating the trim "IBM look" in every employee from factory worker to vice president was simple. Tom Watson, Jr. explained it this way: "In those days it was easy to tell who the first class corporate citizens were; The managers with their suits, ties, and starched collars. And it was just as obvious who the second class people were; The factory workers with blue collars and dirty coveralls. Our management has long believed that sharp contrasts between blue and white collar people in the business had to be avoided. In IBM there will be no second class citizens." From this belief also came IBM's unique policy of subordinates formally rating their managers, the famous open-door policy as a "deterrent to the possible abuse of managerial power," an incredible amount of training for all employees, a strong promote from within policy, and yes, even some company hoopla. Sixty-five years of the no-layoff policy, followed even during the darkest days of the great depression (inconceivable in today's IBM) didn't hurt company loyalty and morale either. And, of course, IBM's consistent record of paying top dollar and top benefits was the cement for all the above. Yes, it sounds quaint all right. Especially when compared to the values displayed toward employees by the Enrons of the world and today's crop of *Fortune 500* CEOs who pull down 531 times the pay of their average employee!

Value number three at IBM was where the rubber hit the road, so to speak. It was stated as: "IBM expects and demands superior performance from its people in whatever they do." T. J. Watson was an unabashed believer in striving for perfection, telling his people: "We believe an organization will stand out only if it is willing to take on seemingly impossible tasks. The people who set out to do what others say cannot be done are the ones who make the discoveries, produce the inventions, and move the world ahead." Reading between the lines, it's a safe bet that T. J., like many other great entrepreneurs, wasn't the easiest guy in the world to please! But this striving for perfection did feed into his natural optimism and can-do attitude. During the Depression for example, Watson was asked how in the world IBM could still be hiring salesmen while the rest of the industry was cutting back. His answer: "Well, you know, when a man gets to my age, he always does something foolish. Some men play too much poker, and others bet on horse races, and one thing and another. My vice is hiring salesmen."

The bottom-line message from Watson on creating a strong, supportive culture is crystal clear. The rationale for their value around people is a good example. While recognizing his father as a compassionate person, Thomas Watson, Jr. once bluntly described the business purpose of the IBM value on respecting people: "Our early emphasis on human relations was not actually motivated by altruism, but by the simple belief that if we respected our people and helped them to respect themselves, the company would profit."

And finally, compared to some of the nonsense today in big business that gets passed off as corporate culture (beautifully framed mission statements that nobody believes in), the most unique thing about how the values at IBM were implemented is the amazing fact that nobody even bothered to write them down for 50 years! The first written description of IBM's values came from Thomas Watson, Jr., in 1963, half a century after his father founded the company. As a matter of company history, Watson, Jr. produced a marvelous 33 page booklet titled: *A Business And Its Beliefs—The Ideas That Helped Build IBM*. This, by the way, would make a great companion piece to Matsushita's 23 page booklet for every business school library in the world!

The fact is, the IBM values were instilled and kept alive by T. J. Watson's unremitting personal commitment and example. He had no "values" consultants telling him how to do it. He had no corporate culture department producing long lists of motherhood and apple pie slogans. And for sure, no one was racing around the IBM offices plastering framed copies of his beliefs on every wall. We call it creating values the entrepreneurial way—and it's the best advice you'll ever get on how to instill a powerful and competitive culture in your new business.

Of course, the epithet to this great story is not so great. Big Blue ultimately became living proof that the dreaded life cycle of all organizations plays no favorites. By 1980, IBM had become a complacent, muscle-bound, slow moving, giant bureaucracy totally unprepared for the technology explosions that rocked the computer industry in the

1980s and 1990s. The joke in Europe at the time was the only organization more bureaucratic than the EC in Brussels was IBM. It was clearly
time to reassess the market need and their competitive position, but IBM
just lumbered on, oblivious to the entrepreneurial revolution taking
place in their own industry. If they had replaced, or even added to, their
three-time honored values with an all-out crusade to become the fastest
moving, most innovative high-tech company in the world in the eighties, could they have avoided the near total collapse they experienced in
the early nineties? We'll never know, but it would have been worth a try.
It clearly couldn't have been worse than the ten years of bitter downsizing (180,000 loyal employees terminated) and massive cost reductions
that were forced on them over the next decade. The moral of the story:
When your business strategy has to change, by your own choice or by
market forces, it's probably also time to change your business culture.

Creating Entrepreneurial Business Values

If planning is the most overused management practice in business, creating and maintaining values is surely the most misused. A couple of
decades ago the whole subject of corporate culture and values burst on
the scene. It was quickly co-opted by industrial psychologists, wild-
eyed motivational speakers, HR gurus and various other corporate
do-gooders. It also became a new, lucrative area for management consultants to make another buck. Every big corporation worth its salt had
to have a mission statement and color posters of holier-than-thou core
values began popping up on office and factory walls everywhere. Being
good to customers, employees, shareholders, communities, and anyone
else the values task force could think of, passed as evidence that you
were an enlightened and presumably successful company. A lot of otherwise good managers seemed to believe that business values were
things you dreamed up in a staff meeting, plastered on every available
wall, and then went back to your real job. Of course all this was, and is,
downright ridiculous.

Such shenanigans are not only silly, they are also quite damaging. As
discussed earlier, the purpose—the only purpose—of creating and maintaining business values is to make sure you focus on, and get very good at,
those few operating factors critical to the accomplishment of your business plan. Pursuing values that are unrelated to the company plan is a
fundamental disconnect for any business.

Your strategy and your culture must be connected. Set your strategy in terms of products and markets, and then determine which operational activities or skills are most critical to achieving the strategy. One of the great modern examples of the power of that connection is 3M. 3M's reputation for product innovation is well known. It has, in fact, the highest ratio of new product revenue to total revenue of any big company in the world. On average, 3M produces an incredible 30 percent of its revenue from new products. And how does 3M achieve this remarkable performance year after year? First, they plan to do it—by making new product revenue the core of their growth strategy. Second, and here's the part so often missed by casual observers, they have built their entire corporate culture around product innovation. They have made innovation the main, in fact the only, corporate value of their worldwide company. Everything at 3M reflects this value: Their planning, their hiring, their reward systems, and even their hoopla. And at 3M, everyone knows the surefire way to get noticed and promoted: "Invent something!" This is both very smart and very effective. Would 3M hit their strategic goal year after year if, for example, they simply copied the values of say, Wal-Mart, or Singapore Airlines, or Mercedes Benz—all great companies? Of course not! It's called connecting the culture to the strategy. And not doing it is the biggest mistake you can make in maintaining your sense of mission as you grow your business.

Entrepreneurs have to get this right. Concentrating your energies on becoming the best in the world at one or two key things will give you powerful, competitive advantages. This is why focusing on a few performance defining values that directly support your market/product plan is so important. Nowhere is this more true than with the young start-up venture. In the do-or-die world of the entrepreneur, it almost seems to come naturally with the territory. But be forewarned. Your entrepreneurial values won't sound anything like the beautifully crafted platitudes of the Fortune 500. For example, if you're a small player in a very competitive, low-margin business, you quickly learn that letting up on cost control, from salaries to paper clips, is a one-way ticket to bankruptcy. But cost control rarely makes it onto a big company's list of values. The reasons are clear: The value statement has nothing to do with the real product/market plan and anyway, cost control doesn't have that warm fuzzy ring big business PR departments like to promote. Fortunately, the start-up entrepreneur doesn't have to carry any of that big business baggage, and the question of "what should our business values be?" can be answered directly and simply.

First, it has to be answered by you, the entrepreneur of the business. It can't be delegated. It's essentially your answer to, "How am I going to go about my business?" Your answers will determine what's important to do and not to do in the enterprise, how your employees should behave toward customers and products, and ultimately the company's overall mission. The values you choose must be tested against no-nonsense criteria such as: "What actions will give us the most competitive advantage and what behaviors must we personally commit to—without compromise?"

Along the way, don't ever forget that the overarching reason for fostering a particular set of values is to support your business plan and therefore improve your competitive position. And those values will never take hold without the binding, personal commitment of you, the entrepreneur, and your future employees. To find and create the values that will maximize your competitive prowess, consider the following points.

✔ Focus on Raising Your Competitive Advantage.

What values, behaviors, or practices in the daily operation of your business will most powerfully raise your competitive position? Is it product quality? Innovation? Employee relations? Customer service? Cost efficiency? Fast action? How might each of these, plus all the other possibilities that you can think of, actually help you rise above your competition? Carefully think through which of those operating values are absolutely critical to the successful accomplishment of your market/product plan. Whatever those few areas are, they must become the cornerstones of your business.

✔ Get Yourself and Your People Committed.

Becoming the very best in the world at those few practices most critical to raising your competitiveness requires an uncompromising, emotional commitment from you as the leader. Ultimately, it will also require the personal commitment of your entire workforce. For you as the leader, there can be no wavering on the commitment issue. You absolutely must lead by example. Your personal, daily behavior will set the standard for your entire company. This is the entrepreneurial way to bring business values to life in an organization—and the best way ever invented to get groups of disparate people to come together to achieve a common goal.

✔ It's Your Behavior, Not Your Words, That Count.

Your behavior is more eloquent than your words. Believe this if you believe nothing else in this book. The moral for the entrepreneurial leader:
don't expect others (employees, suppliers, clients, etc.) to believe in and
commit to your business values until and unless you are the best example
of those values.

✔ Don't Make It a Big Project.

As with setting your future strategy, the entrepreneurial approach is to
keep it simple. Creating a strong and lasting set of business values does
not include setting up a culture department, hiring consultants, or packing your managers off to Hawaii to vote for their favorites and approve
the look of the new wall plaques. Creating a powerful set of values is
truly an ongoing, on-the-job task.

✔ Choose Only a Few Values and Keep Them Simple.

How many things can you be the best at? Try for three and maybe you
can hit one or two. The values of the company have to guide the daily
behavior of your employees. This means they have to be carried
around in their minds and hearts. They can't be buried in a 1,000 page
policy manual.

✔ Never Compromise.

Unfortunately, compromises are more powerful than principles in the business values arena. One well-placed compromise can reverse years of princi-
pled effort. So, never means never when it comes to violating or
compromising your values. And why is that? Your customers and employees
will be the first to know and they'll never forget that when push comes to
shove, you don't really stick to your principles. When sales are bad, you let
some junk go out the door. When times are tough, you are never the one to
take a reduction in pay. When both customers and employees stop trusting
you, the end can't be far behind. On the other hand, can you ever change
your values? Sure. If your business environment changes, creating real shifts
in your markets and your competitive position, you darn well better be
prepared to reassess and change your operating values. Go back and review
the epithet of our own historic example, IBM, to remind yourself how

dangerous it is to rest on your cultural laurels—even if the underlying values have served you well for half a century.

Fostering an entrepreneurial business culture, underpinned by the specific values which will give you the most competitive advantage, has little to do with those feel-good platitudes you've seen decorating the walls of big business—and big government. Entrepreneurial business values are, instead, the most powerful weapon ever invented to beat your competitors and ensure the success of your customer/product business plan.

Keeping It Alive

Creating an entrepreneurial culture is half the battle. Maintaining it for generations can be even harder. And keeping it going when the going really gets tough, is more than most can do. The question remains: Once you've got it, how do you keep it? And especially interesting, how do a handful of enterprises, like the great German company founded by Gottleib Daimler and Karl Benz, keep it alive for over a century? How does Mercedes Benz still get its workers to really believe they are making the best car in the world, every year? A big part of the answer is that this is a company where the values have been set on the factory floor since 1885. The company is full of managers and workers who absolutely love their product and love making it. The work is demanding and the worker's pride is unparalleled. As a Mercedes Benz line-foreman in Stuttgart told me: "This is the strictest, toughest place in the world to work. But we're the best in the world and I wouldn't want to be anywhere else." Now that's worth all the fancy corporate mission statements ever written! And that's exactly what you should be creating from day one in your own company.

Of course you have to get the business going before you start worrying about keeping it alive. But in the spirit of "an ounce of prevention," this final thought on your business culture and values may be worth its weight in gold. Obviously, your core business values have to keep working day in and day out, year after year, to make your company great. Indeed, if your values truly are: "those few operating factors critical to the accomplishment of your business plan," as Thomas J. Watson, Jr., said, then letting them die is exactly what you can't afford to do.

Say, for example, you believe that all employees should behave like you; that they should have a strong sense of ownership of the company and perform their job in a highly entrepreneurial manner. You believe this will be so critical to your company's early growth, that you decide being entrepreneurial should be a core value of the business. Now fast-forward five years, and we see that there's still no employee stock ownership program and the pay for performance plan is a joke. Plus, the promote from within policy doesn't seem to apply to any job opening above mail clerk, and everyone has learned the fastest way to get in trouble is to try something new without first getting your approval. And finally, not only are there no rewards being handed out for being entrepreneurial, but it's crystal clear that there's no penalty for *not* being entrepreneurial. You don't have to be a rocket scientist to answer the "what if?" question. Anyone could figure out that the being entrepreneurial value never got off the ground in your company.

For your future reference, the following are the three greatest influences on keeping your business values alive. If these all-important culture influencers support your company values, you can be sure the values will stay alive. If they don't support your values, or even worse, subvert them, your values will be quickly lost—and with them, the best insurance you could ever have for achieving your entrepreneurial dreams.

✔ **Your Daily Behavior.**

It's not a fair world. The founder is "on stage" every minute of every day. Your personal, daily behavior will set the standard for your entire company. Your most insignificant behavior is of intense interest to employees, customers, suppliers, and shareholders. It seems today you can't fool anyone any of the time. So, surprise everyone and actually behave, all the time, as the best example of the company's values. It may not be a fair world, but it's a price most entrepreneurs gladly pay.

While such attention may give you a feeling of great power, it also carries serious responsibilities. For example, if customer service is a core value of the company, you had better be first in line to show your love for customers. If product quality is the value, you have to be the one who never, ever, allows junk to go out the door. If you choose cost control as a company value, you're the first one that has to start flying economy. The fact is, the single most powerful factor in keeping your company's values alive, is your personal, daily behavior. As the company grows, this will also become true for the senior management team you put in place. So if you, or your top lieutenants, violate the company's stated values, you may as well close up shop and move on. The company culture you said you want and need, will already be dead.

✔ The Rituals and Practices You Follow.

Everyone knows the written policy manual is not what the culture is all about. Your company's true values only reveal themselves in the mundane rituals and practices of daily operations. How do you actually treat workers on the line? How much service is really given after the sale? Do you take the first pay cut in bad years? Do your employees take extra care to make sure the product is perfect? Does such behavior get rewarded, or even noticed? And what's the reaction to losing a customer: Does everyone just shrug their shoulders or does all hell break loose to regain the client? It's at this level that the culture of any company lives or dies.

Suppose you decide that innovation has to be value number one in your business. You announce it to the staff, and it's even noted in the mission statement posters you've hung around the premises. The initial hurrahs are all good. But for the next five years, the rank and file don't hear about it again. Innovation isn't an item in anyone's plan or budget. It's not written into anyone's job description or measured in their annual performance review. It's not discussed in meetings. No one has read a book about innovation or attended a seminar on creativity. The company newsletter has never had an article about it there are no awards handed out for good ideas. There's not even a suggestion program in the company. Where do you think the innovation value is going to be after five years? You're right. Nowhere.

These are damaging things. You are sabotaging your future. You are actively destroying the very thing that you say will give you enormous competitive advantage in the marketplace. To be kept alive, the values you select have to be woven into the daily rhythm of the business. If the values are not part of the life of the company and don't impact the ongoing routine of employees, they will be as dead as yesterday's newspaper.

✔ What You Reward and What You Penalize.

How do I get promoted around here? And what does it take to get fired? Your answers to those eternal employee questions will directly and powerfully set the values of the company—for all employees. The maintenance of a set of values ultimately depends on what actions get rewarded and what actions get penalized. Unfortunately, this is the most frequently violated practice in keeping values alive. Most companies simply forget to make them a part of the organization's reward and penalty systems.

Say, for example, you decide that "loving the customer" should be the big value in your new enterprise. Employee X is widely recognized as Mr. Customer Service who will do anything to satisfy the customers. He comes in on the weekend to make sure the shipment gets out, or whatever. Employee Y, on the other hand, hates customers and everyone knows it. He would be the happiest worker in the shop if it weren't for those demanding customers always wanting something else. At the end of the year, you give both X and Y a slap on the back and an 10 percent raise. Say good-bye to "loving the customer" as a company value.

Some companies still depend entirely on penalties and punishment to control employee behavior. Others, striving to be progressive, have gone berserk with rewards, positive feedback, and all manner of hoopla for just showing up. And certainly the great majority of big companies, raging bureaucracies all, do absolutely nothing. No rewards and no penalties whatsoever. Here the message is clear: It really doesn't matter how you behave. But, of course, we know that to maintain a set of values, designed to achieve the company's plan, it matters very much how you behave. Most of us have learned the hard way, from million dollar CEOs to lowly paid clerks, *it really does matter.*

It should be clear by now that having an entrepreneurial sense of mission isn't rocket science. It's all straightforward, simple stuff: Creating simple plans, picking markets and products you really care and know about, determining the few critical values needed to support your market/product plan, and then keeping those values alive and well year after year. It's simple stuff, but it's also powerful stuff. So whether you're an entrepreneurial dreamer, or do'er just starting up, or one of the dazzling few already on your way, it's absolutely critical to remember that having a powerful sense of mission about your business is entrepreneurial practice number one.

Our final suggestion for creating and instilling an entrepreneurial sense of mission in your business, is to take a long, hard look in the mirror. The mission of your company, for better or for worse, rests squarely on your shoulders. When the mission is fully on your shoulders, there's not a lot of room for other hands on mission control.

This means you have to lead, and the best way, the only way, for an entrepreneur to lead is by example. You have to lead by example to inspire others: your customers, your employees, your suppliers, and your investors. All entrepreneurs can feel a sense of mission about what they, personally, are doing. But the lesson of the truly great ones: the Watsons and Matsushitas of the world, is that they inspired others to feel it as well. And as you're about to find out, so did master entrepreneur Buel Messer, one of the truly unforgettable characters I've ever known.

The Mission of Buel Messer

How can a blind man rustle cattle? Not very well. That's why I got caught.

—Buel Messer, Founder,
Messer Landscape, Inc.

It's 1980. A snowy Friday in the Shenandoah Valley of Virginia. It's the kind of day fathers knock off work early to be home with the family. Buel Messer was already home with the family. Knocking off early was not an option. He didn't have work. There weren't a lot of career possibilities for a convicted felon. A cattle rustler. Out of boredom and frustration, he grabbed his two young sons and a shovel. "Let's go shovel some snow." He needed the boys to be his eyes. Buel Messer is also blind.

Hardly the stuff of a great story of enterprise? Think again. It's just a little more earthy than you'll find in the *Harvard Business Review*. From shoveling snow and mowing lawns, always with his boys, Messer has created a multidivision empire. Today, Messer Landscape has thriving retail operations, a booming wholesale business moving thousands of plantings and multimillion dollar commercial landscaping projects are taken in stride. Not bad for a business that grossed $5,400 23 years ago.

Welcome to the mission of Buel Messer. I first learned of Messer from a newspaper story about a blind landscaper in Virginia. I was overcome with curiosity. How can a blind man be a landscaper? It sounded pretty amazing, so I decided to go meet him and get his story for my book. During that first interview, it also came up that he had served time in prison. I asked him what his crime had been. He answered matter of factly: "Cattle rustling." Naturally, I had to ask him the obvious next question: "Mr. Messer, how can a blind man rustle cattle?" His classic answer: "Not very well. That's why I got caught. And in a round-about way, that's why I ended up in landscaping."

Buel Messer's story has a lot of lessons. The one we're interested in here is all about building a business. Building a business to feed your family and regain your name. Without resources. Without theories. With absolutely nothing but a driving sense of mission. Messer was born dirt poor in the impoverished hills of eastern Kentucky. He was also born with optic atrophy, leaving him with a sliver of sight, about 5 percent, in one eye. He struggled through grammar school and was finally admitted to a state-supported high school for the blind in Ohio. School didn't interest him a whole lot, but athletics did.

On a sports scholarship, he went on to college. To see if he could do it, he made the Dean's List his first and last semesters in college. In between, he was an intercollegiate wrestling champion, and set the state record for the mile in Ohio. In a moment of glory, he ran in Madison Square Garden on national TV, against the world record holder, Jim Ryan. Ryan blew the field off with one of the first under four minute miles on an indoor track. Still, not a bad day's work for a poor, blind kid from Kentucky.

Because of his boundless energy and personal example in overcoming his handicap, Messer was a natural as a role model for handicapped students. He threw himself into his first job at The School for the Visually Handicapped in Wisconsin. There he became interested in helping those with multiple handicaps and started graduate study at night. In Wisconsin, he met and married his now wife of 25 years, also a sightless person. From there, Messer transferred to the Virginia School for the Deaf and Blind. He completed his Masters Degree at the University of Virginia and enrolled in the doctoral program.

Being an academic in the challenging and specialized world of teaching the handicapped wasn't the only thing Messer thought he could do. Consequently, along the way, he dabbled in other things that he knew. Like farming. He started a small cattle and hog operation. For several years, he taught by day and worked the farm all night. Being a farmer entrepreneur became more and more the passion of his life. He expanded the business. Financing was relatively easy to come by. His reputation was excellent. He expanded again, and again. He was getting in deeper and deeper financially—until one black night, his world fell apart. In one fell swoop, one act of desperate dishonesty, Buel Messer's hard-earned accomplishments and his family's modest but honorable way of life, came crashing down.

Despite the novelty, (how *does* a blind man rustle cattle?) judges and peers weren't amused. In rural Virginia, stealing livestock is as much a sin as a crime. Not only do first offenders do hard time in prison, they can do hard time forever back in their community. This was the bleak outlook on that snowy Friday in 1980. The family was wiped out financially. Messer was *persona non grata* in the academic world. And decent jobs didn't go to ex-cons. An eventual full pardon by the Governor restored his voting rights, but not his dignity.

Never one to feel sorry for himself or blame others, Messer says of that period: "I didn't hold it against anybody. I was the one who created it, and I recognized that. I think the fact that I had, through my own bad judgment, committed the criminal acts way back there early . . . forced me . . . that if I did anything the rest of my life I was going to prove, not to everybody, I still know that I'll never convince everybody . . . to do things honestly and forthright and that I'm honest at what I do. It's a challenge and a driving force for me."

Let's take Buel Messer at his word. The overarching mission of his life became the redemption of his honor. He had few options but to reach for it through his own enterprise. How has he done it? What are the business beliefs arising from the character, experiences, and convictions of Buel Messer? What exactly is his sense of mission?

To get in sync with Messer's approach to business, it's necessary to re-learn plain, blunt English. You'll find no corporate-ese here. Backward integration becomes: "we had to have our own trees to sell" and market segmentation gets translated as "little old lady types versus fussy lawyer and doctor types." Once you get the language down, you begin to understand that Messer speaks with a passion and focus rare in business. He knows his markets, he knows his products, and he knows exactly what it takes to beat his competitors. This is the no-frills version of *mission*. This is *strategy* and *culture*, entrepreneurial style.

Starting with the snow shovel back in 1980, Buel's description of the start-up is pure passion: "I had to completely liquidate . . . while I was in prison, which was real depressing and demoralizing . . . it really was rock bottom for me. I'm thinking all the time that there's got to be some way back to something. And I'm always, I've always got a lot of plans and thoughts. But my mind is fatigued.

"So my two young sons, who were about nine and eleven years at that point, and I went around neighborhoods shoveling snow for people. Boy, that looked lucrative. At any rate that gave me an idea in that snow shoveling was lucrative and it was a public service oriented type thing. But when spring came around, the work was over. Well, I figured the next thing we could do would be to mow lawns together—for the same people we were shoveling snow and maybe some others. So I stuck a small ad in the paper, just wanting to get something for the two kids and me that we could do together while I'm being house daddy. We ran the ad: 'Wanted, In The North End, Lawns To Mow For The Season.' This was in the first week of March now. So we get about 25 or 30 responses to an ad that ran two or three weeks. And so we selected 15, between selecting and people deciding whether they wanted us, about 15 lawns in our neighborhood that we could ride a small riding lawn mower to and pull a small cart behind since I didn't drive and the boys weren't old enough. So that's the way Messer Landscape began. And that was 23 years ago this past season.

"I thought it'd be just a little something to really keep the boys occupied and out of trouble. That's what I thought about. I got tired of cooking and cleaning house pretty quickly. But I didn't know there were so many related things to doing those lawns that summer—that one thing we did, just led on to another. And I had more time now to think about things. You know, to really let some creative imagination take place.

"At any rate, the boys and I, we did some sidelines. A lot of them were retired people or little old ladies that we were working for. Those were the types we thought would be best, rather than work for doctors and lawyers and people who had lots of money. We felt they might be a problem for us. They'd be too fussy, and we didn't know what we were doing anyway. We thought that little old ladies would put up with what we had better. I might as well say, I thought that, because the boys didn't really have much input at that point. It was hard enough keeping them working at it. And they were my eyesight of course, even early on then, since I didn't see well enough to do what we were doing. But I did, I actually mowed them myself and so forth. So there was this lady that said: 'Would you prune my shrubbery?' And I said sure, we'll try it. We'd never pruned a bush of our own before but got to doing it and got to reading articles and things about how to do it. It just seemed pretty natural, after that.

"I guess the next kind of major step was a realtor/builder type person that I knew. He had two spec houses that he'd built. He wanted to know if we'd be interested in taking some rakes and trying to rake the rough ground out and put in some grass for him. That was our second year. We'd expanded to the point where we had this one part-time guy with his own truck. I think he might have had his own wheelbarrow too. Anyway that's how we got back and forth to the job to do those houses. We did rake it out, planted some grass, put in seven or eight shrubs in front, mulched them, and miraculously the grass and shrubs grew and everything did well. So I thought, wow, we're landscapers! My mind started going kind of wild at that point with all the possibilities. That first year we had a gross income of $5,400 and it just kept growing every year after that."

Enterprise doesn't get any more basic. And what's behind it? Doing something of value. Something worthwhile. Pursuing an honorable mission. This is what drives people to create miracles in all walks of life. It's what enables groups of people to do the impossible. Value driven missions are personal. They don't come out of the mouths of consultants. Your's will be uniquely yours. Buel Messer's meant overcoming incredible odds to redeem his dignity: "It gave me an opportunity to prove that I was not all together dishonest. Probably I've bent over backwards trying to prove my honesty all along the line. I will say this quite frankly, I've not knowingly or intentionally done one other dishonest thing since. In fact I've probably bent the other way a whole lot . . . I think I was trying to prove something. I was trying to prove . . . that despite this terrible reputation that I had developed, that I still could be a success and a viable entity in the business world and this community—which I feel like I have done by now."

Messer's description of his company's strategy and culture is unadulterated common sense. It has none of the management consultant's conceptual elegance. It's not "big picture" stuff. It's a bunch of snapshots about where he's headed and how he's going to get there. His strategy comes straight from the marketplace. Where he's headed with customers and products underscores his knowledge of and respect for the market. He turns almost reverential when talking about it: "It's not me dreaming it up . . . it's the need in the marketplace! There's strong need out there. I've been able to see areas where there's a strong need, or will be in the future, that I can capitalize on." His sense of gratitude toward customers borders on the Japanese: "I just feel really fortunate that we were able to convince the public that we would give them their money's worth and if something went wrong we'd make it right."

The values are a direct reflection of Buel Messer's eternally, optimistic view of human potential. He sees employees as great contributors to a great cause. His greatest responsibility is to make this happen: "I love taking people that have not maybe had a good opportunity or something of that sort and motivating them, seeing them grow. And through their growth, the business is going to grow. I've always had the theory that you don't necessarily need all the highly trained personnel that some people might see a need for. I feel like I'm a good teacher. I can teach people. I thrive on being able to develop people to help them to be better than they were. . . . You've got to make people feel strong about themselves and be motivated. I would say being able to manage people might be the secret to everything."

Messer Landscape's sense of mission hasn't come from sophisticated strategic planning—which they don't do. Nor has it come from intellectualizing their culture—which they don't do. Their sense of mission and astonishing growth, has truly come from "the character, the experiences, and the convictions of a single person." And like Mr. Watson at IBM, Messer's mission has been sewn into the daily fabric of the business. Will it last? Probably as long as Buel Messer is around. Will it stick after he's gone? It could, but nobody knows. But if you want to see it in action, Messer Landscape is a living, breathing, example of a business built and operated on a powerful sense of mission.

There's a lot of Buel Messer in all of us. Everyone is missionary about something. The trick is to direct it into your entrepreneurial start-up. This really isn't so difficult—especially if you're doing something you love, as most entrepreneurs do. It's probably easier than spending two years of your life getting an MBA. It may even be easier than slogging through another dozen books on how to manage. All you have to do is get your entrepreneurial juices flowing about—*what* you want to do and *how* you're going to do it. If it can work miracles for a blind landscaper in Virginia, just imagine what it could do for you!

APPLICATION 3
Creating Entrepreneurial Business Values

Much has been written about company cultures and core values. But the real purpose of creating and maintaining business values is to identify and focus on those few things (values) that will ensure you achieve your market/product plan. What do you have to focus on? What do you have to be really good at? What operating practices do you have to do better than all your competitors?

This two-part application on values, won't guarantee your entrepreneurial success, but it will ensure that you have asked the right questions about what you have to get very good at to succeed in your entrepreneurial venture. Those questions are listed below.

- What operating values should we have to achieve our business plan?
- Which values will give us the most competitive advantage?
- How will we get everyone committed to the values?
- How can we keep them alive over time?
- What actions can I take today and what actions must I plan for the future?

There are many operating practices, or functions, that you will need to do to run your business: marketing and selling, product innovation, customer service, employee motivation, cost control, and so on. But no company can be the best at everything. The key to success for any entrepreneurial start-up is to figure out which two or three of them will give you the greatest competitive advantage over your competition. If you can figure this out, and truly become dominant in those few operating areas, you will be on your way to becoming a powerful force in your chosen product and market. This is exactly what Application 3-A and 3-B are all about. So go for it!

APPLICATION 3-A
What Values Should We Have?

Values determine what you focus on, and become great at, operationally. Therefore, the values you select must be things that give you competitive advantage in products and markets and will have the commitment of the bulk of your employees.

What Values Do We Need to Achieve the Plan?	What's the Competitive Advantage?	How Will I Get Everyone Committed?
1.		
2.		
3.		
4.		

What Actions Can I Take to Implement These Values?　　**When**

1.

2.

3.

APPLICATION 3-B
Keeping Them Alive

What can you do to ensure that you focus on and maintain your selected values? The three greatest influences on keeping them alive are shown below. For each, jot down one or two ways in which that particular factor could have the greatest impact on supporting each value.

Values	Management Behavior	Rituals and Practices	Employee Rewards and Penalties
1.			
2.			
3.			
4.			

What Actions Can I Take to Keep These Values Alive?   **When**

1.

2.

3.

Customer/Product Vision

My Customer, My Product,
My Self-Respect

Vision of What?

The computer is the most remarkable tool we've ever built. The most important thing is to get them in the hands of as many people as possible.

—Steve Jobs, Founder,
Apple Computer, NeXT, Pixar

Every book ever written about entrepreneurs says they have vision. But vision of what? Think about it. Imagine you're starting your own small business tomorrow. What will you be thinking about? What do you absolutely, positively have to be racking your brain over? If you're going to get to day two of the enterprise, you'd better be thinking about: "What can I make or do that someone will pay me hard money for?" In the mundane world of day-to-day entrepreneurship, the vague notion of vision can only mean one thing. The single most critical vision all entrepreneurs must have is a clear picture of a specific set of customers who need and will pay for a specific set of products and services. Nothing could be more basic to the entrepreneur. This is the sine qua non of enterprise. The vision is precise. It is intense. All else revolves around it. Entrepreneurs are blessed and obsessed with this integrated vision of customers and products. It's not really so surprising when you think about it. What else could you be thinking about? Business can take many forms, but there's never been a business, or at least a business that survived, without a product or service of some sort and a customer somewhere willing to pay for it. If you really want to get back to basics, this is where you start.

Now here's the underlying truth that so often gets lost in the shuffle: Great entrepreneurs are not product inventors alone. Nor are they just great promoters. Was Walt Disney a product person or a marketing person? Did Ray Kroc at McDonalds have a great product concept or a great customer concept? Is Steve Jobs a scientist or a salesman? The truth is, all great entrepreneurs are both! Jobs, for example, had a powerful vision. A vision of "the most remarkable tool we've ever built." A computer junkie from the word go. Sounds like a product guy doesn't he? But then he says: "the most important thing" is to get them used in every office, in every home, and by every child in every classroom. Like no other computer maker, Jobs understood the needs of naive users. That's why Apple made them inexpensive, easy to learn, and fun to use. Now he sounds like a customer guy. What's going on here? The obvious answer—he's a product person *and* a customer person all wrapped up in one. He's an expert on both—a make and sell craftsman—with the classic customer/product vision of an entrepreneur.

The Functional Organization—Death Knell of the Craftsman

Great entrepreneurs, by necessity, have an inseparable vision of customer and product. Like the craftsman of old, they have to make and sell. This vision produces focus, expertise, and respect for both customers and products. It also produces great competitive advantage over the competition. That your start-up business will require this intense focus on both customers and products—customer/product vision in our words—is a simple, obvious truth. But this simple truth about enterprise has the drawback of most simple truths. It's so obvious that over time you begin to take it for granted. It's easy to do, especially when more progressive and sophisticated ideas come along.

In the late nineteenth century, as companies got bigger and bigger, just such an idea came along. It was the famous pyramid, still used today, to diagram the structure of a company. We call it the modern, functional organization. It was designed with two goals in mind: To create a hierarchical management control system, and a horizontal specialization of employee tasks, or functions. On paper at least, creating a clear chain of command and organizing it by function seemed to meet a lot of objectives. Control could be maintained by a few at the top. Specializing would produce higher levels of specific employee expertise. It was efficient. Economies of scale were possible. And a professional bureaucracy could handle any rough edges. Such a rationally designed organization, it was claimed, could grow bigger and bigger with ever increasing efficiency. Thus was born the pipe-dream of infinite economies of scale and mass produced enterprise. What happened? A lot.

Early on, some of it was helpful—like driving down the cost of Henry Ford's Model T and other mass-produced commoditites. With these impressive cost reduction examples, companies, over time, began to organize themselves more and more into separate functions. Factories, for example, began to be built far away from the headquarters and the sales and marketing folks who had to sell what came out of the factories. These functionalized groups, in large companies, actually began to look like separate businesses with separate cultures. Employees such as scientists, assembly line workers, design engineers—would spend their entire career working with the product. They were the company's product people and never had to meet, much less sell or service, a customer. Other employees—salespeople, service personnel, market researchers—by the nature of their jobs, spent all of their time thinking about and working with customers. They were clearly the company's customer people and never set foot in a factory. And amazingly, huge numbers of employees didn't seem to be close to either customers or products. These were the people that cut the payroll checks, wrote the leases, and handled personnel—all the administrative functions. What ultimately evolved was that all organizations became more or less divided into three super-functions: the product function, the customer function, and the administrative function.

So what's the message for you and your start-up business? Just this: Dividing up your company into highly specialized functions and controlling everything from the top may still look terribly efficient on paper. But it doesn't work out so well in a world where impeccable service and quality, lightening fast innovation, and employees with entrepreneurial instincts are all more important competitive factors than just being a low cost producer. Too much control at the top produces inertia at the bottom. An all-out push for economies of scale destroys the personal touch that produces high quality. And professional bureaucracy, the lubricant intended to keep the gears moving, becomes the biggest, frozen gear in the place.

Extreme functionalizing is particularly damaging to employee commitment and performance. Henry Ford's Five Dollar Man, as he liked to call his production line workers, slowly began to realize that they faced the dreary prospect of tightening the same nut on the same bolt for 45 years. Or, as they still say at GM, working the assembly line there is like flunking high school the rest of your life. Or, to bring it right up to the high-tech world we live in today, the Dilbertesque nightmare of working forever in your tiny cubicle has become the high-tech equivalent of flunking, if not high school, then maybe junior college, the rest of your life.

But nothing in the functional form of organizing will be more damaging to your company's future than separating and pigeonholing your product and customer people. And to really complicate matters, the functions in a company almost never self-correct. Like giant glaciers, they tend to drift farther and farther apart. Allowing your employees to become product people, or customer people, or administrative people is highly anti-entrepreneurial—and in our experience—is the single most damaging thing you can do to the entrepreneurial spirit of the company.

The Modern (Dys)Functional Organization

**Product
People**
**Admininistrative
People**
**Customer
People**

The supremely efficient company ultimately finds itself in the absurd situation of having product people who have never seen a customer, customer people who know nothing and care less about the product, and administrative people hopelessly out of touch with both customers and products. So at the end of the day, the number one casualty is the entrepreneur's number one strength—the old-fashioned passion of the craftsman for both customer and product. What you get in its place, is a very large and very rigid *dysfunctional* bureaucracy. The craftsman, the original make-and-sell entrepreneur, will simply be wiped off the organization chart. Heading down this path is a proven prescription for boredom, bureaucracy, and killing off the entrepreneurial spirit in even the best employees.

Xerox: Billions in Lost Sales between Palo Alto and Stamford

The most famous example in history of the disasterous effects of functionalizing and separating product people and customer people is Xerox. Its Palo Alto Research Center (PARC), founded in 1970, virtually paved the golden road to the modern computer industry. The only trouble was that none of the gold ended up in Xerox's hands. You may recall that in the seventies PARC invented the Alto, the world's first personal computer, and never marketed it. Not so well remembered is the fact that Xerox also invented the world's first fax machine, called the Telecopier, and just let it die. The complete list of technologies created by PARC that made others rich is truly astonishing. *The New York Times* sampling that follows is enough to make any Xerox shareholder cry.

A Sampling of Technologies Conceived at Xerox PARC

Technology	Later Developed By
Personal computers	Apple/IBM
Facsimile machines	Canon/Panasonic
Modern chip-making technology	VLSI Technology
Silicon compilers for chip design	Silicon Compilers
Portable computing	Grid Systems
Bit-mapped screen displays	IBM/Apple
Mouse and icon-based computing	Apple
Laser printers	Hewlett-Packard/Apple
Drawing tables	Koala
Ethernet office network	3Com
Graphics and computer animation	Pixar

Database retrieval systems	Metaphor Computer
"What you see is what you get" word processing	Microsoft
Small-talk language, object-oriented programming for computers	Park Place Systems/ Digitalk
Postscript language used in high-end printers, or desktop publishing and typesetting	Adobe Systems

The New York Times, October 6, 1991, Sec. 3, p. 6.

How could this possibly happen? Here's a hint. When PARC developed the Alto, Xerox marketing executives, sitting 3000 miles away at the Stamford, Connecticut headquarters, simply refused to market it. The customer folks refused to sell what the product folks had been working on for years. If R&D and marketing couldn't get together on the hottest electronic product since TV, the rest of the list is easy to understand. The one thing everyone can now agree on is this: Completely separating your product development and marketing functions, physically locating them 3000 miles away and permitting very different cultures to flourish in each, is a recipe for disaster!

It didn't start off that way, of course. Back in 1946 in Rochester, New York, Chester Carlson made and sold the world's first photocopier and founded Xerox. By the 1960s, Xerox produced only two major products, but dominated the world in both: photocopiers and electronic typewriters. Being dependant on just two products, albeit the market leader in both, seemed risky. So Xerox came up with a smart strategy on *what* to do. The company would embark on an all-out attack on developing new technologies and new products. Unfortunately, they weren't quite as smart in determining *how* to go about doing it. Xerox, like most other blue-chip companies at the time (RCA, GE, IBM, AT&T), got caught up in the "lab in the woods" theory of doing product innovation. That notion was to set up large research facilities in remote, serene places, far from the annoying interruptions of people like company salesmen and customers. They were also caught up in the wonders of functional specialization and couldn't imagine that the great and mighty Xerox couldn't gather together the great scientists and researchers to come up with blockbuster products.

They were right, of course. Xerox created PARC, located it in sunny Palo Alto, and stuffed it full of young, bright and very hip California scientists. They only forgot one thing: They left all their young, bright, and very pin-striped marketing people in their Stamford, Connecticut headquarters. These two groups were not exactly made for each other. The product people were the brilliant, hippy scientists with long hair and gold chains in California. The customer people were the high-flying, two martini, marketing and sales chiefs with their Ivy League MBAs—sitting 3000 miles away. The two groups not only didn't share the same company culture, but they didn't seem to come from the same universe. The result was the Palo Alto scientists came up with one great idea after another that the marketing people in Stamford mistrusted and just never got around to selling.

Tens of billions of lost sales later, what is Xerox doing about it? Not enough it seems. Apparently they tried overbooking revenues, but the SEC recently discovered their little accounting trick and forced the company to take a massive, negative adjustment to earnings for the past several years. Even so, it's hard to not feel some sympathy for the company and hope they've learned their lesson. After all, it only seems fair that, for a change, Xerox should start making a buck or two off its own mighty technology contributions to the world.

The Real Magic of Disney

Of course you will encounter lots of organizational problems as your company grows larger. But, believe me, none will cause you more trouble and more lost revenue than the slipping apart of the key functions in the business. Once isolated in their functional cocoons, it's very costly and darn near impossible to get customer people, product people, and administrative people back on the same page. That's the page that says: If all of us together don't start making more products that more customers want to buy, we're all going to be history.

The good news is that it doesn't have to come to this. Some companies, such as Toyota, simply never allowed functionalizing to get started in the first place. They weren't about to let anything destroy their customer/product vision. And a few, like GE, have even been able to transform themselves into a more entrepreneurial company by knocking down the organizational barriers and getting all employees to refocus on customers and products. Some newer, entrepreneurial companies, such as Dell Computer, have taken the customer/product connection to a radical, new level. Michael Dell's *direct model* is a revolutionary attack on the whole concept of organizing around functions. And then, there is the real magic of Disney, which I think provides the simplest and most basic illustration of all. Let's consider a few of these great customer/product examples. They will give you proven ideas for creating and maintaining a powerful customer/product vision for your own business and avoid the deadly Xerox disease.

Toyota: Those Amazing American Supermarkets

There are some large companies that never fell sway to the "functionalize everything" craze. Take a look at Toyota. Judged against any standard in the automobile industry, Toyota is simply the best car maker in the world. Their operating margins are the highest. They can assemble a car in 13 hours versus about 20 for Honda, Nissan, and Ford, and GM is farther behind. They regularly match or beat Mercedes quality using one-sixth the labor of their luxury class competitor. And a completely built-to-order car can be in the hands of the customer in an amazing week to ten days. Nobody else even comes close.

What is the secret of their success? It can all be laid to the customer/product vision of Eiji Toyoda (with a "d"), the founder of Toyota (with a "t") Motor Company. He started making cars in 1933 and had assumed early on that the car business, like any other enterprise, had to be built around customers. In 1947, as Toyota was trying to rebuild after the devastation of World War II, Mr. Toyoda made his only trip to the United States. He wanted to learn how the Americans did things. Toyoda didn't see much of interest at the giant U.S. automakers in Detroit, but he became fascinated with the new style American supermarkets. What he observed was that supermarket chains were operating in a lightening fast turnover environment where customers literally pulled products through the stores. For example, he was amazed at the rapid delivery of fresh milk from the cow to the customer at the dairy counter. He joked that it was as if there was a farmer and a cow behind every counter filling the milk bottle just in time for the customer.

With these new American methods in mind, founder Toyoda and his legendary production boss, Taiichi Ohno, decided to try this customer driven production approach for making cars. They established horizontal units, put design, production, marketing and sales together under one engineer and started a counter-revolution in the auto industry against the functional method of organizing. Under this system, for every activity from design to after sale service, the customer called the shots. What emerged was a total business philosophy that says when the customer speaks, everyone all the way back to R&D, has to jump. They called it *kanban*, or just-in-time production, and the rest is history.

Many companies rushed to install this latest Japanese management technique. Predictably, such efforts usually missed the forest and crashed into the trees. Why? Kanban is not a technique—it's a mind-set that says customers truly drive the business. You get organized at every step of the car-making and selling process, to provide the product when the customer wants it. It's like pulling a gallon of fresh milk out of the dairy counter that starts a chain reaction all the way back to the cow. Whether it's cows making milk or people making cars, the kanban mind-set produces exactly what the customer wants, and exactly when he wants it.

This mind-set makes it a little difficult to get too excited about functional prerogatives. And it makes it impossible for design people to disregard production people, and for production people to disregard marketing people, and so on. Obviously Toyota is organized. People and groups of people have specific tasks to perform. But the *kanban* culture, constantly tracking the customer, overrides the entire organization. Their famous *chief engineer system*, for example, says all new models have the same boss from start to finish. The chief engineer has enormous authority from design to production through the marketing of the new model. It's all driven by the mind-set that says that the entire company jumps when the customer speaks. This is what keeps Toyota number one—and it's what will give your new business exactly what you'll need to succeed: super competitive customer/product vision!

General Electric: Neutron Jack's Scientist/Salesman

The Wall Street Journal headline trumpeted: "GE's Latest Invention: A Way to Move Ideas From Lab to Market." The thrust of the story was how GE scientists have also become GE salesmen: "They still sit in chaotic offices surrounded by books on computational logic and esoteric journals, but now they also have to be entrepreneurial. GE is turning around the equation of U.S. business. Instead of pushing marketers to come up with ideas and then asking scientists to make them work, the company increasingly gives researchers wide berth to imagine and invent—and then shop the invention around GE's divisions.

The result: GE and its scientist-salesmen regularly and rapidly manage to transfer technology from the laboratory to the market, a transition that frequently baffles other American businesses." This story, from the early 1990s, was simply reporting on the latest in a string of stunning organizational innovations General Electric was implementing under Jack Welch.

But we need to back up a few years to get the full story. By 1980, after nearly a century in business, GE had become just another big, bloated, micromanaged bureaucracy, on the downside of its life cycle. Leading business journals were already writing about the demise of another American icon. GE had long carried the dubious honor of being called "the Harvard of corporate America." The company had single-handedly invented much of what passed as twentieth century management science. They essentially invented long range strategic planning. The GE strategy model was later popularized by the Boston Consulting Group and is widely discredited today. They pioneered hierarchical management, systematic market research, sensitivity training, and even right brain/left brain profiling of employees. They also created a highly functionalized organization. GE was a corporate think tank on how to manage or, as some claimed, how to keep it complicated! In fact, GE got it so complicated that by the time Welch took over in 1981, it was an overmanaged, muscle bound behemoth, going nowhere fast.

General Electric was clearly in need of an entrepreneurial overhaul. In 1981, it got just that. Enter Jack Welch, a straight talking GE engineer, who was not impressed by MBA theories and jargon. In the biggest and most dramatic corporate turnaround in history, he drove GE's market value from a sluggish $12 billion to become number one in the world with an astounding value of over $400 billion when he retired 20 years later.* No other company is even close to GE's market capitalization: Rounding out the top five in the current *Fortune 500* are: Microsoft at $331 billion, Exxon Mobil at $295 billion, Wal-Mart at $277 billion, and Citigroup at $251billion. When he took over, he

---

*Welch unfortunately ended his career as living proof that even great leaders of companies, who we all admire for their performance, can get damn greedy. Paid $125 million his last year at the helm, over a thousand times the average pay of GE employees, Welch still negotiated an outlandish retirement package that included a 5th Avenue apartment for life with butlers and maids and free food, and free travel for life, and . . . well, you probably know the sordid sotry so there's no point beating a dead horse or another very rich ex-CEO.

was quickly dubbed the man who wants to run GE like a small business. *Fortune* magazine said: "The scrappy CEO has mounted a radical assault on the canons of modern management—which GE largely wrote. What's happening at GE now . . . is an explicit rejection of many of the old principles. Welch has tried to infuse the company with a sense of entrepreneurship, and in doing so has become the country's most admired CEO."

Here's what "Neutron Jack" did. He flattened GE's nine levels of management, cut pay levels from 29 to 5, obliterated the massive corporate staff and got rid of all product lines that weren't first or second in their market. And, he took dead-aim at the old functional structure with GE's scientist/salesman idea to get more products to more markets faster. Instilling this concept has been an important part of GE's remarkable success. Welch recognized the inherent problems a highly functionalized company has in maintaining a powerful customer/product vision. As he concluded in his interview with *Fortune*: "Even in a horizontal structure you'll still have product managers, still need accountability, but the lines will blur. The functions will go away, if you will . . . teams will move together from left to right, from product idea to product delivery. . . ." Amen.

If GE's scientist/salesman approach can help turn around a dying dinosaur and transform it into the most valuable company in the world, you might want to take special note of this point. Making sure you never fall into the functional trap could be the best advice you'll ever get if you hope to move your fledgling company beyond a mom and pop operation!

Dell Computer: The Power of the Direct Model

Kanban has been brought to a new level in the twenty-first century by companies like Dell Computer, Amazon.com, Ebay, and B2B pioneer Commerce One. As an example, let's take a closer look at entrepreneur Michael Dell's amazing company, which he started in his dorm room while still a student at the University of Texas. As a footnote to history, while Dell was assembling and selling computers from his room, he was also violating a hundred year old university rule against "conducting commercial activity" in UT dorms. Now that Michael Dell is the third richest person in America, and the pride of Texas, we assume UT has modernized it's dorm rules in this age of student-entrepreneurs!

It seems that Michael Dell has always been a rule-breaker. Even a cursory look will tell you that Dell Computer does things differently from other *Fortune 500* companies. First and foremost, the company is totally driven by its fully integrated customer/product vision. Of course, Michael Dell is the guy who eliminated the middlemen and put his entire company into direct contact with their customers—who are primarily sophisticated, corporate buyers. He literally invented selling computers direct to customers and enabling them to custom design their purchase over the phone and now via the Internet. Talk about bringing your product and customer functions together—it doesn't get any more integrated than this.

At Dell it's impossible to be just a salesman and still expertly assist every customer to custom design his computer. Conversely, you can't be just a scientist and spend eight hours a day talking to customers. Michael Dell himself says the company's mission is to bring to bear all its human and technology resources to better serve customers: "We're always looking to see what we can do to make our customers' lives easier or save them money. It pervades every part of the company."

Like kanban before it, Dell's approach, which the world now knows as the "Dell direct model," is revolutionizing how business operates in many key areas—particularly in business to business ("B2B") selling. The Internet, which Michael Dell calls the "ultimate direct model," accounts for 20 percent of Dell's sales and is rapidly growing. Dell predicts it won't level off until it hits at least 50 percent. Dell's model of selling custom-made machines directly to buyers, gives it some hard-to-believe competitive advantages. Aside from obvious things like tons of direct customer feedback and no re-sellers to deal with, it also means Dell carries no finished goods inventory. Dell's total inventory costs are running less than 2 percent of sales. What oldline manufacturer wouldn't die for that kind of inventory management? Dell has not just taken Toyota's just-in-time game to a new level, they've created a totally new ballpark in which to play the game. When you hear Dell people say, "Our only religion is the direct model," you can believe they mean it!

All of this is pretty radical stuff when you think about it. Even *Fortune* magazine, not prone to hyperbole, calls Dell "customer obsessed." They also call it the "stock of the decade." The results of Dell's blending together of the traditional customer and product functions does appear to be good for Dell's clients—and very good for Dell. It's not only the top performing computer company in the world today, it is racking up some eye-popping records among *all* companies. According to the latest *Fortune 500* list, Dell ranks number seven in earnings per share growth (35.6% per year) and number one in total return to investors (58.8% per year) for the past 10 years. Now those are numbers any new entrepreneur could live with! Which brings us to the greatest customer/product story of all—and the *real magic* of Disney.

Disney: The Real Magic

Ever have a management course on Walter Elias Disney?* Probably not. Why would anyone want to study the business practices of a cartoonist called Uncle Walt? Of course he did create the second most recognized product in the history of the world. Coca Cola is number one and a mouse named Mickey is number two. So on second thought, and since you're starting up your own business, it just might be useful to find out what it actually takes to create the second best known product in the world.

Some observers say Uncle Walt was a lot more than just a cartoonist. And of course they're right. The fact is, he's the greatest product creator in the history of the entertainment business. The list of product achievements is long. He produced the first talking cartoon, a 1928 black and white cartoon about *Steamboat Willie*, (later renamed Mickey). He also produced the first technicolor cartoon, *Flowers And Trees*, in 1932. Through the use of multiplaned cameras, Disney introduced the earliest version of 3-D movies in 1937. Disney later perfected true three-dimensional animation through his Audio-Animatronics electronics system. The year 1937 also marked one of his greatest product achievements and the beginning of a new era in filmmaking. In the face of great Hollywood skepticism, Disney Studios released *Snow White and the Seven Dwarfs*, the first feature length animated cartoon. Fifty-five years later,

---

*Through diligent research, I located the only Disney case study we had at the Harvard Business School. It covered the long-range financing for Walt Disney World in Orlando. Of all the rich lessons to be learned from Disney the entrepreneur, long range financing strategy is hardly the place to start. But of course no one ever accused HBS of being overly practical. For dedicated Disney afficianados, I suggest two fun seminars at Disney University in Orlando: "Management, Disney Style" and "Service, Disney Style." I've attended both and highly recommend them.

Snow White still makes millions for the company every time it's re-released. *Fantasia* in 1940 was the world's first stereophonic movie, and in 1955 Disney unveiled the world's first 360-degree projection at Disneyland.

Moving into television, Disney simply created the longest running (1954–1983) prime time television series ever. *True-Life Adventure's* remarkable 29 year run on TV will probably never be matched and it single-handedly revolutionized the TV documentary. Along the way, in addition to Mickey Mouse, Disney was busy creating an entire family of world famous characters such as Donald Duck, Pluto, Goofy, and of course, Minnie Mouse. From these lovable characters, licensing rights and products like the Mickey Mouse Watch continue to fill the coffers of The Walt Disney Company. The amazing fact is, most of Walt Disney's original products continue to produce profit like timeless pixie dust. The vaults at Disney Studios contain reel after reel of pure platinum. Film classics like *Snow White, Pinocchio, Cinderella, Peter Pan, Sleeping Beauty*, and *Alice In Wonderland*, add up to a perpetual profit stream unparallelled in business. These film products alone would earn Disney a place in anyone's business hall of fame, but hold on, the best is yet to come!

The capstone of Disney's product vision came in 1955, with the opening of Disneyland in California. The number one lesson from the instant and incredible success at Disneyland was that it was way too small. Disney determined to insulate future theme parks from the tacky development of motels and fast-food joints that had rapidly engulfed Disneyland. Before he died in 1966, Disney had laid the groundwork for Walt Disney World in Florida. With 27,500 acres, it would be 150 times bigger than the Califonria property. Once underway, Walt Disney World became the largest private construction project in the United States. Under the careful eye of Roy Disney (Walt's brother) it opened on October 1, 1971. Only 10,000 people showed up for opening day. A nervous ripple of doubt went through the company. By Thanksgiving Day, the cars were backed up for miles and the biggest theme park in the world has never looked back. That first year it drew an unprecedented 11 million customers, making it, overnight, the biggest tourist attraction in the world. Today, this 43 square miles of land built on a Florida swamp, draws close to 30 million guests a year. It dwarfs the number of tourists visiting entire countries like Germany and Great Britain. Today, Disney's "dreams come true" theme parks are far and away the top entertainment product in history. The money just pours in from Anaheim, Orlando,

Tokyo, and Euro-Disney near Paris. The combined parks entertain over 100 million guests a year. Not bad for a simple cartoonist with no management education! The fact is, Disney's record of product creation and picture perfect implementation are simply unparallelled in business. Surely then, Walt Disney is a great product person—a creative scientist par excellence!

Other Disney watchers, however, call him the greatest promoter in the history of entertainment—perhaps the greatest in all business. They make a good case. In hindsight, he certainly looks like a marketing genius: A customer person through and through. The cartoons and films show Disney's magic touch in pleasing customers. But it's the theme parks that most dramatically illustrate his extraordinary care and understanding of what customers want. The opening of Disneyland in California was the culmination of a 20 year dream for Disney. In his own words, the idea came straight from a customer—himself: "The idea came along when I was taking my daughters around to those kiddy parks. While they were on the merry-go-round, riding 40 times or something, I'd be sitting there trying to figure out what I could do."* From these simple thoughts of a slightly unsatisfied parent–customer, he eventually came up with the idea for a great outdoor entertainment center for the whole family. He wasn't thinking about an amusement park or another seedy carnival. Rather he wanted to create fantasies or themes in which the customers (he called them *guests*) would not be spectators, but would actually participate in the show. The development process was slow: "It took many years. I started with many ideas, threw them away, and started all over again."† Disney had no specific business strategy in mind other than creating something fun for everyone.

It was there in Disneyland, that Walt Disney's real magic revealed itself. He loved his *products* for sure, but the one thing he loved even more was seeing the faces of his *customers* using his products. In the early days, Disney spent a lot of time in the park. He could be seen leaning against a fence, watching the children whirl around in the Teacups—with a big smile on his face. He seemed to enjoy it as much as the kids! This passion for making customers happy still works today. Disney's theme parks do exactly what Walt Disney said they should—

---

*Walt Disney World, The Walt Disney Co., 1986, p. 6.
†Ibid.

they really do make people happy! Disney said it best himself, "Give the guests everything you can give them. Keep the place as clean as you can keep it. Keep it friendly, you know. Make it a real fun place to be."* Was Uncle Walt a great customer person? A great marketeer? A super salesman? You better believe it!

Creating themes and fantasies requires perfect products and perfect service to guests. And Walt Disney understood that requires perfect employees—or as he called them, *cast members*. Employees, from janitors to Snow White, aren't service providers—they're performers, members of the cast. When they work, they're on stage. They relax and eat lunch backstage. A cast member's sole reason for being is to make the guests happy. They must treat guests with the same courtesy as they would friends in their own home. Guests with questions are never avoided, they're sought out. All this helps to keep them happy. In this very special relationship between cast members and guests, little is left to chance. Cast members are not sent out into the parks unprepared. Disney training is intense and absolutely explicit on how to make guests happy.

Disney may have been the first person in any business to really understand that caring for the customer and the product is every employee's responsibility. He certainly had no peer in making this work. In an extraordinarily frank employee pamphlet, *The Disney Look*, appearance and grooming for cast members is covered in excruciating detail. From the length of fingernails to the use of effective deodorants, it's all covered. And the opening message to employees makes it absolutely clear that commitment to Disney's customer/product vision is a condition of employment:

Each guest who makes up our audience is our boss. He or she makes our show possible and pays our wages. If we displease our guests, they might not return, and without an audience, there is no show. For this reason, anything that could be considered offensive, distracting or not in the best interest of our Disney show, even a conspicuous tatoo, will not be permitted.

The lesson from Walter Elias Disney? Keep your eye on the customer/product show. And don't be timid or afraid to demand that all your em-

*Ibid.

ployees do the same. In this environment, functionalizing is a non-issue. Xerox style warfare between *customer people* and *product people* simply doesn't happen. Employees understand that they all have products/ services to offer—and users/customers to serve. This is profoundly simple, but as we said earlier, simple ideas have a way of getting lost in the shuffle. In your business, allow that to happen at your peril! No start-up company can afford to take its eye off the customer/product ball for a second. The following graphic will help you keep this in mind.

Creating the Customer/Product Mind-Set

The real magic of Disney was simple. He was a product expert and a customer expert at the same time. A scientist and a salesman. An unbeatable combination. It's the beautiful balance between these two basics of business that made the world of Disney what it was. Focusing on both is the key. How could it be otherwise? Well, unfortunately it can, and often is, *otherwise*! There are at least three other possible styles: the Scientist, the Salesman, and the Bureaucrat.

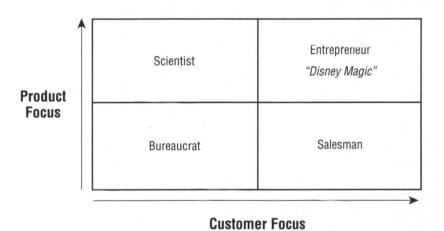

The Scientist

Ever come across people, or even whole companies, who are so into their technology or product, that they forget they're creating it for someone else to use? (Think dot-com industry.) We call this the *scientist syndrome*.

In the world of Disney, it could be the filmmaker who loves to make films but doesn't care if anyone pays to watch them. In the world of Steve Jobs, it's the computer scientist who builds the world's most elaborate machine, but it takes an Einstein to figure out how to use it. This is more common than it may first appear. It ranges from user unfriendly products, to simply unusable products, to the adding of so many bells and whistles to a product that no one can afford it. The scientist often has a peculiar disdain for the need to sell and satisfy customers. He tends to actually look down a bit on salespeople and customers. Of course, there's nothing wrong with being a scientist for science's sake—if someone else is paying for it. The trouble comes when you're paying for it—and you end up with a ton of exotic products that nobody needs or wants. That's the scientist syndrome—or loving your products but hating your customers—and it isn't exactly the focus you're going to need to grow your new business.

The Salesman

Is it possible to love your customer but hate your product? You bet it is. Most of us run into the *salesman syndrome* everyday. This is the I-can-sell-anything type. The professional salesman who loves to sell but doesn't give a damn what he's selling. Cars last year, computers this year, and Mexican real estate the next. It has probably never worked and certainly doesn't work today. The fact is most salespeople know how to sell. They're trained *ad nauseum* on how to sell. But that's the problem. They know ten times more about selling techniques than they do about their product. The number one customer complaint about salesmen today is not that they don't know how to sell. It's that they can't explain their darn product! Substituting courtesy for competence is a common variation on this theme. It's the ever courteous voice on the phone who never solves your billing problem. Or the smiling baggage attendant at Kennedy airport who announces that your luggage just went to Karachi. The bottom line is customers don't want or need more selling and smiling. The harsh fact is, nobody even wants to see a salesman. They want real product and service experts—the ones who really care about the product and really know how to make it work. For the entreprenuer about to fall into the salesman trap, forget about more marketing and sales training, and start spending a lot more time making yourself into a product expert.

The Bureaucrat

If you hate both your product and your customer, consider going to work for the government or at least a really huge company. You'll never make it as an entrepreneur, but you'll be a perfect bureaucrat. The *bureaucrat syndrome* is painfully commonplace. It's so common that some of us believe it's the driving force of most of the large organizations we deal with. Bureaucrats demonstrate zero excitement about customers or products. They seem to have little interest in even being around the people who make the products and sell the customers. This is a crazy state of affairs—but it may not be entirely their own fault. There are plenty of hardworking employees who have never talked to a customer or touched their company's product. It's a little difficult to get excited about things you've never seen. Unfortunately, most bureaucrats spend their 45 years in their cubicles passing papers and e-mails back and forth and praying for 5 o'clock to come. In the bargain, they miss out on the joy of working with customers or products—the two, really exciting things about any business. So, maybe they're bored with good reason. As a new entrepreneur, you might think you won't have to worry about the bureaucrat syndrome until you are much larger and several years into the business. But be warned, it just ain't so. In my experience, any company with three or more employees can become a raging bureaucracy. So it's best to stay vigilant on this, and make sure you and *all* of your employees, stay intimately involved with both customers and products.

The Entrepreneur—Disney Magic

How about loving the customer *and* loving the product? The entrepreneurial mind is locked on an inseparable vision of customer and product. Of course, entrepreneurs are close to their products. They're intensely interested in the design, manufacture, and usage of their product/service. They take it personally. They're ashamed when the quality is bad and they're proud when they get it right. They love their product and make no bones about it. Entrepreneurs are also close to their customers. They have to be. They know their paycheck depends on it. They never forget they need the customers a lot more than the customers need them. They push themselves and their company to their limits to meet special requests of customers. They listen carefully to customers, not because someone told them to, but to pick up any new idea to improve their product or service. In your start-up business, if a customer is unhappy, it will be a major crisis. If your customer is really happy and tells you so, it will make your day. Yes, entrepreneurs clearly love their customers. Of all the characteristics of entrepreneurial behavior, this dual focus on customer and product best illuminates the difference between entrepreneurs and professional managers. Like the craftsman of old, entrepreneurs are intimately involved in both making *and* selling. This entrepreneurial vision produces appreciation, expertise, and even respect for both customers and products. It also produces great competitive advantage in the marketplace.

So what does it take to produce such a powerful customer/product vision or mind-set? Even great entrepreneurs don't usually come to the task naturally. Creating a strong customer/product vision is most often the result of necessity. It comes with the territory in a start-up business. As we said at the beginning of this chapter, if you're going to get to day two of your start-up enterprise, you'd better figure out how to make something that someone will pay you for! A few famous examples illustrates this point.

Karl Benz

What does it take? It takes some of Karl Benz's fascination with engines, meshed with his belief that customers deserved and wanted real improvements in each new model of his automobile. The notion of turning out a new model every year never occurred to Benz. For him, the rule was to turn out a new model when you had significant improvements to offer the customers. This is quite a different vision of the world from the "planned obsolescence" concept hatched in Detroit many years later.

Sarah Walker

It certainly requires some personal understanding of what products customers really need. America's first self-made woman millionaire was a poor African American housecleaner who was losing her hair. In an effort to concoct creams and shampoos to specially treat black women's hair and cosmetic needs, she invented and marketed the first line of specialty products for African American women. By the dawn of the twentieth century, Walker Manufacturing Company had 2000 franchisees and Sarah Walker was a millionaire—by inventing and selling products she and her friends desperately needed.

Soichiro Honda

It may even take some heartfelt passion for products and customers. As a young man, Soichiro Honda was passionate about driving high-speed race cars. He was no less passionate, in his self-annointed mission, to provide post-war Japan with much needed, cheap and reliable, transportation. Designed down to the simplest of machines, his first product, the Honda scooter, still stands as a modern symbol of giving customers exactly what they want. Meeting very simple needs, very perfectly, may in fact be the first lesson of customer/product vision.

Ray Kroc

It could also require a bit of the salesman's instincts of Ray Kroc (McDonald's founder) blended with his personal obsession for delivering quality and cleanliness a million times a day. From traveling salesman of milk shake machines to product zealot who preached, "You gotta see the beauty in a hamburger" Ray Kroc epitomized the value of keeping your eye on the customer and the product at the same time. His greatest customer/product invention however wasn't the hamburger: It was the beauty of the clean toilet. We'll never know how many billions of Big Macs have been sold just because parents want to get their kids to a clean toilet—but you and I could retire on it. Ray Kroc's success came from knowing exactly what customers wanted and delivering it over and over and over again.

Estée Lauder

Josephine Esther Mentzer grew up in a poor immigrant family in New York City. As a young girl, she yearned to be one of the beautiful high society women she saw in salons and department stores along Fifth Avenue. She became a sales girl in several of those same stores until she recreated herself as Estée Lauder and started her own small cosmetics business. The company had one overriding mission: to make women beautiful. For years she personally applied her products on customers, honing both her product knowledge and her considerable customer service skills. Eventually she employed 7500 "Beauty Advisors" (not sales girls) and trained them incessantly to give the same personal attention to customers that she did. The one lifelong lesson she learned: "Women really do want to be beautiful—and helping them do that is the way to succeed in the cosmetics industry." Up until her eighties she gave final approval on all new products after testing them on herself and her friends. This intensity on customers and products has paid off. Today Estée Lauder, Inc. is the world leader in fine cosmetics with nearly $4 billion in revenue and over 15,000 employees. It accounts for an amazing 37 percent of all cosmetics and fragrances sold through department stores. Not bad for a poor immigrant girl who only dreamed of being beauiful—and helping other women to do the same!

Steve Jobs

The modern American symbol of the customer/product mind-set may very well be Steve Jobs and his user-friendly computers. Jobs is the true example of an entrepreneur who loves his product, but loves seeing it used by customers (especially school children) even more. With all the management drama that occurred in Apple Computer the past two decades, it's easy to forget that Jobs is the original "user friendly" computer guy. More than any other person, he is responsible for the revolution in computers that took them out of the esoteric mainframe world of corporate IT departments, and moved them into the kitchens and bedrooms of nearly every family in America. Steve Jobs is an American legend who understood the way to get computers used by everyone was to make them easy and fun to use. After founding three great companies, Apple, NeXT, and Pixar, with the same passion, Jobs is living proof of the almighty power of the customer/product mindset.

Kevin Grauman

And finally, does a customer/product mind-set produce growth? Ask Kevin Grauman, a South African by birth, who founded the Outsource Group in California in the mid-1990s. According to the most recent *Inc* 500 listing, his firm is simply the fastest growing private company in America. With 6000 employees and $300 million in revenues, the business has a five year growth rate of an astounding 54,330 percent! Grauman absolutely hated the government red tape and petty bureaucratic procedures he observed in the corporate world. He reasoned that big companies were spending a lot of time and money on such things, especially in the Human Resource areas of managing the payroll, coordinating benefit packages, complying with all kinds of government directives, and so on. That's where he saw the need for an outsourcing firm that would handle all these time-consuming, mundane operations for clients. So he founded Outsource Group, and he's never looked back. The company manages the entire HR back-office function for its clients and represents them as a single group in purchasing employee insurance and benefits. In the process, they save their clients big headaches and big bucks. It's obviously a winning formula—all derived from actually feeling a need in the marketplace and designing a service to expertly answer that need.

The examples could go on and on, filling this entire book. In all of these cases, the early customer/product mind-set was driven by a sense of necessity. That produced a constant interweaving of product possibilities and customer desires—a daily shifting between the scientist and the salesman. Unfortunately, there's nowhere to learn all this. You won't find it in a management course at your local business school. And you certainly won't get it working for a big company. But there is a simple, powerful way to instill customer/product vision in every employee in your new business. It's so simple, you may be inclined to pass right over it, but please don't. It's guaranteed to give everyone a customer/product driven mind-set. We call it *My Entrepreneurial Job Description* and it's conveniently laid out for you in Application 4.

APPLICATION 4
My Entrepreneurial Job Description

Walt Disney believed that everyone in The Disney Company had a definite role to play in the delivery of the product or service to the ultimate, paying customer. It is in this spirit that you should use this application. The Disney Company lays it out simply on the first day of orientation training for new employees at the theme parks. The training manual says:

> While a department may not deal directly with the public, it is imperative that each department within an organization view its customer or "public" as the person/people who actually benefit from the service

of that department. For example, at Walt Disney World, the wardrobe department's actual "client" is not the guest, but the host and hostess who will be interacting with that guest. Or, the accounting department can view their "clients" as a variety of internal departments. The people in any department might be three or four layers removed from the guest who purchases a Magic Kingdom park passport. Nonetheless, their attitudes toward service will ultimately affect the quality of service the guest receives—a real domino effect!*

In addition to, or even instead of, using the standard type job description for your employees, consider a truly customer/product centered definition of every job. The typical job description is a convoluted, five page dissertation on how many nuts you have to screw onto how many bolts per hour. Well, it's not quite that bad perhaps, but the bottom line purpose of the enterprise, making great products for great customers, rarely finds its way into a modern job descripiton format. Why not start your employees out with three questions entrepreneurs live and die by: who are my customers, what are my products, and what do I have to do to satisfy my customers? The message is very clear and very entrepreneurial: Everyone has a product or service to provide and customers or internal users to serve. This simple addition to everyone's job description won't solve all your customer and product challenges, but it may be the single most powerful tool you have to instill an entrepreneurial customer/product vision in your people and throughout your company.

APPLICATION 4-A
My Entrepreneurial Job Description

Everyone in your company, from you to all your managers and workers, has to be absolutely clear on who your customers or users are, what your products or services are, and exactly what you have to do to satisfy those customers or users. As the entrepreneur yourself it's obviously critical that you focus on these basics in your own job. However, our strongest suggestion is that you use this entrepreneurial job description for every employee you ever hire. If you want to maintain an entrepreneurial company with entrepreneurial employees, this is where you start!

---

*Service, Disney Style, Walt Disney Company, (undated) p. 5.

	Internal Users	External Customer
Who Are My Customers or Users?		
What Are My Products or Services?		
What Are My Customers' or Users' Exact Requirements? • Quality • Quantity • Timeliness • Other		

Creating a Passion for Customers and Products

The most expensive MBA in the world can't give you entrepreneurial passion. The entrepreneur's timeless adage says it all: "My customer, my product, my self-respect." The success of the business is a defining factor in their life. And they really believe customers and products are the heart and soul of the enterprise. It's not an overstatement to say they are obsessed with customers and products. This passion for customers and products will give you enormous competitive advantage against your entenched competition—particularly those big bureaucracies who think they own your market. So use your passion and instill it in every employee you hire. It's what's going to make you win!

When you have real passion for your customers and products, simple things that a *Fortune 500* CEO never even thinks about take on monumental importance. For example, customer requests get an immediate response—not "pretty soon" or "I'll get back to you tomorrow," but right now! Old-fashioned courtesy is not a rare event, it's the only way customers are ever treated. Really listening to customer suggestions changes from sloganeering to a daily reality. Individual responsibility for quality is the norm, not a pipe-dream of the corporate quality assurance program. No compromises on quality are suggested, let alone tolerated. Endless product planning is replaced by a true sense of urgency in producing real inventions that meet real needs, real fast. And if you lose a current customer, no one stands around and shrugs their shoulders. All hell breaks loose in a mad scramble to get the customer back. You don't need a Ph.D. in business to figure these things out. They're all common sense ideas—and they're things entrepreneurs do all the time.

Creating a passion for both customers and products is the driving force of great entrepreneurs all around the world. And so it should be for you and your company. There are hundreds of things you can do to create and maintain this passion. Here are several of the most important and common ways entrepreneurs do just that. We call it loving the customer and loving the product.

Loving the Customer

> *I solemnly promise and declare that every customer that comes within ten feet of me, I will smile, look them in the eye, and greet them, so help me Sam.*
>
> —Sam Walton's Employee Pledge,
> Founder, Wal-Mart Stores

Loving customers comes from seeing them as the only means of putting food on the table. It's hard to hate people who do that for you. It also comes from appreciating the people who admire and use your own creation: your product or service. It's also hard to dislike folks who admire your work. None of this means entrepreneurs are genetically more friendly or treat their fellow man better than others. But when it comes to customers, they do have a very special feeling for them. As an up and coming entrepreneur, you will have a lot of built-in motivation to love and respect your customers. The really nice thing is that every minute you spend on doing this is money in the bank. That's certainly been true for a down-home retailer from Bentonville, Arkansas: an amazing customer-friendly outfit that has become the largest company in the world—in only 40 years!

One day during the year 2001, Wal-Mart Stores, headquartered in tiny Bentonville, Arkansas, became the biggest company in the history of the world. That recession year, with sales of $219 billion, Wal-Mart galloped past its rivals for the top spot with an impressive 13.7 percent revenue gain. To really drive home the point of who's on top, the next four largest revenue producers, Exxon Mobil, GM, Ford, and GE, all registered revenue declines for the year. But there's more: Wal-Mart, just 40 years old, still covers less than half of the U.S. market, and only a fraction of the global retail market. They've gone from one store in 1962 to nearly 4000 today, and they're just getting started. As amazing as it sounds, this is a company with a lot of room to grow.

How did all this happen? How could a five-and-dime retailer from Arkansas become the biggest business ever? We've all heard about Wal-Mart's super-duper information systems and its hard-nosed purchasing. But those are not the reasons I go to Wal-Mart. And they're not the reasons why millions of others go either. After all, Target, K-Mart, Costco, and a dozen more discount chains have about the same information and purchasing systems. What I, and I suspect the millions of other customers, really like about Wal-Mart is: It's the one big company that really and truly makes you feel welcome. Like the famous Wal-Mart employee pledge quoted earlier, everyone and everything at Wal-Mart says: "We love our customers!"

Take the official Wal-Mart job of People Greeter. The idea, which came from an employee, is that when you visit a Wal-Mart store, it should be like visiting a friend's home. So there's a People Greeter to greet every visitor, at every door, of every store. Essentially what they do is smile, say hello, give you a cart and wish you a good visit. Each of the 4000 big stores must have seven to eight People Greeters. That's about 30,000 employees standing around, doing nothing but saying hello to customers who enter the stores. They don't sell, stock the shelves, check out customers, or even sweep up. They just say hello. There's no doubt the first thing any efficiency consultant or cost-cutter would do at Wal-Mart would be to get rid of all these "nonproductive" employees. And in one fell swoop, they would cut the legs out from under Wal-Mart's number one competitive advantage.

Loving the customer, along with loving the product, is the sine qua non of entrepreneurial behavior. But it becomes a cliché in so many companies. Imagine what it would be like if all your employees actually behaved as if they loved customers. It would be like . . . well . . . it would be like Wal-Mart. Of all the ways you and your future employees can show love of customer, here are four of the most important.

✔ Knowing Your Product.

The driving force of the entrepreneur's relationship with customers is the customer's reaction to his product or service. Loving your customer has everything to do with knowing (and loving) your product. After all, how can you really take care of your customers if you don't know how your product works, how to fix it when it's broken, and how to squeeze more out of it to make life easier for your customer?

Behind this broad thought, there's a very practical point to be made. No one really wants to see a salesman. In fact, people go to extraordinary lengths to avoid them. This may come as a big disappointment to the pure salesmen of the world, but it's a fact. And who do potential customers want to see? They are actually dying to see people who can really solve their problems. And that takes a product expert, not a salesman with an order form. This little entrepreneurial twist, virtually forgotten by the marketing gurus of the world, could be the most powerful sales tool you will ever have. Think of the last time you chose a doctor, or wanted to buy a car, or needed to acquire outside help to solve a business problem. Who did you want to see? An expert, of course. Someone who really knew the ins and outs of solving your problem. But certainly not a salesman—no matter how friendly he might be or how many lunches he might buy. The fact is, potential customers will clear their calendar in a second to get their hands on a real product expert. This is why *knowing your product* is the first step to really loving your customer.

✔ Responding Immediately.

The most visable difference between entrepreneurs and bureaucrats is the priority they place on responding quickly to customers. Fortunately, for you as a start-up entrepreneur, most of your competition will be just plain awful at it. Think of the last five times you made a complaint to a manufacturer. How long did it take them to resolve your complaint? Are you still waiting for an answer? And how about your last visit to a large department store or hotel, or God forbid a government agency? Did it seem the staff behind the counter knew every trick in the book to avoid making eye contact and getting sucked into waiting on you? If you had a dollar for every minute you've waited at airline counters, hotels, department stores, gas stations, on the phone with parts and service departments, not to mention renewing your drivers license, you wouldn't have to read this book. You'd already be sitting on the Riviera clipping coupons! I've come to the conclusion that most of these service people are either deaf, or blind, or have fused spinal cords which keep them from looking up from their desk.

Responding quickly to customers is a standard part of all customer service training. It's taught over and over again and nothing changes. Why? Because giving customers an immediate response is not a systems problem or a training problem. It's a deep seated problem with the priorities of the service giver. Waiting on customers is simply a pain in the neck to most people in most companies. This is never a problem for entrepreneurs. When customers are the only way to feed your kids, you don't need a training seminar to get yourself in gear. It simply wouldn't occur to successful entrepreneurs that anything could be more important than responding immediately to customers' requests, questions, and complaints. This is why Sam Walton insisted that every new Wal-Mart employee take the "So help me Sam" pledge. It at least gets them off to the right start. It's also why he put a Wal-Mart People Greeter at every door of every store. It's not very scientific, but it's the kind of customer care that's made Wal-Mart the number one company in the world—and can do the same for you in your world!

✔ Being Courteous and Competent.

"When we answer the phone, we're very courteous. That's the good news. The bad news is we don't answer the phone." These are famous last words from Ramon Cruz, CEO of Philippine Airlines, lamenting the lousy telephone system in Manila. What he was really saying was that courtesy without competence will get you nowhere. The most courteous airline in the world (which Philippine may well be) can't overcome chronic lost baggage problems and reservation systems that don't work. The opposite is also true. Competence without courtesy isn't exactly going to get you in the winner's circle either. The planes may run on time, but you're being served by the cabin crew from hell.

Entrepreneurs have a huge advantage in this department. It comes with the territory. Courtesy has a certain ring of sincerity from people who run their own shop. When they thank the customer for making a $200 purchase, you get the feeling they just might really mean it. And if the product doesn't work, they take it personally—and know exactly what to do to get it fixed. This double-barreled behavior, so rare in big companies and government agencies, is just another area where entrepreneurs and their young companies have a built-in advantage over the bureaucracies of the world.

All bigger companies seem to have sterling intentions around courtesy and competence, but it's tough. There's the old problem of functions and specializing. The nice folks who made this marvelous machine and know how it works are never the ones you get to see. The young sales clerk may smile, but he doesn't know diddly about the gas-powered garden tiller you need, or what software is really best for the kind of graphics you produce. At another level, it's just not easy to remain courteous to customers who are already screaming mad about the abominable service they just got from your colleague over in aisle 8. And it's humanly impossible to be an instant expert in computers this month and garden equipment next. No, in the larger companies you will be competing with, it's not easy for employees to be both courteous and competent. And if it's not easy, you can be sure such noninspired bureaucrats won't make it happen—especially when they know in their heart of hearts, it is going to make no difference at all to their weekly paycheck. This is the real nub of your entrepreneurial advantage: Even a little bit of courtesy and competence can give you a huge competitive edge because you will be the only place in town providing both!

✔ Keeping Current Customers Forever.

Your most important prospect for future sales is a current customer, always, always, always! The priorities are clear when your company is young and small. Losing one or two current customers is an unmitigated disaster—to be avoided at all costs. All the annual profit sits in the current customer base. So why, at *Fortune 1000* companies, does everyone scream and cheer over getting a new customer and simply shrug their shoulders if one of the current customers slips away? Why do 99.9 percent of all sales compensation systems pay a premium for new business and nobody gets penalized for losing old business? Why are the best people thrown at new clients and the 10 year old client ends up with the B team? And why, in so many companies, is marketing still the champagne and caviar side of the business while spare parts, repairs, and ongoing service feeds on a diet of warm beer and grits?

By far, the most important marketing job in any business is to resell and expand those current customers. This is not an argument against new business—just a common sense look at growing your revenues and profits. Reorders are golden. Repeat business literally keeps you alive. Unfortunately, this idea seems to lose its punch as a company gets bigger. If this happens in your growing company, you will have committed the cardinal sin of entrepreneurial enterprise. You will not only be putting at risk the most profitable piece of your business, you will be a sitting duck for every new and hungry entrepreneurial competitor around. Don't let this happen. Make sure keeping current customers forever is your first priority, not the last, as you grow your business.

Loving the Product

> *Her name is Mercedes.*
> —Gottlieb Daimler, Co-Founder,
> Daimler Benz Company

If you have to boil it all down to one thing, the single, most critical element in any successful start-up is the entrepreneur's ability to come up with a better mousetrap. The mousetrap could take the form of a breakthrough product, an innovative new service, or even a new and improved version of an existing mousetrap. But here's the catch: The final judge of the worth of your product will be the market, not you. So if you want to become a great product company, you'd better be prepared to also become a great customer company.

A famous case in point: Gottlieb Daimler is usually hailed as a great maker of engines and cars. It's true that the Daimler automobile set the world standard at the beginning of the 20th century. But in reality, he was a near-fanatic on knowing exactly what his customers wanted. It was Daimler, more than his partner and technical genius Karl Benz, who understood that knowing your customer is the essential first step in producing great products. He was technically competent to be sure: He produced the first fire engines, motorcycles, motorboats, engines for rail vehicles, and motorized airships. But he was first and foremost, a salesman who loved his product. For Daimler, the whole point of making cars was to please and even astonish the customer. Everywhere Daimler went he saw a great market for his wonderful machines. He went to Paris and licensed his engines to a young man by the name of Peugeot. He went to Coventry and made his engines the envy of Britain. He personally opened the branch in St. Petersburg where he enthusiastically, and a bit optimistically it turned out, judged the sales prospects to be enormous.

Even the great brand name *Mercedes* came about to please a customer. In the early 1900s the largest distributor for the Daimler automobile was in Vienna, Austria. This dealer threatened to switch to another car maker in France so Daimler rushed to Vienna and promised him the company would do *anything* to keep his business. As a joke the dealer told him he'd only stay with the Daimler car if the company would put his 11 year old daughter's name on the hood. And what was her name? You guessed it. Her name was Mercedes and the rest is history.

Probably no customers will ask you to put their names on your product, but then again, maybe you should. If not that, you'd better at least find another dozen ways to show you really care about what your customers want and need—and be prepared to deliver it. Here, straight from the entrepreneur's handbook, are five of the most basic, common sense, practices for loving your products and getting others in your company to love them, too.

✔ Knowing Your Customer.

There has never been a great product company that didn't give its customers what they wanted. It's definitional. Can you imagine a great product that no one wanted to buy or use? As with the Daimler-Benz Company, knowing exactly what your customers want, and actually delivering it, is the crucial first step in becoming a world-class product company. This is a lesson many entrepreneurs have to quickly learn during start-up. It's especially true if you are starting out from a strong scientist mentality.

Any artist, for example, will tell you that no one values their work as much as they, themselves, do. They will also tell you that trying to sell their first work of art can be an ego-smashing exercise. All of a sudden, what matters most is not how beautiful the artist thinks the painting is, but rather how beautiful the customer thinks it is. This gives rise to the most powerful emotion in all enterprise. The anxiety producing, face-to-face trauma of customer judgement. The judgement is aimed right at the ego of the entrepreneur. It can send you to the heights of glory or it can shatter your self-esteem. Successful entrepreneurs learn to accept this, and make it work to their advantage by becoming customer experts as well as product experts. Both of these notions—loving your work and accepting that beauty is always in the eyes of the beholder—are central to creating an entrepreneurial passion for product.

✔ Feeling Old-Fashioned Pride.

I've never met an entrepreneur who didn't believe that his product was important and that it was doing great things for customers. Entrepreneurs obviously have a strong sense of personal ownership in the products they make and the services they deliver. These are entrepreneurial givens for creating old-fashioned pride, and it's an enormous advantage you will have over your competition. The important question for new entrepreneurs is how to pass their feelings of old-fashioned pride on to their employees.

We know that employee pride in the product depends on having a sense of ownership of the product, the belief that their inputs to the product are important, and that the product is really satisfying customers. If you want your employees to have old-fashioned pride in your company's product, you simply have to pass on to them some level of your own involvement with the product. At minimum, employees have to have some measure of psychological ownership of the product. They also need to know how and why their work contributes to the success of the product. And they have to believe and actually see that the product is doing great things for customers. This means all employees should meet customers, hear their positive comments about the product, and even listen to their complaints.

Big company managers often say that pride in product went the way of most old-fashioned things—down the tube. Well, that just isn't true. What is true, is that all people in all jobs need to share to some degree in the entrepreneur's natural pride in the product. This means that one of your most important jobs will be to make sure your employees acquire some entrepreneurial feelings about the company's product. Take these things out of the equation, and you'll be in danger of ripping all pride out of your employee's work—and quite possibly the growth out of your new company.

✔ Making It Better.

Lord Charles Forte grew Trusthouse Forte from one sweet shop on Oxford Street to over 800 hotels worldwide. He knows something about entrepreneuring and how to make it better than the competition. When I first met him several years ago, he gave me the best definition of "making it better" that I've ever heard. Forte said that when his managers proposed opening a hotel in a new city or country, which they did all the time, he asked them just three simple questions:

1. Can we make the hotel cheaper and better than the competition?
2. If not cheaper and better, at least better?
3. If not better, at least cheaper?

If he didn't get a convincing "yes" to at least one of those three questions, the conversation was over. That simple system seems to have worked rather well over the years for Europe's largest hotel chain.

Most entrepreneurs, like Charles Forte, don't get all caught up in academic and consultant definitions of quality. They typically see popular concepts such as Six Sigma, TQM, and the ISO 9000 certification as a lot of bureaucratic poppycock. The missing link in many theories and techniques on quality is the word *competitive*. The entrepreneur makes his living by beating the competition. And, as Charles Forte knows, you can beat the competition three ways: higher quality, or lower costs, or both. And lower costs can be just as good a way as higher quality. This very competitive approach explains why Trusthouse Forte is equally comfortable with owning low cost chains like Travelodge in America alongside some of the ritziest properties in the world such as the glamorous Savoy in London.

In an age when the life cycle of products can be six months or less, we may have to add one more question to Lord Forte's simple list: Can we make it faster? And that leads us to the next entrepreneurial practice for loving the product.

✔ Making It Faster.

Speed is truly the entrepreneur's secret weapon. And as Akio Morita, the founder of Sony, liked to say: "The best thing about it is it's free." This should be sweet music to your ears. It's no secret that entrepreneurs love to compete with big companies. The reason is simple: Breaking the tape first is practically guaranteed!

In high-tech fields like electronics and software, the competitive advantage of making it faster is well known. But it may not be so obvious in other twenty-first century industries, especially those with long research and development cycles such as biotech. Ed Penhoet, the co-founder of the hugely successful Chiron Corporation, is one of the superstars of the biotechnology industry. He says the entire biotech market has been a horse race: "Everyone in the industry is smart so you don't get much of a competitive edge with just brains. . . . The winners are the ones who get to the finish line first with FDA approved products. In biotech speed is most important—even more important than cost. . . ." So even here, in the super hi-tech field of biogenetics, making it faster is what gives you the competitive edge. Once you're in the race, speed becomes a bigger competitive advantage than either brains or costs. This is a lesson no 21st century entrepreneur can afford to forget.

Making it faster can also separate the winners from the losers in giant, old-economy industries such as auto making. Ross Perot, that quintessential entrepreneur from Texas, really hit the nail on the head on this point. After selling EDS to General Motors and becoming their largest stockholder, he was stunned and dismayed at how slowly everything seemed to happen in what was then the biggest company in the world. He saw from the inside why GM was forever losing market share to smaller rivals. He called it GM's biggest problem and went public with this famous complaint: "I just don't get it. It took us four years to win World War II—but it takes these people seven years to produce a new Buick. Surely World War II was a tougher challenge than producing a model change in Detroit." Touché!

The real lesson here from the world's great entrepreneurs is: It's simply impossible to go wrong spending time on customers and products. To get you started now, the upcoming Application can be used to record your first brainstorming session on loving the customer and loving the product. But before you do that, here's one final thought on growing your business the old-fashioned way.

Growing the Old-Fashioned Way—
Creating More Products and Selling More Customers

> *My mind started going kind of wild at that point with all the possibilities.*
>
> —Buel Messer, Messer Landscaping

Providing more products to more customers used to be the way all companies grew. But a lot has happened since we all went to business school and got our MBAs. Today, there seems to be a lot of ways to grow.

There's the Enron way, the dot-com/new economy way, the AOL/Time Warner way, and so on. Mergers, acquisitions, asset stripping, pushing accounting rules to the limits, and outright fraud, are some of the current day favorites. So yes, we have lots of ways to grow a business today. On the other hand, some big companies have simply given up on growth altogether. The strategy here is to make a virtue out of not growing. With great fanfare, companies announce they are returning to their core business, which is really a corporate euphemism for admitting that their current strategy has run into a brick wall. Have you noticed that companies that are growing by leaps and bounds never announce they're returning to their core business? And in a classic "same clowns, new circus" routine, it's never quite explained why mergers and acquisitions were such smart strategies last decade—but now it's even smarter to do the opposite.

The old-fashioned way of growing is easier to understand. All you have to do is make more products and sell more customers. To do this, you don't need M&A specialists, investment bankers, lawyers, or accountants. You do, however, have to know the answer to a very important question: Where are our opportunities for growth?

Fortunately we have the answer, which was inspired by that all-time master of keeping it simple, Buel Messer. You'll recall that he is the blind cattle rustler turned landscaping entrepreneur in Chapter 1. It struck him one day that the most important reason to focus on customers and products is that they hold the key to all future growth of the business. Here is Bruce Messer's commonsense analysis of how to grow any business.

Current Products to Current Customers

Messer actually started out shoveling snow with his two small boys in the winter of 1980. He had a small group of customers lined up for the entire season. He quickly realized that in his existing business, his income was going to be determined by how many times he could provide this same service to the same group of customers. It didn't take a genius to figure out that the more it snowed, the more money he would make. Messer discovered the first way to grow any business: selling current products to current customers more often. Creating growth this way, which can eventually become fairly limited, requires a tremendous amount of attention to the ongoing servicing and selling of your existing customers.

New Products to Current Customers

By March of 1981, the snow shoveling business was finished and Messer wondered how he would make a living during the summer. Since he had developed a good relationship with his snow removal customers, he asked a few of them if he could mow their lawns during the summer. They liked his work and quickly agreed to employ him for the summer. So, Messer discovered that another way to grow his business was to sell a new service to his satisfied, current customers. Growing this way, constantly producing new and improved products for your current customers, typically requires focus on, and investment in, new product research and development.

Current Products to New Customers

Once he was up and running with year-round work, he got the expansionist bug. He began to look around for new market areas in which to offer his existing services of snow shoveling and lawn maintenance. He advertised and lo and behold, he acquired several new customers in other parts of town and even in nearby communities. Messer was now pursuing the most common method of growing any business: offering current products to new customers. Growing this way typically involves geographic expansion, new distribution channels, exporting, and so on. It requires a heavy dose of solid marketing and selling.

New Products to New Customers

Finally, Messer hit his stride and became a full service landscaper. What it meant was developing completely new products and services for new, large corporate and government clients. Managing tree farms, creating large tracts of shrubs, buying land-moving equipment and dozens of trucks, was a far cry from owning a snow shovel and a lawn-mower. Likewise, bidding for multimillion dollar landscaping projects for government offices and corporate headquarters is hardly the same as becoming friends with a few homeowners in your end of town. What Messer did of course, was to use the fourth way of growing his business: offering new products to new customers. This avenue to growth, similar in most respects to actually starting a new business, requires intense focus on both new product development and new customer marketing and selling.

In pursuing all the possible ways to grow his business, did Messer once think about mergers, acquisitions, strategic alliances, or fancy accounting techniques? Of course not. Messer and virtually all entrepreneurs grow their businesses the old-fashioned way: making more products and selling more customers. Since we now know there are only four possible ways to do that, it isn't all that complicated. Here, graphically displayed for you to ponder, are your four options for growing your business.

Growing the Old-Fashioned Way

		Current	**New**
Products	**New**	New Products to Current Customers	New Products to New Customers
	Current	Current Products to Current Customers	Current Products to New Customers

Customers

Growth possibilities abound when you completely focus your thinking on customers and products. To cover all those possibilities, Buel Messer's simple recipe for growing the old-fashioned way is exactly what you need. In that spirit, we'll close this chapter by taking a look at a company that thinks of little else *other than* customers and products. Welcome to the beautiful sights and sounds of Taylor & Boody.

The Sights and Sounds of Taylor & Boody

When you buy an organ from us . . . you can be sure we've never built that same organ before.

—John Boody, Co-Founder,
Taylor & Boody Organbuilders

You'll find a Taylor & Boody pipe organ in the chapel at the Harvard Business School. You'll also find one at majestic St. Thomas's Cathedral on Fifth Avenue in New York City. You'll even find five of them installed in Japan. And at their wood mill and workshop, you'll find young apprentices from Germany, the center of the universe for hand-crafted organs for hundreds of years, learning their trade from two Americans, George Taylor and John Boody. This is an industry enjoying a global renaissance, and Taylor & Boody is leading the revival in the United States. There are about 40 Taylor & Boody pipe organs around the world, each one custom-designed, handmade, and lovingly installed over the past 25 years. That works out to about one and a half organs a year—and the current backlog of orders stretches five years into the future.

When I saw their client list, my first thought was about the missed opportunity at Harvard. What a shame the powers-that-be at Harvard Business School didn't have the good sense to invite Taylor and Boody to give their students a lesson on the art of loving customers and products. It's a safe bet that the young MBAs will never hear, at any business school in the world, anything even close to the passion that Taylor and Boody bring to their business.

To learn about that passion firsthand, I scheduled an interview with co-founder John Boody. The hard part of interviewing Boody was finding him. Just over the Blue Ridge mountains, a half hour down county highway 254, and then five miles east on route 708, I found myself in the most beautiful countryside dotted with white farm houses and cows. There were few signs. I drove right past an old two story red brick school building with no markings of any kind. After seeing nothing but more cows for another couple miles, I backtracked and went to the school building to ask directions. I walked up the main stairs, opened two very large doors, and saw stretching upward through a large opening in the ceiling, the biggest, most magnificent organ I'd ever seen. Behind it was another, about half the size, but equally beautiful. I figured I had found John Boody.

The first thing I learned from Boody was that handmade mechanical pipe organs have a long history—dating back to the fifteenth century in Europe. They are among the oldest surviving technical inventions in the world. Many, built as long as 400 years ago, are still in regular use and are revered for their superior aesthetics and dependability. Historically, the center of gravity for handmade organs was in Europe, more specifically, Holland and Germany. But shortly after Word War II, that began to shift. John Boody explained the history: "That shift started because so many American servicemen, who were musicians, ended up in Europe at the end of the second world war. They discovered there were a lot of historically based organs still in Germany and Holland and France, and these organs had more musicality and more sensitivity than the big electric action organs that were being built in the United States. They said: 'Well, how can we get back to this music? How can we reestablish this craft in America?' Now it's completely flipped around. There are about five companies, all in this country, who are leading the pack worldwide in the quality of the large, million dollar plus instruments that are being built today."

Since George Taylor and John Boody's company is part of this elite group, an obvious question comes up. What does it take to become one of the five top companies in the world making and selling large, traditional pipe organs? Where do you even learn the business of organbuilding? I asked Boody how he and George Taylor got into such an enterprise in the first place: "George and I came at it in slightly different ways. George went to Washington and Lee in Virginia. He was a sociology major, but he was an organ student also. So he played the organ and was familiar with organ technology. The school had a Henry Irvin organ built just after the Civil War. The organ was threatened with a modernizing reworking and George went to the President of the University and said 'if you let them change this organ you're doing the wrong thing.' The President was impressed and George basically got to oversee the work that was done. That was his introduction to organbuilding. Actually we've just recently rerestored that same organ. After he graduated, George received a Ford Foundation grant to go to Hamburg, Germany and do a three year apprenticeship with Rudolph Von Beckerath, a very well known organbuilder. He got his German journeyman papers and then went on to get a Master Organbuilder rating. There are very few people who have done that—learning the organbuilding business in the German way from top to bottom. He came back to the U.S. and began working in a partnership in Ohio for an organbuilder named John Brombaugh.

"All through high school and college I sang in choirs, a capella groups, and even a barbershop quartet. I've also always been interested in making things, particularly in woodworking. I even took Shop class in school which none of the other college track kids were interested in. Of course that was great training for a future organbuilder. I liked working with wood well enough that I went to the University of Maine and entered their forestry program, which is one of the best in the country. It was good training for me, but after a year I decided my heart was really in music and I changed my major from forestry to music. I ended up getting a BA in music—with emphasis on voice and choral conducting. That also turned out to be a great experience for becoming an organbuilder. At the University I worked for the FM radio station and two things happened: First I started a program called Organ Masterpieces and I learned there was a whole genre of European organs that were original, historic instruments. I got interested in that and wondered if anyone in the U.S. was building organs that way. Another thing that happened was I was given a couple of pipe organs that came out of old Maine churches that were getting electronic substitutes. I started putting the organs together and fooling around with the parts. Because of my interest, I even managed to spend my summers apprenticing for Fritz Noack, a great organbuilder in Massachusetts. We have a saying that you can catch the 'organ bug' and I really did. There's just something special about pipe organs being mechanical and musical at the same time. I graduated from college in 1968 and was quickly drafted into the Army and went to Vietnam for 13 long months. When I returned home I got a job with John Brombaugh and Company in Ohio. Of course the day I walked in, there was George Taylor."

So there you have it. Business 101 for entrepreneurial organbuilders. It's a far cry from the management pap that business schools serve up. It's George Taylor's love of organs and his years in Germany and the United States learning to be one of the world's masters at building them. And it's John Boody combining his love and skills in music and woodworking, to give the business a worldwide reputation for the high quality of its wood and the fine decorative style of its organ cases. This is how entrepreneurs who love their products and respect their customers prepare themselves for the business world.

The next thing I asked was why and how Taylor & Boody Organbuilders got started? What was the impetus to take the entrepreneurial plunge and create their own company? Boody continued: "John Brombaugh was part of that group of organbuilders who, after the second world war, got interested in making historically based organs. They studied the old German organs and learned how to revive a craft that really had been lost for a hundred years in this country. So John was in the first generation of the revival—and George and I are a half generation removed because we worked together with John for seven years. In Ohio we did a lot of pioneering work in metallurgy, metal technology, and pipe making and kind of returned to the historic mechanical action way of building organs. That time was the perfect incubation for us because we were young and inspired and wanted to change the organ world. And we were willing to work for no money—for the opportunity to learn. I think the first year we made 35 cents an hour. We built some really good organs and a number of those organs were very influential to other people.

"We were building a big organ in Eugene, Oregon and while we were working out there Brombaugh fell in love with the West Coast. He just announced one day he was going to move the company to Eugene. John was a little bit on the crazy side, and he didn't worry about how much money he made. George and I decided we didn't want to do that. We had been starving for a number of years so we decided to try starting our own business. In 1977 we took one contract from our partnership with John as a start-up. When we started we were still young. I was only 31. It took us more than a year to build that first organ. It was very low priced by today's standards, and we took progress payments to survive financially. Of course we had a very slim organization. We actually built that organ in the garage behind my house in Ohio. George and I, with our bare hands, added on to the garage roof when we needed to set the organ upright. By the time we were through with that organ we already had secured another contract and since that time we've never, ever lacked for work. We've had one contract after another and right now we're running with a five year backlog of contracts.

"We've been very fortunate that we've had some very prestigious jobs. We built the organ for St. Thomas Church on Fifth Avenue in New York, which is one of the premier music churches in the country. Now we're going to build a second organ for them, a small portable instrument, so we'll have two organs at St. Thomas'. We've also built for Christ Church in Indianapolis, which is very well known for its musical work. The Harvard organ is a small, portable instrument. The business school has a nonsectarian chapel which has three musical instruments— a very fine grand piano, a very good harpsichord, and now a Taylor & Boody organ. Then there is the huge organ we made for Holy Cross College, which has been recorded numerous times. And of course we're very proud of our five organs in Japan.

"By now, we've kind of worked our way to the top of the heap. A lot of our contracts now come to us without any competition. People come to us and say: 'We want to buy a Taylor & Boody. When can you do it for us?' So I guess in business parlance we've developed something of a brand name. We've been able to provide the quality our customers are looking for and also the business structure that people have come to depend on. They know we will deliver the quality and service they expect." It seems clear that no matter how much business success George Taylor and John Boody attain, they remain craftsmen to the core. Like all craftsmen, they have to both make and sell. And like all successful entrepreneurs, they are very good at both. It's fair to say that they are indeed, masters at loving their customers and loving their products. So let's zero in on what John Boody has to say about their customer/product vision.

Listen first to Boody expound on the Taylor & Boody relationship with customers: "A big organ is the only musical instrument that's tied to its room. It's not like a harp or a piano that you tote in there and take what you get and then tote it away. So it's very critical that we get good spaces. We can't work with a lot of new churches and music buildings because they're so flimsy, thin walled, and just bad acoustically. So we have to work hand in glove with our customers, going out and hammering these projects into line and then servicing the instrument over the years. We always say that when you buy an organ from us, we're going to join your church or join your family. Our customers become our friends. They call us up all the time and we're in constant communication with them. Every year we go around and visit our customers, including those in Japan—and 'lay our hands' on the instruments and keep them in good condition. We oversee the constant maintenance and tuning of all our own organs. As the years go by this is getting to be a bigger and bigger activity for us as we have 40 out there now. In any event, we are exceptionally close to our customers. There's no other way to do this work.

"We've developed a motto here of 'just say no.' This is because our reputation rides on the success of each instrument. If we don't see any possibility for success for the customer, then we shouldn't build the instrument. The first organ we built in Japan was for a university in Yokohama. We were thrilled with this opportunity. They were designing a music auditorium and we went there to consult about the building of the organ. Their building design was so bad that we came back here, and with some acoustical designer friends, conceived of a building, made a cardboard model, and sent it to them. We told them: 'The building you're designing is all wrong. It's not going to be a success at all unless you do it our way—and we won't build the organ unless you do it our way.' There was a very long silence and we were sure we had lost the business. Then, they came back to us and said Okay. They changed the whole design of the building, making it very tall and open in the interior, with galleries around three sides, and so on. All things that had never been done in Japan. We built and installed a big, three manual organ for them, and today this auditorium is a very influential music room in Japan. The university is delighted and of course this was our entree into the Japanese market. I suppose if we were starving, maybe we'd have to say yes, but we've been really fortunate up to now in that we can say no. The bottom line is people don't just buy our product, they buy Taylor & Boody. Of course the product has to be good but all that aside, when people are looking to purchase a very high dollar item they have to be able to look you straight in the eye and know you can get along. They have to like you and they have to trust you."

John Boody could talk for days about the Taylor & Boody approach to their product. Here's a sample: "We're a craft business. We're not a manufacturer in the sense of someone who makes toasters, honing their product and turning it out one after another. George and I, and everyone in our company, are essentially hand-craftsmen which is a very unusual thing in this day and age. We know the music that we have to play on these instruments. And we know what it takes to make the pipes work really well. And we've become very well known for our architectural ability to do the designs, the moldings, the carvings, the very look of the instruments. You have to couple the musical training with the craftmanship to build a great musical instrument. Of course this is all very labor intensive. Ninety-five percent of our costs are directly in labor—hand work. There's no production line. Every organ is handmade and custom-made. When you buy an organ from us, like the big one you see out on the shop floor now—you can be sure we've never built that same organ before."

The process of organbuilding is both time-consuming and incredibly demanding. To illustrate, here's Boody's description of just one of the important steps—the preparation of the wood: "We cut all our own timber and saw our own lumber. Because a pipe organ is a big wooden machine, we found early on if we didn't have strict control of our materials we couldn't get the quality we want. So now we control the preparation of the wood from start to finish. The drying is very critical and we have a dry kiln so we can dry our wood to specification. We have our own wood storage warehouse at our mill so we can keep wood over a long period of time, which gives us very good stability and very good quality. We're known now worldwide for the quality of our wood and we actually supply about ten different organbuilders around the country with our surplus, so the wood business has become sort of a sub activity of our organbuilding business."

After all this tender loving care, it's not surprising that Taylor & Boody's end products are simply awe-inspiring to look at and listen to. As I was leaving the interview with Boody, he handed me a CD titled *Great Organs Of America: Modern Landmarks*. This was obviously something pretty special. He explained: "This is a recording of the largest organ we've built. It's at Holy Cross College in Massachusetts. Listen to it. I think you'll like it." I did listen. Several times. Even to my untrained ear, it was glorious and powerful. I can only imagine what it must sound like live. There was a printed message on the CD's inside cover from George Taylor and John Boody: "The Holy Cross Organ represented a pioneering effort to construct a large contemporary organ conceived in the high Renaissance tradition of Dutch organbuilding. The organ's main case is 32 feet high and 16 feet wide. Together with its 3822 pipes, 12 windchests, bellows and Rückpositiv case of solid American white oak, it weighs some 9 tons. Building The Holy Cross Organ was a daring adventure. From the outset it has been a challenge to builder and player alike in understanding a great tradition. From a builder's perspective this organ presented, above all, an opportunity to enter a world of rarely-heard sounds and practice our craft on an unprecedented scale. The rewards have been great."

And indeed they have. George Taylor and John Boody, master organbuilders and new millenium entrepreneurs, are living proof that a small company can do great things in the world. When you consider the customer/product vision for your own company, remember the Taylor & Boody example. You're going to need the same passion for customers and products to survive and succeed in your own entrepreneurial venture. To help keep this in mind, we'll close with one of the most powerful statements of customer/product vision I've ever found. Here are the words of George Taylor and John Boody at the dedication of their 24th organ in 1994:

> In conclusion, one may well ask why we build organs in an age which is ever less interested in objects of lasting worth. Obviously the construction of traditional musical instruments is an anachronism in our time. Not only is a fine organ difficult and time-consuming to build, when compared with machine-made goods, it is costly indeed. Furthermore, learning to play an organ requires years of devoted practice. Given these facts, it is tempting to settle for less expensive alternatives to the traditional organ. But the truth remains

that there is a value to the work done by human hands which is sacred. The spirit of those who have contributed to this organ will breathe through its music, a message of peace and goodwill. Herein lies the real meaning of this investment. In return may it bring to life the musical treasures of ages past together with the talents of our time. Let it stand as a sign to future generations of our confidence and faith in God who has blessed us so richly.

APPLICATION 5
Great Ideas for Loving Customers and Products

Application 5 is designed to give you a jump start—even a mighty leap forward—in keeping customer/product vision alive in your entrepreneurial venture. Whenever and however you plan to begin your business, you can get started now on the lifetime road of loving customers and loving products. As you tackle Applications 5 and 6, use the following questions about customers and products to get your entrepreneurial juices flowing.

- Are you overfunctionalized or in danger of becoming that way? What can you do to prevent this from happening?
- How clear are your employees on who their customers are, what their products are, and what it takes to satisfy those customers?
- How can you use the four key practices in Loving the Customer discussed in this chapter?
- If you significantly raise your company's focus on customers, what would the major effects be?
- How can you use the four key practices in Loving the Product discussed in this chapter?
- If you significantly raise your company's focus on products, what would the major effects be?
- How good are you and your employees at focusing on your customers and products "with obsessive consistency?" Do you in fact love your customers and products?

Here's a final suggestion that might help you and your employees maintain your focus on customers and products over the long haul. Hold monthly brainstorming sessions using Application 5-A as the format. One hour on finding new ways to improve what you do around customers and products could be the most valuable hour you spend each month. It's a simple way to maintain your customer/product passion—and give you a constant source of great ideas.

APPLICATION 5-A
Great Ideas for Loving Customers and Products

Great ideas abound when you focus on *customers* and *products*—the two most important words in business! A few ideas may have been around for a while waiting for a champion. Many will come from customers, competitors, and frontline workers. Others may come to you in the next five minutes. It's worth the effort. As the leader of the company, creating a passion for customers and products may be the most important job you have.

Great Ideas for Loving the Customer   **When**

1.

2.

3.

Great Ideas for Loving the Product   **When**

1.

2.

3.

APPLICATION 6
Growing the Old-Fashioned Way

There are only four possible ways to grow or expand any business. Where are the major opportunities for growth in your new, entrepreneurial venture? Identify the most promising actions you can take. Remember, there are no other ways—this is it! You should use this application over and over again, every time you want to come up with new actions to grow your business.

	Current	**New**
New	New Products to Current Customers	New Products to New Customers
Current	Current Products to Current Customers	Current Products to New Customers

Products (row axis label)   **Customers** (column axis label)

Actions   **When**

1.

2.

3.

4.

CHAPTER

3

High-Speed Innovation

When Your Life Depends on It

Anybody can be innovative if his life depends on it.
—Akio Morita, Founder, Sony

A landmark study of California companies found that the cost of innovation, as measured by new products and patents, is an astounding 24 times greater at large companies than small companies. If you're the CEO of a giant bureaucracy, this statistic could keep you awake nights. If you're a start-up entrepreneur, it's the best news you'll ever hear.

The examples of new, small companies riding to success on the wings of their own innovative actions could fill this entire book. But few people today need stories or statistics to convince them that speed and creativity are major competitive factors in our global economy. The evidence is indisputable that young, entrepreneurial companies can and regularly do, simply beat the socks off their larger, more mature competitors. And almost always, their number one competitive advantage is that they move faster and they're more creative than their larger rivals.

Akio Morita, the founder of Sony, Japan's most innovative large company, called moving quickly the entrepreneur's secret weapon. He went on to say that the really nice thing about it is, it's virtually free. Most things companies do to create competitve advantages cost a lot of money. But it doesn't take money to make decisions a little faster than your competition, to try new ideas before anyone else, and to operate day in and day out with a sense of urgency. Morita also believed that innovation and fast action are natural human reactions to facing a crisis or being challenged. He called it being obsessed with survival. Morita learned this from his own experience in post-war Japan. He saw that all people, and all companies, can move quickly and be creative if their survival depends on it. It's a lesson he never forgot. And it's the central lesson you need to learn to create and maintain high-speed innovation in your new company.

Most people think that Sony's first product was the transistor radio. Hardly. In Japan in 1945, products had to be much more practical. Akio Morita was a young, returning lieutenant from the Japanese Navy. He obviously had to start looking for a new career. What he and everyone else discovered upon returning from the war was shocking. Tokyo was a devastated, burned out city after 400 straight days of allied bombing. There were no jobs, no money, no raw materials to make anything, and little food. Surviving was a day-to-day challenge. In this chaos, Morita thought that making something to sell or barter might be the best thing he could do. He and a small band of friends asked themselves: "What can we possibly make that the Japanese people still need and will buy?" Someone mentioned that everyone was still going to eat rice. But they weren't farmers, they were unemployed engineers. The group eventually came up with the idea that people would need something to cook their rice in—so they decided to try to make an electric rice cooker. But they faced an immediate problem. There was no finished metal available anywhere. Then they remembered all those American B-29 Superfortress bombers that had flown thousands of bombing missions over Japan. The B-29s had American fighter escorts which, because of the great flying distances, had to carry extra fuel tanks under their wings. Before returning to their bases on Okinawa and the Philippines, the fighter pilots would release the empty, extra tanks to fall to the ground. So in fact, there was a lot of available metal all over Japan. The group scavenged the hills around Tokyo and brought back all the fuel tanks they needed. They heated them, cut and reformed them, and added an electric wire. Voilá! Sony had its first product: A Japanese rice cooker made from the fuel tanks of American fighter planes!

Sony's first high-tech product came in 1950. Morita wanted to make a giant leap forward and get into more sophisticated products. He was keen to try magnetic tape which he reasoned he could at least sell to the Ministry of Education for classroom use. Again he encountered a major roadblock in raw materials. There was no plastic available in Japan and making recording tape without plastic seemed impossible. Morita and his colleagues tried cellophane but it didn't work. They tried standard newsprint and found it was more stable. On their hands and knees, Morita and his team cut long strips of the paper. They coated them with ferric oxide, a compound they found at a local chemist—and lo and behold—it recorded sound. By 1965, just 15 hectic years later, this little known firm in Japan had gone from making recording tape from newsprint to becoming the great IBM's main supplier of magnetic computer tape.

Morita always chafed at the criticism that Japan is a nation of imitators, not innovators. And who could blame him? Sony has produced thousands of great product innovations over the years. In any event, Morita knew a thing or two about high-speed innovation. He described it this way: "It is said the creativity of the entrepreneur in Japan no longer exists. I disagree. Big companies like Sony are doing all they can to think small. From a management standpoint, it's very important to know how to unleash people's inborn creativity. My concept is that everybody has creative ability, but very few people know how to use it. So we are trying to promote innovation within our own large company by the way we manage. It's the only way to stay competitive."

Which brings us back to the powerful, most basic lesson of Morita: Innovative action is not a mark of genius. And it's not a skill you learn in management school. It is a normal human reaction to crisis and challenge—and it can disappear in a hurry if people and organizations lose their sense of urgency and crisis. In your own organization, your gravest threat may not actually come from your competition—it may come from your own growing bureaucracy and self-satisfied complacency. Recognizing these internal threats, and knowing how to beat them off has to be your first line of defense in keeping high-speed innovation alive in your company. Of course you can do it. After all, anyone can do it if their life depends on it.

The Seven Deadly Sins Against High-Speed Innovation

Everything that can be invented has been invented.
—Charles H. Duell , Director,
United States Patent Office, 1899

Charles Duell is one guy you wouldn't want running your new product development unit. From hiring "Mr. Duell" types to letting your company become a bumbling bureaucracy, there are a lot of ways to kill innovation and action in your business. We call them the *deadly sins,* and here are seven that you should avoid like the plague.

✔ **I'm Okay, You're Okay.**   Mr. Duell's "I'm okay, you're okay" complacency is at the top of the list. Insisting we're all okay breeds terminal inaction for companies in the heat of competitive wars. Mr. Morita's point is, we're *not* okay, we're *never* okay! Crisis and stress may have become politically incorrect words in modern management thinking, but the fact remains that more gets done in an hour of crisis than in a month of complacency.

✔ **One Best Way—Silencing Workers Forever.**   If you really want to kill off innovation in your workers, there's no better way than to instill a one-best-way-to-do-the-job mentality in your company. This ranks as the original sin of modern, scientific management.

✔ **Out of Touch with Customers and Competitors.**   There are three proven sources of great ideas for any business. The first source is your own company—your people, your ideas, and so on. The next two sources, however, are external: your customers and your competitors. If you're out of touch with customers and competitors, you'll be missing two-thirds of the great ideas for your business.

✔ **Centralized Everything.**   Centralizing everything is the one-best-way approach applied across the entire company. It's the death knell to employee autonomy and experimentation. Whenever and wherever it's applied, you can be sure that the trade-off is going to be innovation and fast action.

✔ **Research Labs in the Woods.**   This is the Xerox story—and the millions that get wasted by corporate scientists toiling in idyllic research centers. Remember this frightful quote? "The cost of innovation is 24 times greater at big companies than small ones." Maybe all those stories about inventors in garages are true after all. And just maybe, the lab in the woods is the last place you'll ever find high-speed innovation.

✔ **Let the Marketing Folks Take Over.**   Here's the opposite extreme to the Xerox "Lab in the Woods" mess. Marketing and sales people always complain about "engineers in ivory towers" so why not turn product innovation over to them? Great idea except for one thing— they don't have an ounce of deep product knowledge in their bodies. They'll give you bells and whistles, but no product breakthroughs.

✔ **Senior Management Disconnected.**   Finally we come to the biggest deadly sin new entrepreneurs absolutely have to avoid. It's harder to avoid than you might think. The road from entrepreneurial innovator to managerial control freak can be a short one. The bottom line is: If you disconnect yourself from the innovative processes and potential of your new company, the game will be over before it's even begun.

Let's fast-forward now from post-war Japan, and the deadly sins, to an amazing example of high-speed innovation, going on as you read this, in the amazing land of Iceland. Dr. Kari Stefansson and his band of 300 genetic researchers are racing against time to find cures for the world's 12 major diseases. They are living proof that entrepreneurial innovation can and often does come from the most unexpected places.

Decoding the Viking Gene Pool

We are studying the most sacred information that exists. The information that goes into designing you.
        —Kari Stefansson, Founder,
            deCODE Genetics

In 1980 there was not one biotech company in the world. Late in that year, the U.S. Supreme Court ruled that genetically engineered organisms are patentable—and one of history's most important, fastest growing entrepreneurial industries was born. Today there are over 1000 biotech firms around the globe. *Fortune* estimates biopharmaceuticals will soon surpass the traditional pharmaceutical industry's total worldwide sales of $250 billion. And that doesn't even include the biggest potential market of all for biotech—agriculture. This is the ultimate *high-tech/high-touch* business, and for more than 20 years the venture capital has poured in and the pace of entrepreneurial start-ups has been staggering.

The biotech revolution is now moving from childhood to adolescence, or in our terms from the start-up phase to a period of sustained high growth. It's been a story of tiny, scientist/entrepreneur led firms literally stealing the market from right under the nose of the world's mature, cautious, and slow moving pharmaceutical industry. By all rights, the world's giant pharmaceutical companies, with their very deep pockets and a hundred years of global experience, should own this new market. But they don't. The owners are companies no one had even heard of 15 years ago like Genentech, Amgen, Chiron—and now deCODE Genetics, a fabulously interesting and innovative member of today's biotech elite, founded in that far away Viking land called Iceland.

Iceland is one of the most homogenous populations in the world. It's made up entirely of the original Vikings from Norway and a few Irish slaves they brought with them in the 9th Century. There has been virtually no new migration into Iceland since then. This twist of history is at the heart of Iceland's greatest entrepreneurial company, deCODE Genetics, one of the fastest moving and most innovative companies I've ever come across.

deCODE Genetics and its founder Kari Stefansson have certainly received great press. *The Wall Street Journal* headline read: "If This Man Is Right, Medicine's Future Lies In Iceland's Past." The *Financial Times* in London reported: "Iceland Cashes In On Its Viking Gene Bank." The *New Yorker* ran a full length feature article titled: "Decoding Iceland" with this lead-in: "The next big medical breakthrough may result from one scientist's battle to map the Viking gene pool." What's all this noise about? And just who is Kari Stefansson? And how did this happen in little Iceland, a country with a grand total of 270,000 people?

Well, here's the scoop straight from Reykjavik, Iceland, where Stefansson graciously submitted to a long interview on a very cold January afternoon. (The Icelandic people are always wonderful, but if you ever visit their country in the dead of winter, you'll find out why nobody has immigrated there for 1100 years.) To put the story into some context, it's worth noting that Kari Stefansson has become Iceland's richest person in just the six years since he left his post at Harvard Medical School. He's gone from living on a professor's salary to an estimated net worth of $400 million today. This is because his start-up firm has become Iceland's most valuable company with a market valuation of approximately $1.5 billion. Not bad for six years effort. Of course, the underlying asset driving deCODE Genetics' amazing success has been over a thousand years in the making.

That asset is Iceland's unique, homogeneous population. There are pockets of inbred populations around the world, but there is only one country, Iceland, with an entire population of homogeneous families. In fact it's the only country in the world that prints its phone directory by people's first names! As the geneology is incredibly well documented all the way back to 874 A.D. and there has been no new migration since, Iceland is a geneticist's dream laboratory. The whole premise that deCODE Genetics is based on is that the only way to discover the genetic basis of complex diseases like cancer, Alzheimer's, schizophrenia, and multiple sclerosis, is by finding the genetic mutations in a homogeneous population, thereby eliminating the wide genetic variability found among different racial and ethnic groups. Only by comparing the DNA of people with the particular disease to very similar people who don't have the disease, can we hope to isolate the disease causing genetic mutations. Iceland is by far the best place in the world to do this. Not only is Iceland's population uniquely homogeneous, the country has also maintained extensive genealogical records dating back to the Viking sagas, has a high quality health care system, and serendiptiously has accumulated an extensive bank of human tissues from biopsies and autopsies. On top of this, scientist/entrepreneur Kari Stefansson has assembled 300 top genealogists, geneticists, and DNA researchers in Reykjavik to work for him. They have identified and are currently working on finding the critical genetic mutations for 12 very tough diseases. Stefansson is therefore sitting atop an array of priceless and unique assets for unlocking the secrets of the world's major diseases. They are also assets that make giant pharmaceutical companies drool and bring the international investment community pounding on the door. It's one of those rare and happy intersections in life of doing something really great and being able to make an honest buck at it.

Like so many great entrepreneurs I've interviewed, Kari Stefansson is passionately articulate about his mission. Listen to his description of what deCODE Genetics is up to: "Let's take my discipline which is genetics. I mean what is genetics? Genetics is the study of information that goes into the making of man, and the flow of this information between generations. It is basically pure bio-informatics. We are studying the most sacred information that exists. The information that goes into designing you. So you could argue that what we are studying is the quintessential 'IT.' And what we basically do is that we gather very, very large amounts of data on genetics, and we put it into the mechanism of modern informatics. And what we have done is that we have sort of approached our society as a system of data—that we then mine with the use of the informatics technology. It is by far the most powerful way of looking for new knowledge in medicine and new knowledge in biotech and it has worked wonders for us. And we are convinced that this is going to be the mechanism whereby we institute a new revolution in medicine.

"One of the things that you have read about a lot or seen a lot in the media in your country, is the discussion of the Human Genome Project. This is Francis Collins and Craig Venter and all of those guys. Now Collins is very bright and he has been a wonderful leader of the Human Genome Project. But that project is focused on sequencing the entire system of the human genome. And once you have done that, how are you going to turn those data into knowledge? And that is where a company such as ours, deCODE Genetics, comes in. We take this human genome data, and look for the correlation between variances in the genome and variances in human nature. Variances like specific diseases, health problems, longevity, and so on. So we are in an ideal position to actually use the human genome data. We can plough into it and we can deliver knowledge that can be turned into solutions. We are already doing this in fact.

"The basic approach to what deCODE Genetics is doing, is to look at the society as sort of a system of information. And the Icelandic society has an advantage when it comes to that. One of the principal advantages is the wealth of knowledge on genealogy here in Iceland. I have the genealogy of the entire nation going 1100 years back in time on our computer database. If you think about human genetics as the study of the flow of information, what the genealogy gives you are the avenues by which the information flows. And therefore it allows you to sort out what information goes where, what are the consequences of this variance and that variance. So we have an extraordinary resource in this genealogy database. Another resource we are beginning to construct these days is a centralized database on the health care of the entire nation. So you have the genealogy, which basically tells you who is related to whom, and then you will have the health care information on everyone. Then you can begin to figure out exactly what is inherited and what is not, what is transported and what is not. So I think that we are in a particularly interesting position in an exciting field and in exciting times—and we have exactly the right data."

By this point in our discussion, it was clear that Kari Stefansson and deCODE Genetics were on to something significant. But the question that hadn't been answered was how this little miracle of a company got started? I knew that Stefansson's last job was teaching at Harvard, and while prestigious, that seemed a very distant reality from the man I was facing—this world-class entrepreneur and the wealthiest man in his country. So I asked him how all this had happened in so short a time? Stefansson's personal story goes like this: "It happened in the following manner: I was a professor at the Harvard Medical School and was sitting in Boston studying the genetics of multiple sclerosis when I first started to see the confluence of two very important things. One of them was the times—technology was being produced to allow one to study genetics in a systematic manner. And then I began to think about these incredibly important qualities of the Icelandic nation that would be possible to mine once this technology was in Iceland. Secondly, I began to sense the danger that foreign companies and universities would start to come to Iceland and do 'helicopter science.' By that I mean transporting the material abroad from Iceland for the studies.

"So I started to look at the possibility of setting up a facility in Iceland. And I put together a business plan and it took me a few weeks to raise enough money to start the company. We raised $12 million. We started the company in the fall of 1996—and now the company is valued at about $1.5 billion. So things are going very nicely. When we started our company we had 20 people and now we have in excess of 300 people. In February of 1998, we signed the largest corporate deal that a biotech company has ever signed in genetics. The deal, with Hoffman La Roche in Switzerland, is valued between $200 and $300 million. This is basically a research alliance where we are working on the discovery of genes that cause 12 common diseases. We share the intellectual property with Hoffman La Roche and they pay us royalties and licensing fees and fund the work. So things have gone very nicely."

It's always interesting, I think, to find out what people think is responsible for their entrepreneurial success, and especially those people who don't really consider themselves entrepreneurs or even businesspeople. Kari Stefansson fits this bill so I asked him, "If a person who didn't know anything about starting a business, let alone a biotech business, came to you and asked the reason for your pretty amazing success, what would you tell them?" The surprising reply, "What I think characterizes the successful entrepreneur, or the successful start-up which is the extension of the entrepreneur, is in addition to having a good idea, and willingness to work extraordinarily hard, is the love of the risk. It's not only that you shouldn't spend an awful lot of time avoiding risks, I think you should actually seek out the risk. It's the quintessential component of this—to thumb your nose at the risk. Sure everyone is a little bit afraid of risk. But what gives you the courage to look the risk in the face—is the fact that you believe in your idea. First you have to put together an idea or a concept. And the concept has to be good and you have to believe in it. Once you believe in your concept, the risk that others perceive is basically irrelevant. It isn't there. Because you believe your idea is so great, you'll be able to go through anything.

"But it is also the willingness to sacrifice everything for what you're doing. And it's not because the amount of contribution you can make is in sort of a linear correlation with the amount of time you spend on it. It isn't. There is an exponential contribution when you begin to live the concept, rather than just work on it. You elevate yourself up to a higher level. You begin to see things in a way that no one else sees. You begin to understand in a way which no one else understands. I think it is the question of being able to put all of this intensity into it. And if you cannot do that, if you don't do that, nothing is going to come from even the best of ideas. Nothing can possibly come out. This is the modern crusades. This is the modern Viking, you know. You go in and sacrifice everything. And if you have a good concept, and you have good people, you come out a winner. If you don't the first time, never mind. If you are still consumed by your work, the following morning you rise out of the ashes like the Phoenix, and begin again anyway."

I also wanted to get Stefansson's thoughts on our notion of the organization life cycle. This should be particularly relevant to a company so dependent on maintaining its speed and innovation. Stefansson thought for a moment and answered, "Everyone has to face this. And I will tell you, this is a particularly difficult problem for a discovery based company like ours. Because the fact of the matter is, chaos is essential for the creative process. Of course I know this is the opposite of 'good managment,' but we must find the way to remain creative. I'm going to tell you a secret, which shows the importance of failing to do this. The only reason the biotech industry exists today, is that the pharmaceutical industry failed so terribly at doing this. We exist because the pharmaceutical industry has been incapable of maintaining a creative spirit within their labs organizations. I recognize the difficulty of doing this if you grow beyond a certain size, but these are exciting challenges you must deal with. I am absolutely 100 percent convinced that we can succeed at it, but it's going to keep us on our toes. I am already thinking that in our 'stuff,' because of this very problem, we may spin off new projects into small, separate companies to try to maintain this creative spirit which we know is so much easier to maintain in the smaller organization."

The following Monday I took up Kari Stefansson's offer to visit his offices and the marvelous lab he was so proud of. Joining me was my partner in Iceland, Arni Sigurdsson, and his associate, Olli Olafsson. Our tour guide was Laufey Amundadottir, who has a Ph.D. from Georgetown University and was doing research on breast cancer at Harvard before she returned to Iceland to join deCODE. She is currently the division head at deCODE for cancer genetics and personally runs the subprojects on lung cancer and prostate cancer. The first stop on the tour was the work station of Thor Kristjansson, deCODE's senior programmer and the architect of the firm's genealogical database. After a few introductory comments, he suggested a simple demonstration might be the best way to understand his job. He turned to Olli Olafsson, a complete stranger to him of course, and said, 'Let's see how you and I are related. What's your complete name and date of birth?" Olli told him and Thor typed it onto the screen:

Olafur Thor Olafsson–26, 11, 1953

Next he typed in his own name and birthdate:

Thordur Jon Kristjansson–03, 04, 1965

Then he clicked on a few icons and the page began to scroll with separate columns of the names and birthdates of generation after generation of both his and Olli's direct line of ancestors until—bingo! A single name popped up, centered in a box, above the two lists:

Jon Thorsteinsson–born 1687/died 1762

Just beneath the name and dates were a couple of indecipherable lines of Icelandic, obviously giving some details about great, great, great, great, great, great, great, great, great, great grandfather Thorsteinsson. "There," Thor proudly announced, "is my and Olli's most recent common ancestor!" Olli almost fell over. My partner Arnie was beside himself. And I, who have spent three decades trying to construct my own family tree back just two or three generations, stared at the screen in stunned silence. The computer had jumped 313 years and 11 generations back in 10 seconds. Laufey, our guide and cancer expert, simply said, "This is why Iceland is a good place to do genetic research."

High-speed innovation is obviously the name of the game in biotech. Kari Stefansson knows his company is racing against time— with an insatiable need for innovation. He and deCODE Genetics have these two qualities, speed and innovation, in spades. And what about you? Coming up next are the critical steps you can take to ensure you and your company will have them too. We call them the Golden Rules of high-speed innovation.

The Golden Rules of High-Speed Innovation

Akio Morita said that high-speed innovation is the entrepreneur's secret weapon. So as a start-up entrepreneur, the key question becomes how can you make sure that high-speed innovation is working in your new company? What is it really that creates and drives such behavior? And if you have it yourself, can you pass it on to your employees? These are critically important things to know. Fortunately, unlike decoding the human genome, entrepreneurial practices are not so complicated. At the heart of all high-speed innovation, are just two golden rules: feeling the necessity to invent and having the freedom to act.

Sony may be Japan's most innovative big comany, but the world champion in this category has to be the Minnesota Mining and Manufacturing Company, known around the world as 3M. This great company has shown the world that entrepreneurial speed and innovation can be maintained—even in a *Fortune 100* company. From the beginning in 1906, when six miners invented sandpaper to avoid going bankrupt with their worthless gravel pit, this has been a business built on a single-minded strategy—to grow by inventing new products year after year. And do they ever! 3M has the highest percentage (around 30%) of new product revenue of any large company in the world. They define *new products* as those invented within the past five years. With $16 billion in revenue and 58,000 different products, this is a tremendous record. How does 3M do it?

It's important to note, up front, it isn't from throwing massive amounts of money around. 3M's R&D budget as a percentage of its revenue, is only average for its industry. They do it, first and foremost, by *aiming* to do it. Their most important strategic goal each year is in fact hitting the 30 percent new product revenue target. Next, they have created an incredibly focused corporate culture, in direct support of that strategy. Their corporate culture has only one value: product innovation. Everyone in the company understands the most important thing to do at 3M is to invent something. It's the way to get big bonuses, big kudos, and most importantly it's the way to get promoted to the top. So after nearly a hundred years, the culture of innovation at 3M is pervasive. Indeed, the company is run by people who love science and products, not MBAs. This means that all senior executives push like crazy to get new products in their divisions. And if you invent a product, you get first crack at running that product business, a highly unusual and motivating factor for company scientists. In other areas of the business, you can't miss the importance of innovation. Every 3M ad for years has talked about innovation or used the tag line "Borne of Innovation." Inventing a product is the basis of the most important employee awards, including being invited to present your ideas at the prestigious 3M Inventors' Forums held around the company. And day-dreaming is an official activity. Engineers and scientists are given 15 percent of their time to day-dream about new and different products, away from their official projects. And perhaps the most important thing of all is the company mantra that "failure is a good thing." At 3M you don't get demoted or fired for making honest mistakes in your efforts to invent new technologies and products. Of course, 3M learned this lesson long ago since it was founded on a mistake—that worthless gravel pit—that forced them to invent sandpaper as the company's very first product.

If you ask 3M people for the secret of their success in inventing new products, they're likely to come up with some vague answer like: "Accidents, or failures, or mistakes." They'll tell you about the laboratory accident that led to the discovery of Scotch Guard for example. Or you'll hear about the repeated, failed attempts to make a super light glue that failed to stick permanently—and ended up as one of 3M's great all-time products, Post-it Notes. But, of course, all companies have accidents and failures. What makes 3M so different is that after their accidents, mistakes, or failures, they ask a naive question: "Have I come up with something here that anyone in the world might need?" They then put together a make-shift marketing team and go find out if anyone wants to buy this unplanned concoction from the 3M lab. The beauty of it is, the answer comes back yes often enough to give 3M the greatest record in the history of business for inventing new products and racing them to the market.

When you look at the speed and innovation of entrepreneurs, and the few highly innovative big companies such as 3M and Sony, you will see that it's not a system, or a process, or a management technique that is producing these super competitive practices. If you look very closely, and peer a little below the surface, it's clear that they are being propelled by a couple of basic, powerful forces. First, they all have a passion for, and belief in *the necessity to invent*. For them, innovation is not icing on the cake. It's the cake. And second, they are simply brimming over with *the freedom to act*. From the CEO to frontline workers, experimenting and trying new things is part of the job. It's expected of everyone. These two common sense practices, the necessity to invent and the freedom to act, are the entrepreneur's golden rules of high-speed innovation.

The Necessity to Invent

> *We did it because we believed we had to.*
> —Larry Hillblom, Co-Founder, DHL

Remember this bit of old-fashioned wisdom: *Mater artium necessitas*. If your Latin is a bit rusty, it says "necessity is the mother of invention." We've all been saying it since the time of Caesar because it's absolutely true. And nowhere will you find a better illustration of it than Larry Hillblom,* the red-headed rebel and ringleader of the young trio who invented the worldwide courier business.

Larry Hillblom was a young law student in northern California who worked as a free-lance courier on weekends. At the time there were no courier companies. Hand delivering time sensitive documents, cash, and travelers checks around the world was an individual and disorganized business. It had been done that way for decades. For Hillblom, it was also a great way to spend a weekend. He got a lot of studying done and pocketed a few bucks. On his long flights across the Pacific, he began to wonder why no company provided this valuable service. On one of his 20 hour trips he scratched out an idea to create an international courier company. He got two of his law school buddies, who were also freelance couriers, to join him. They called it DHL (for Dalsey, Hillblom, and Lynn), and they literally invented an industry.

There was certainly a need. Everywhere Hillblom went he found interested prospects. After all, he was offering something revolutionary. Business documents from Tokyo to Milan could take 10 days. From Lagos to Mexico City forever. In a world where postal delivery times between Philadelphia and New York had gone from three days by Pony Express to five days by the U.S. Post Office, overnight delivery anywhere in the world had a terrific appeal. But the three young entrepreneurs quickly learned that big banks and shipping firms weren't about to contract out their worldwide courier needs to three students who didn't have business cards, let alone a single overseas office to serve them. Hillblom saw that creating a DHL global network was an absolute necessity to getting the business up and running. In fact, they had to have most of the network in place *before* they could get the big clients they desperately needed. A half-built network wouldn't be very interesting to the Deutschebanks and Toyotas and IBMs of the world. DHL had to be everywhere they were. This meant that DHL would have to create a worldwide network of offices overnight. But how could three students with no business experience and no money possibly do this?

---

*Larry Hillblom was killed a few years ago while flying his own plane. It disappeared without a trace into the Pacific Ocean near his home on the island of Saipan. Larry shunned publicity all his life and became a virtual recluse by the time he was 40. He died as he lived—doing his own thing in his own way. I only met him twice, but like everyone who knew him, I was fascinated by this rebellious business innovator.

Hillblom told me that they pulled it off for one reason only: "We did it because we believed we had to. No network, no business. And we didn't know there was any other way than bootstrapping it, which was lucky for us. If we had spent our time writing business plans, lining up bank financing and venture capital, and using headhunters in 50 countries, there would be no DHL today." And what a network they built! They opened an amazing 120 country offices in the first 10 years of DHL's existence (1972 to 1982) which is still the fastest international expansion of any company in history.

Their method was pure *mater artium necessitas*. They started in Asia, built the company on the run, and never looked back. On every courier trip each of them took, they signed up anybody they could find to be their local partner. They weren't too discriminating. They got a taxi driver at the Sydney airport, the manager of an A&W Root Beer stand in Malaysia, a toy salesman in Hong Kong, and so on. They offered generous terms, up to 50 percent ownership, and in return the local partner had to ante up an address, a phone and fax number, and a promise to pick up and deliver the DHL pouch every day at the airport. Using this seat-of-the-pants approach, the DHL network began to grow country by country, gaining momentum with each new location. By the late seventies it was like a thunderbolt roaring across the globe. There were no plans or systems or procedures, and zero external financing. Handshakes sealed all the deals. Most important, Hillblom was able to show the big banks and other prospects an impressive, rapidly growing list of worldwide DHL locations. It worked. The business exploded and the rest is history.

Thus was born the worldwide network of DHL partners and mini-entrepreneurs—based on a level of high-speed innovation bordering on the unbelievable. Larry Hillblom (Dalsey and Lynn opted out early) did indeed create quite a network without resources or experience because he had to. In the process he also created a $3 billion company with 40,000 jobs. These things can happen when you truly feel the necessity to invent.

Right now you may be saying, "I'm not clawing my way out of the rubble of World War II in Tokyo, my company isn't looking for cures to the world's great diseases, and I'm not contemplating a worldwide network of *anything*. Anyone could be fast moving and creative in those situations. My business is more normal, perhaps even a bit mundane. Maybe nobody is going to feel a great need for speed or innovation. So where's our feeling of necessity and our sense of urgency going to come from?" Unfortunately, there's no free lunch on creating the idea that innovation is a necessity in any business. It has to come from you, the founder. You have to build it into your business. It comes from your own perceptions of the challenges you face and what needs to be done to succeed. Regardless of your circumstance, whatever your business, doing it better and doing it faster has to be made into an exhilirating race. Beating your customers' expectations and beating the competition is a noble challenge for any company. Even beating your own personal best can be thrilling—and sometimes more important than beating the next guy. For sure, you can't just sit around hoping something big and exciting happens to your business.

Fortunately, you *can* make it happen. You absolutely *have* to make it happen if you expect your people to respond with great speed and great ideas. To make sure the spirit of *mater artium necessitas* is alive and well in your new business, the following are three fundamental conditions you should create and maintain.

✔ Feeling the Heat of the Marketplace.

This is a problem most big companies don't have. Inside a bureaucracy, you can't find anybody who feels much heat about anything. From clerks who shrug their shoulders when customers complain to faceless big-shots who haven't seen a customer since 1970, absolutely no one seems to be accountable. This is unfathomable behavior to an entrepreneur. When it's down to putting food on the table, someone has to be personally accountable.

Feeling the heat has to start at the top. Visits to the headquarters of companies can provide contrasting, if symbolic, examples of this. I first met Fredy Dellis when he was President of Hertz International. He had done a magnificent job of keeping Hertz number one in the wildly competitive international car rental business. Dellis was right for the job and the place he worked, Hertz International's headquarters in London, was right for the business. For starters, the Hertz headquarters was physically located on heavily trafficked Bath Road, right at the entrance to Heathrow Airport. Heathrow is the busiest airport and the number one car rental location in the world. This is ground zero for the international auto rental business. The Hertz building itself was one of those ghastly, plastic looking, 1960s British office structures and the noise and fumes of the Heathrow traffic overwhelmed the reception room. Hertz cars were jammed into the side and back parking lots of the building. It looked more like a rental location than a corporate headquarters—the upside of which was that real customers were forever dropping in with problems or questions. The constant roar of planes taking off and landing at Heathrow replaced the quiet pitter patter of other, more stately corporate headquarters. There was no carpeting to soften the sounds and busy looking staff in Hertz uniforms were coming and going. All the big name competitors—Avis, Budget, National—were just a stone's throw away at the airport and everyone knew exactly what their competition was up to. From President to clerk, no one could miss this daily reminder that Hertz has a ton of tough competition. All in all, these were down and dirty digs, but they delivered a strong message. As Dellis himself put it, "We're in the thick of the battle here. Everyone in this headquarters knows what customers and competitors look like, smell like, and what they think of Hertz."

The last time I saw Dellis, he had a bigger job and a bigger challenge. As the new President of Burger King International, his mandate was to close the gap in the chain's eternal, and losing, market share battle with McDonald's. He certainly had a bigger and fancier headquarters to do it from. A first visit to Burger King's headquarters is indeed a stunning experience. Located somewhere outside of Miami, through what seems like miles of orange groves, an enormous pink coliseum takes shape in the distance. Driving closer you get the feeling you're approaching a grand fortress on the scale of Corinth or Persepolis. Eventually the structures square off, revealing wide drives and a beautiful man-made lake at the rear. There are actually three or four large pink buildings in a gigantic clearing ringed by citrus orchards. It's a breathtaking sight really. The interior is more of the same—a spacious mausoleum look—with thick carpeting. Everything is picture perfect right down to the manicured gardens in the multistoried lobby. It's large, elegant, quiet, and very few people are in sight. The staff cafeteria, the only place to eat for miles around, is sort of the Russian Tea Room version of a fast food joint. Eating there is definitely a different experience from the Burger King you and I know. As I said, a stunning experience—and a stunning sense of isolation from the real world of Whoppers and Big Macs.

The contrast between Hertz on Bath Road and Burger King in the Florida orange grove is striking. My first thought was, how could anyone working in this idyllic paradise have the foggiest idea of what it will take to steal market share from McDonald's and Wendy's? What in the world does this place have to do with serving thousands of impatient customers and cleaning dirty toilets at a Burger King in downtown Chicago or on Orchard Road in Singapore? When a headquarters appears completely untouched by the marketplace—by customers or competitors—you have to wonder where the innovative ideas for great new products and radically improved services will come from.

It doesn't have to be this way. It can't be this way if you expect to have a company full of fast-moving innovators. The best way to instill the idea that innovation is a necessity for your business is to make sure that everyone, from your headquarters staff to the frontline, feels some personal heat from the marketplace. Dealing with customers face-to-face, and obsessively benchmarking competitors, is the surest way to start this process. At the end of the day, all employees have to understand that their own economic survival, as well as the company's, is on the line every day. Having your and your employee's feet to the fire, may in fact be the very first necessity.

✔ Create Crisis and Urgency.

The entrepreneurs I know would not do well in a management course on reducing stress in the company. I've never known an entrepreneur who operated without pretty high levels of emotion and without a strong sense of urgency. Entrepreneurs have a tough time not getting upset when things go wrong. They also find it impossible to not get excited if things go well. They are impatient people who love winning and hate losing. This may be politically incorrect in some quarters, but these qualities, it turns out, produce a huge entrepreneurial advantage—at least when delivered in reasonable doses. Some great entrepreneurs really stand out in this category: Steve Jobs, Richard Branson, and Soichiro Honda come to mind. They are all well known as masters of instilling a sense of urgency and crisis in their companies. They are also company leaders who are unabashedly idolized by their workers. It may not always be pleasant but at the end of the day, most employees love and admire leaders who really care and don't mind showing it.

One of the best I've ever met on this score is Jimmy Pattison. He's the founder and sole owner of The Jim Pattison Group. With over US$3 billion in revenues and 22,000 employees, it's Canada's largest company owned by a single individual. As you might guess, Jimmy Pattison has a knack for getting people's attention. A couple of years ago he called my office (from Frank Sinatra's house in Palm Springs which he had just purchased) to invite me to address his annual company conference which was to be held at a beautiful site in British Columbia. Naturally, I agreed.

Several months later, upon arrival at the conference site, I noticed the printed schedule showed that I was to open the conference the next morning with my talk—at the bewitching hour of 7 A.M. At dinner that night, to make sure it wasn't a misprint (which I secretly hoped it was), I asked Jimmy if 7 A.M. was really the starting time. He said matter of factly, "Yes we like to start all our meetings by 7. And by the way, would you mind showing up a little early because I really don't like to start late." I said, "Of course," went to my room and set the alarm for 5 A.M. to be safe. I got to the large meeting room about 6:40 the next morning and noticed everyone was already seated waiting for the conference to begin. I'd never seen that before. Jimmy grabbed my arm and started walking me toward the stage saying, "I think everyone's here so let's just start now." I cleared my throat, took a quick gulp of water, and started presenting to the 300 managers in the audience. I glanced at my watch. It was 6:41 A.M. and The Jim Pattison Group annual conference was rolling! Jimmy was center aisle, front row, taking notes. I'll never forget it as long as I live.

And that's the point of course. What I later learned that makes this little tale worth telling, is that Jimmy Pattison never starts a meeting on time. He always starts them early. He's sending a powerful message. One of his VPs told me, "It's Jimmy's way of getting our attention, of telling everyone we have to keep moving—that we all have a lot to do and we can't sit around wasting time! I can tell you one thing, nobody in this company ever shows up late for a meeting." Well Jimmy certainly had the attention of his top 300 managers—and he had mine, too.

Everyone knows that more gets done in a day of crisis than a month of complacency. And few great leaps forward have ever resulted from careful planning. They almost always come on the wings of crisis. But creating a sense of crisis and urgency doesn't mean screaming at the top of your lungs (well, once in a while probably won't hurt) or threatening to fire everyone in sight. It does mean establishing deadlines, sticking to them, and as in the case of Jimmy Pattison actually trying to beat them. It also means taking it very hard if a good customer is lost. And it certainly means that all your employees know you are dead serious about making the business a success. The trick is to dole out these messages in small, regular doses. Creating tiny tremors, not giant earthquakes, if you will. It still may not please the all-stress-is-bad crowd, but the entrepreneurial message is clear: A little crisis a day keeps complacency away.

✔ Do Something, Anything, Better Each Day.

Wouldn't it be wonderful if every employee you ever hire comes to work each day thinking, "What can I do today a little bit better than yesterday?" But of course they won't—unless you tell them it's the most important part of their job. Finding a way to do something better, faster, and cheaper every day requires continuous innovation. And making sure this philosophy is worked into the daily performance of all employees could be your core competitive advantage.

It certainly was for our old friend Larry Hillblom at DHL. Getting DHL started was obviously a landmark event, but keeping that innovative spirit alive for the long haul was an even tougher challenge. DHL set out to do what had never been done before. No one really knew if it could be done, especially by young, inexperienced students with no money. One thing was certain: To pull it off, high-speed innovation had to be the very basis of the business—and it had to be built into every employee's job from day one.

But to be brutally honest, how exciting could it be to be a courier? It's all about carrying documents you never get to read from people you don't know to other people you don't know. It doesn't sound all that interesting to most people. Well, Larry Hillblom made it incredibly exciting. Hillblom's brilliant technique was to transform the company's brash promise of overnight delivery anywhere in the world, into a daily, heroic challenge for every courier in the company. Every delivery took on the aura of breaking the four minute mile. Getting the document anywhere in the world, overnight, became the ultimate challenge.

Just delivering the contents on time wasn't the only challenge. It was often getting them there at all. Nobody was particularly helpful in the early days. Not the international airlines who never seemed to fly on time. Certainly not the customs officials with their bureaucratic schedules and demands for "baksheesh." On top of this mountain of inefficiency sat the national post offices. Most resented anyone delivering "their mail" and they fought DHL tooth and nail around the globe. After hurdling all these institutional roadblocks, the real fun began. DHL couriers often found themselves in dangerous situations. Wars, revolutions, natural disasters, and even landing in jail a time or two became part of the courier folklore. So just being fast wasn't enough. A large dose of guile and derring-do was standard issue. To succeed against all these odds, local managers and individual couriers always had the ultimate authority on how to get the job done. Doing something, anything, better each day was not a company slogan. It was an absolute requirement of the job.

Of course continuous innovation doesn't just happen. People like Hillblom make it happen by sensing a need for it in all they do. He consciously set out to make a mundane sounding business an exciting, heroic enterprise. Hillblom's real genius was to involve lowly couriers in the heroic battle. To see a DHL courier racing through the streets of Hong Kong, sweat flying from his brow and a grim determination on his face, is to see living proof that companies can instill in their employees a passion to do their job better and faster each day.

The first time I met Larry Hillblom I got to see some of his genius up close. I was delivering a mini-seminar in London to DHL's Board and top 50 executives. I assumed Hillblom didn't attend such meetings. His reputation as something of an international Howard Hughes, living on the Pacific island of Saipan, was well known. He never granted interviews or made public appearances. However, about two minutes into my presentation, a youngish looking, red-headed American with a beard strode purposefully to the one empty seat at the front. He was dressed in tennis shoes, levis, and a red plaid lumberman's shirt. I'd never seen such a figure at a board level meeting, especially in London. I carried on assuming this wandering lumberjack was crazy or lost. It wasn't long before I found out that Larry Hillblom is far from crazy and is never lost. He took the seminar very seriously. He had more questions and more ideas than anyone else in the room. He got emotionally involved in every point. And when it was over he vanished into thin air. No fanfare or goodbyes. I later learned this was classic Hillblom: He periodically shows up at company meetings, gets everyone passionately involved in improving the business, and then disappears back to Saipan. I must say it seemed to work that day. And Hillblom's legacy of innovative action seems to still be working. Now 30 years old, DHL has 40,000 employees with offices in more countries than there are members of the United Nations.

Larry Hillblom's story is a lesson about raising mundane chores to magnificent challenges for every employee. For new entrepreneurs, it's a lesson worth remembering. While the occasional grand, strategic stroke is always welcome, it's small, daily innovations by all employees that will make your company great over the long haul. That's why it's so important to get everyone, including yourself, to come to work every day asking, "What can I do today a little bit better than yesterday?"

The Freedom to Act

> *The trick is to get to the finish line first.*
> —Ed Penhoet, Co-Founder,
> Chiron Corporation

If you can only follow one golden rule at a time, you'd better make it the freedom to act. Innovation without action might get you a Nobel prize, but it won't get you a customer. Most entrepreneurs agree that fast action is more important than innovation. The fact is, if you try out a lot of new ideas, if you are willing to experiment, and if you make a mistake you come right back to try again, you *will* be an innovative group. The important brand of innovation for business has never been quiet, ivory tower, analysis to eventually come up with a blockbuster idea. It has always been, and will continue to be, trying ten different things and hoping three of them work. It's very much the old story about Amoco, which for many years was the top U.S. company in oil and gas exploration. When the crusty, long-term CEO was asked how Amoco beat all the other, bigger, oil companies in finding new oil, he replied, "We drill more holes. You find a lot of oil when you drill a lot of holes."

Creating a fast moving, action-oriented company requires a high level of freedom within the organization to take action, to continuously experiment, and to make an honest mistake or two. The biotech industry is a perfect place to learn how to do this. And Chiron Corporation is the perfect company to investigate. After 20 years it has emerged as one of the big winners in the biotech race. It's the number three biotech firm in the world—after Genentech and Amgen—with about $900 million in revenues and healthy profits. Their first blockbuster product, which really put them on the map, was the hepatitis B vaccine—now estimated to have prevented millions of cases of hepatitis and hundreds of thousands of deaths. They also have products for the treatment of kidney cancer and melanoma, pediatric vaccines, and blood tests for HIV and hepatitis. Ed Penhoet, the co-founder and CEO, raised half a billion dollars in capital, acquired Cetus, another big industry star, and signed product distribution agreements with the likes of Merck, Johnson & Johnson, and Novartis. Chiron is a charter member of that elite family of biotech firms that have produced big products and big profits.

My first encounter with Ed Penhoet was pure luck. We were both speakers at a conference in San Diego. I listened to this articulate scientist/entrepreneur deliver a dazzling talk about the future of the biotech industry and I knew I had to interview him. A couple of months later, I went to Emeryville, California, Chiron's headquarters, for a tour of their famous labs and a long interview in Penhoet's office. I didn't know quite what to expect. I had never discussed business with a world-class scientist with a Ph.D. in both biology and chemistry. I knew I couldn't speak his language. I hoped he could speak mine. It turns out he can speak

both quite well. I shouldn't have been surprised. The first thing you notice about Penhoet, and others from his industry, is that they're very
smart. And I had assumed, given the incredibly high-tech nature of the
industry, that success primarily depends on how smart your scientists are.
It turned out that I was in for a big surprise: "We're all smart. In our field
we've already been preselected, in the sense that by the time you get to
people who have Ph.D.s from major institutions like Harvard, UC
Berkeley, or UCSF, it's a given that they're smart. They've gotten 99 per-
centile on their SAT scores and all the rest. In this group there are very
few people who are really very much smarter than the rest—damn
few. . . . In the beginning it was just a race. We all knew what had to be
done. We had to be able to hit the ground running and stick with it.
Everyone is now talking all about speed, right? Well, it's particularly true
for biotechnology. It's always been a race. I suspect in today's environment, with the world moving as fast as it is, everything is a race to some
degree. So I think every company has to come to grips with how to move
more quickly and how to cut out the blockages. Certainly in biotech . . .
the trick is to get to the finish line first."

Who would have imagined that speed is a more critical competitive
advantage than IQ in the ultimate high-tech business of biogenetics? After all, this is an industry where even junior staffers have Ph.D.s. Penhoet went on, "It may be that speed is even more important than cost in
the end, because really—you can't save your way into success in this
business. Do you know what I mean? The real value comes when you get
some very valuable products in the marketplace. That creates the margin
so that you can keep the other ones flowing through the pipeline. If our
history has taught us anything—after all these years of being in a horse
race—it is that you have to focus on speed as the key element in building
any organization. I could go through our product portfolio with you, tell
you who the other players were, and what we knew about where they
were at various points of time. I wouldn't want to leave you with the impression that this is a theoretical race—this is a very real race. I mean,
we knew who the other entrants in the race were. We knew when the
the starting gun was fired. We tried to keep track of where they were,
where we were, and whether they were ahead or we were ahead. Take a
number of these projects we were working on like Factor VIII, the anti-
hemophilic factor, or hepatitis B, or IGF, it wasn't, oh gee, we're racing
against the world. No, we were racing against Genentech and Genetics
Institute on Factor VIII. So, it's a very personal kind of race really, and I
think as a company gets larger, the issue is to keep that sort of personal

competition inculcated in the group. You know, it's you and me running to the finish line against each other. I think that has been tremendously valuable to us. Probably it was good for both Genentech and Chiron, for example, that we were competing against each other in several products, because it became very direct and very personal."

It would be impossible to make up a more compelling argument for the competitive value of speed and action than Ed Penhoet's own words provide. That is why Penhoet is one entrepreneur you really must listen to. Unlike many others, he's really thought through *how* he did, *what* he did. His summary on the success of Chiron completes the circle. It's all about having the freedom to act and act quickly—and how that translates into the entrepreneur's most powerful competitive advantage: "The overall competitive advantage Chiron has is speed. I'm measuring speed from the point where somebody conceives of a new piece of biology and it gets commercialized at the other end. It's one thing to move an opportunity which is obvious, but it's another to recognize a new opportunity. So I think where we have special skills is first of all, recognizing new opportunities very early on, grabbing those, and then running with them in a very aggressive manner. The large companies have difficulty competing in a rapidly moving field like biotech. In large part, it's because their bureaucracy requires too many levels of review. By the time you've educated everybody in a large organization about the advantages or disadvantages of a new program, somebody else who has a more light-footed organization has already moved the product so far along that the large company is no longer in a position to compete. Whenever people have visited Chiron over the last 20 years, the number one impression they've left with is a feeling of energy. When you walk by the lab you feel the energy. People are busy. Things are happening. So energy is an extremely important part of our success without question. So it's that sense of urgency, feeling of energy, knowing the competition is there—it's our whole culture if you will."

This is what you want to be able to say about your own company after your first 10 or 20 years in business. If high-speed action is a defining advantage even in biotech, what are the odds that it will also be a critical competitive factor in your business? If you're thinking about a thousand to one, you're probably right on the mark. So your challenge is to figure out, up front, how you're going to make that happen. Remember, entrepreneurs (even the ones in biotech) aren't action-oriented because their genes are different. They move fast because they personally feel the need to act and they don't have to ask six layers of management before they move off the dime. To create such a bias for action, and keep it alive in your company, your people have to have the freedom to act, the freedom to experiment, and the freedom to make mistakes. It's not any more complicated than that. Here are three proven ways to get you started.

✔ Freeing the Genius of the Average Worker.

Entrepreneurs simply don't buy the notion that you have to be a rocket scientist to run a business. It's not the deep intellectual proposition the big name business schools make it out to be. Enterprise runs on common sense and the bulk of the common sense resides in the bulk of the people. In other words, the average worker. Soichiro Honda called it the "genius of the average worker." It's these people who know the product inside and out. They're the ones on first name terms with customers. It's the average worker who has to deal every day with every stupid form and time-wasting procedure in the company. In summary, they have the most intimate knowledge of the workings of the business. None of this is surprising of course. What is surprising is how little we use their genius. We don't expect great ideas or great initiative from this crowd. And if we don't expect it, they ain't going to give it.

So why don't we strip clean this gold mine of good ideas and mass of energy? A big part of the trouble seems to be with the reality of who's average. Average workers come to work on time, go home on time, and in between do their job. They do what we expect them to do. They're not the superstars in the company. They're never going to become a vice president, let alone CEO. The average workers also aren't the bums of the business. They're not drug addicts, thieves, or lazy no-goods. They don't come to work every day determined to wreck the company. Average means average which means most big time corporate executives don't think about them much.

Not only do those larger corporations not tap their genius, they seem absolutely determined to deep-six any ideas or suggestions the average workers have. Putting good human relations aside, what would you lose if the bulk of your people go brain-dead as they walk in through the factory gate? What is the cost of freezing out the action-taking instincts of 90 percent of your people? The answer is obvious. You'll get a company full of "rivetheads"—the half angry, half sad label coined by Ben Hamper, GM assembly line worker turned writer. From his own experience in the factory, Hamper says you get to the place where "Working the line at GM was like being paid to flunk high school the rest of your life."

As an entrepreneur, fighting for your survival, you can't afford to operate this way. You can't afford to silence your richest source of improvement ideas and kill the initiative of the people who know the most about your business. You have to find a better way. Enter Soichiro Honda, Japan's greatest entrepreneur of the twentieth century, and the entrepreneur behind a very different kind of car company than GM. Honda was never part of the blue-blood establishment in Japanese industry. Indeed he was the "working man's man." I met and interviewed Tetsuo Chino, the former President of Honda (USA), and a life-long friend of Mr. Honda, at Honda's headquarters in Tokyo. He told me a wonderful story of how Honda got on with the rank and file: "The workers idolized him. For example, several years ago when Mr. Kume was introduced as the new President, the first to replace the founder, we had a big party. Thousands of employees came. Mr. Honda stood up to introduce Mr. Kume. It was emotional and a little tense because the great founder was stepping down. Mr. Honda started this way, 'This company, Honda, we always seem to have a kind of sloppy person for President. A person just like me. Have you noticed? Well, here we go again. Tadashi Kume is a very sloppy person and that is why he now becomes the President.' Then he turned straight to the audience of several thousand employees and said: 'So I'm sorry to tell you, but because you have such a sloppy President, you will have to work harder or the company will collapse.' And you know, the employees just cheered and cheered. They loved it." Chino covered many other Honda actions that endeared him to the average workers, "You know he built three Honda plants in Japan just for handicapped workers. The rest of the employees really appreciated that. And also, he had a very unusual rule for a Japanese company—neither he nor any top executives could have any of their relatives working in the company. He said he didn't want a dynasty because it would be unfair to the rest of the employees." Chino concluded right on the point of who in a company should be trusted to make decisions and take action: "Mr. Honda really thought the genius of the company was in the workers. And they knew that he trusted them. This was very much appreciated by the employees and it was very unusual in big Japanese companies." I would say Mr. Honda's practices would be unusual in big companies, period.

So who will be the geniuses of your company? Who will have the good ideas and should be encouraged to experiment? Who in your company will have the freedom to act? Honda often said that in any group of one hundred workers, 5 percent will be superstars, 5 percent will be bums, and 90 percent will be average. And he really did believe the average workers were the geniuses of the company. They were the ones that built the cars and literally made the company go. The only problem, as Mr. Honda saw it, was that his managers spent all their time with the superstars and the bums. They were always doing things to try to keep the superstars happy and they expended a tremendous amount of time and energy trying to fix the bums. They simply forgot about the average workers. They never even talked to them. Honda's idea was if you got just one good improvement action a month from each of the 90 percent of the workers, company performance would go through the ceiling. The moral of the story: Free the genius of your average worker and you can create a miracle in your company—a miracle of good ideas and innovative actions that no competitor will ever match.

✔ **Action with Customers, Products, and Inside Your Organization.**

Where should you aim your improvement actions? If everywhere, all the time, sounds too ambitious (or a little nutty) how about focusing on the core of what keeps you competitive? And that, of course, leads us right back to customers and products. We're not talking about silly things like more customer questionnaires that no one bothers to read, or a new advertising slogan about product quality that no one believes. The actions that change your core competitiveness are always the sleeves-rolled-up efforts to make buying, using, and servicing your product a faster and better experience for customers. You'll simply never go wrong by trying things to improve your products and better serve your customers. Of course, every single action may not be a home run, but there's no faster, cheaper way to learn and improve.

Actions directed at the key processes and internal workings of the organization are sure-fire winners also. There is one giant caveat, however: They've got to be connected to the business of making great products and keeping customers coming back for more. We're definitely not talking about marginal activities like who gets the corner office or planning the company picnic. Dozens of committees, a thousand meetings and a million e-mails can go into some projects that have absolutely nothing to do with the core business. It's as if the really hard thinking and the most determined actions are reserved for feathering the nest of the bureaucracy or providing perks for certain executives. Beyond this caveat, there is serious work to do on the internal workings of the company. High on that list would be actions taken to improve the key resource of most companies: the people. It's hard to conceive of any more important improvement. Other resources or processes that might be especially critical for your business—quality, efficiency, purchasing—would also be target areas for all manner of improvement actions.

"I'm always trying to reinvent the way we do things." You won't find better advice anywhere for keeping ahead of your competitors. Welcome to the world of Sabrina Horn, wunderkind of the high-tech public relations industry. Horn was still in her twenties when she founded Horn Group, Inc. (HGI). In just over a decade, HGI has become one of the fastest growing PR agencies in the country. With offices in San Francisco, Boston, and New York, and agency partnerships in Europe and Asia, HGI is a high-speed, innovative example of a totally new kind of PR firm. Or, as they like to remind you with their registered service mark—SMART-PR—the Horn Group is a public relations firm totally dedicated to the high-tech industry.

HGI has been on a super-fast track. It is an "Inc. 500 Company," making *Inc. Magazine's* list of America's fastest growing companies. It was also named "Best U.S. Employer" by *Working Woman* magazine, an unheard of accolade in an industry famous for its high pressure burn out rate. The firm has received numerous other industry awards and tributes. Most important for our purposes here, HGI is on the cutting edge of reinventing the PR industry. Horn Group aims to be as high-tech in the way they do PR as their clients are in their respective businesses. From the simultaneous distribution of thousands of virtual press releases, to using hyperlinks for streaming video and audio trailers, to online press conferences, HGI's high-tech PR services have become a largely paperless business mirroring the cyberspace style of the clients they serve.

I visited the Horn Group in their totally wired, but warm and inviting, San Francisco offices. What follows is an incredibly honest and frank interview with Sabrina Horn. "The market is correcting itself right now. And that's a good thing because somebody had to let the air out of the balloon a little bit. But I think it's going to continue to be a massive growth area of innovation and economic development and prosperity. It was just the beginning of it and it just got so hot that the pressure valve needed to be opened up a little bit. So I think it's going to continue, but not at these crazy, crazy levels. You know, companies going public that had no business going public, that didn't have the infrastructure, and with individuals running those companies who were more interested in personal wealth creation than building a company that would last. That is the downside to all of this. Because, let's face it, God created man with a couple of bad traits and one of them is greed. So, you know, we have to fight that. But I think the growth is going to continue for at least an-other 10 to 20 years."

Everybody knows that high-tech companies move at the speed of light and live or die on relentless innovation. But the very specialized, high-tech PR firms that present them to the world actually have to stay one step ahead of the hurricane that cyberspace has become. Whether it's the unending string of new product launches, or new strategic al-liances being signed, or make-or-break initial public offerings (IPOs), the PR agencies have to be ahead of the e-commerce industry curve every day in every way. In fact, it seems there has never been an industry more dependent on public relations. It dwarfs anything the world ever saw in the old economy.

As mentioned earlier, HGI has already been recognized as one of the fastest growing private companies in the United States, so I asked Horn, "How have you done that? What are the key things you've done to grow HGI?" She didn't hesitate a second. She had the answers ready. "I ini-tially built a franchise of clients around PeopleSoft's technology, and that was a key thing in our growth. PeopleSoft was my first client and I think it's important for entrepreneurs to focus on an area of competence, and not get distracted by opportunities and by too much of a good thing. I think that was really good for us in the early days because we built a reputation for ourselves as being really good in one area of software. Everybody knew we did it and they all called us and we had our choice of the companies we wanted to work with.

"We've always had a focus within high-tech. B2B (Business to Busi-ness) software is where we have worked for several years now. You know, we have so many great ideas. There are so many great companies out there to work for. But you just get so distracted. So we've actually devel-oped a little model to help us get focused in the areas of technology that we want to go after. So that anything outside of the dotted line, we're just not going to do it. And we're very committed to *not* doing it. You always have to be looking at where the technology is going and where you need to go, but at the same time you need to have a core expertise.

"In the service business your product is your people. If we made a product like a TV, we'd have quality assurance, we'd have manufactur-ing, we'd have engineering, we'd have all this infrastructure to support making the product. And what services companies don't do enough of is support their "product," which is their people. So that's what we do. That's certainly our reputation and we've even won awards for it. We won this award last year for *Best Employer in the U.S.* For a PR agency to get that kind of recognition is big stuff because they're usually terrible shops that burn out people. So I think the second thing is, certainly if you're an entrepreneur in a service business, and probably even in a product business, it all starts with your people. If they're happy, then you have a better chance of having happy customers.

"You know, it's shades of gray in PR. Because all of us offer similar services, it's in how we deliver the service that becomes the magic. I think we've always tried to be on top of, or one step ahead of, new ways of doing PR so that our services are never a cookie cutter. I'm always trying to reinvent the way we do things. And it's not just from using better technology in PR, but also in our processes. Just getting more efficient. Whether the client sees it or not, we are always kind of retooling what we do. Currently we call the vision for that SMART-PR. In fact our registered service mark is now SMART-PR.

"So I think that clients come to us because they are a fit with our expertise and our focus, they appreciate our culture around people, and they like what we have to say about innovation and trying to do things differently. I think that would probably be the three key things supporting our growth."

And those three key things are exactly what we're talking about in this chapter. Aim your best improvement actions at the areas that will really make a difference: Your customer, your product (or service as Horn labels it), and the key processes inside your company whether it's people development, continuous innovation, and so on. Sabrina Horn has it down pat—and look where it's gotten her—on the list of the fastest growing private companies in America. Try her advice and we'll look for your name there, too!

✔ Battling Bureaucracy.

What should you, as the boss, be doing about bureaucracy? Plenty! Remember, the fundamental purpose of rapid action in business is to beat the competition to market with better products and services. Anything going on in the company that gets in the way of that goal has to go. In this sense, taking a sledgehammer to any emerging bureaucracy in your business may be the single, most heroic act you will ever take as an entrepreneur. You're the only person who can stop bureaucracy from getting started, and you'll be the only person who can clean up the mess if it does get started.

To see how the day in and day out battle against bureaucracy can be won, go to Dallas, Texas. I first came across Chili's Grill & Bar 10 years ago (now renamed Brinker International) when it was still on *Forbes'* list of "The 200 Best Small Companies in America." As one indication of their growth, Brinker was recently honored again by *Forbes* as one of "America's Best Big Companies" and it just recently made *Fortune's* list of "America's Most Admired Companies." The numbers confirm the accolades: In just 20 years since its start-up, Brinker International's revenues today stand at $3.4 billion. Small or big, and always led by its flagship brand Chili's, Brinker has been one of the fastest growing companies in the United States for the past two decades. And they've done it in the completely saturated restaurant business. Founder, Norm Brinker and his handpicked chairman, Ron McDougall have rewritten the book for high-speed innovation and beating bureaucracy in the food service industry.

Norm Brinker was a farm boy from Roswell, New Mexico, who grew up to single-handedly invent the full service, chain restaurant business in America. Brinker has done it all: worked an entry level job at Jack In The Box, owned a single coffee shop, was chairman of both Burger King and Pillsbury's massive restaurant group, and has created one big name chain after another. Along the way he has become a living legend in the restaurant business. Some of the famous restaurant chains he has created are Steak And Ale (his first in 1966), Bennigan's, Chili's Grill & Bar, Romano's Macaroni Grill, and Big Bowl Asian Kitchen. Today, Brinker International has an incredible eight successful concept restaurant chains running, earning the company the label of the "mutual fund of casual dining."

Ron McDougall has worked for and with Norm Brinker since 1974 and when Brinker asked him to head up a new venture called Chili's, McDougall headed for Dallas. Their odysseys in and out of the corporate world have left Brinker and McDougall with a profound preference for fast moving innovation—and a hatred for bureaucracy.

Norm Brinker, for example, is famous for going straight to customers and employees to tell him what needs to be done. "Before I walk into one of our restaurants or a competitor's restaurant, I wait for a group of people to come out, and I ask them, 'How was it? Is this place any good?' " At company headquarters he almost never calls meetings, but spends a big part of his time just talking to people. He likes to wander into someone's office and explore any new idea on their mind. He tells managers who have just come into the Chili's system to look around and point out anything they think can be done better before they become "'Chilized." Indeed, nearly 80 percent of the current Chili's menu has come from suggestions made by unit managers. Brinker knows the importance of taking good advice from the people in touch with the customer and the dangers of stifling employee creativity and action. "People either grow or shrivel. It all depends on the company's attitude. There's the attitude that says, 'Boy, I've got a great idea, let's try it.' Or there's the attitude that says, 'That's not the way we've done things—you run the restaurant, we'll come up the ideas.' Say that too many times, and employees get the message."

To get the complete Brinker message on battling bureaucracy, I went to their busy headquarters in Dallas for a full blown interview with Ron McDougall. He's a classic medium-is-the-message kind of guy. I was practically overwhelmed by his energy and enthusiasm for everything that's happening. He speaks without commas or periods. Just a continuous flood of exclamation points. "We believe here that if you stay the way you are today, even if you're successful, down the road you're not going to be working so well any more, because you're going to be yesterday's news at some point. So we're not afraid to change here! We're not afraid to challenge! We're all challenging the system! No matter how good this thing is, we *never* think we're in first place. We always play like we're in second place trying to get that extra edge to get back into first place. Our biggest enemy is probably ourselves—that's this company, which is us! And so we challenge the system all the time: whether it's more efficient operating procedures, better quality products, better ambiance in a restaurant, . . . better service systems. Whatever it is, we're always trying to find a better way to do it. So where we are today, that's like your benchmark—now *beat it* somehow—or we fail! You know what I mean?" Well, yes. With McDougall it's pretty hard to miss the message.

Like Brinker, McDougall places great store in the innovative ideas of employees, "The key isn't to change for change's sake, obviously, but to keep looking to find a better way to do it. And we don't care where the idea comes from. Whoever has the idea—bring it up—we're gonna make this thing happen! So a 'not invented here' syndrome hopefully doesn't happen in this environment. I don't think of every idea myself, nor did Norm. You know, a lot of great ideas come from the waitstaff, from the unit managers. You know, employees throughout the whole system because they're actually closer to the firing line, and they can see the opportunity better than we can see it. We try to foster an environment where you can get those ideas up, surfaced, so you can capture the ideas and work with them! Also, everyone in the company including the home office is on profit sharing—*everyone!* All the way down to the person who walks in the first day, they're on profit sharing. So I've got a whole team here that's looking to save money! And you don't need a $100,000 idea to contribute. If you can save $1,000, that goes back into the profit pool. So if someone's going crazy on the copier machine or sending a million e-mails to everyone, we have a lot of policemen around!"

If the best way to combat bureaucracy is to not let it get started in the first place, here's a front-line warning from experienced bureaucracy basher McDougall, "The larger you get, there tends to be a rigidity that sets in—through time, I think. When you're small you're scrambling and flexible—quicker on your feet—because there aren't that many things to change. The larger you get, take a McDonald's with thirty thousand restaurants out there, you change one thing, you've got to change thirty thousand restaurants. You have to change procedures, hundreds of thousands of employees, whatever. And bureaucracy tends to set in, in the larger systems. There's a lot of little links in the chain. A lot of departments. They tend to become little fiefdoms out for themselves, and doing things for their own department. They come up with internal projects that are needed for the department, but won't ever have any impact on the business! Some of the larger companies I've been with—I've seen those things happen. These projects become a project within themselves. They never have an application outside your four walls. Never impact the business. But it's a real neat project to work on—or it's a lot of fun, or you get strokes out of it—but it's not moving the enterprise ahead one centimeter. This you have to fight all the time. Keep your eye on the ball, eliminate the bureaucracy, and don't let the fiefdoms spring up. You know what I mean?"

To McDougall, decentralized action taking is an article of faith and a key to battling bureaucracy. He explains how they keep the faith and deal with the inevitable mistakes. "At most companies it's red tape, or levels. You've got approval levels you have to work your way through to get something through a lot of the doomsayers. A big company is more people saying how you can't do something than how you can do it. And around here, we don't like to fail, but we're not afraid of running hard and hitting the wall once and bouncing off and getting up and going again. It's a belief that you have to try things, and if it doesn't work, don't be a fool and stay with it and drive it in the ground. Try it and, if it doesn't work, back off and come again! We tried a lot of things that didn't work very well; we retreated and attacked again from a different direction."

So there you have it, Brinker International's proven recipe for battling bureaucracy: Implementing continuous improvements, keeping employees involved, decentralized action taking, permitting some failure along the way, and perhaps most important, top executives who make it a priority to never let it get started in the first place!

From day one as an entrepreneur, one of your most important jobs will be to battle bureaucracy. Every time someone suggests a new procedure, a new committee, another system, ask yourself how *exactly* is this going to contribute to beating the competition? If you can't come up with a clear, convincing answer, don't do it. And use your common sense. Often simple things can be the most effective: five-minute meetings, one-page memos, periodic crusades to cut down on e-mail, and annual bureaucracy audits to weed out unnecessary practices, procedures, and forms. Finally, don't fool yourself into thinking you can hold off on this because it couldn't possibly be a problem in your small enterprise. Take my word for it, it only takes three people to form a raging bureaucracy.

Changing the World with a Good Idea

I actually felt guilty wasting that much water.
—Lito Rodriguez, Founder, DryWash

This is the amazing story of Lito Rodriguez, a young Brazilian entrepreneur, who has innovated a technical and business revolution by figuring out how to wash cars without a single drop of water. Given current estimates that half of the world will be facing severe fresh water shortgages by 2025, washing cars without water looks like a business with a big future. In fact, Rodriguez's company, DryWash, has only been in business six years but it has already become the largest chain of car-wash facilities in the world. And Rodriguez has a backlog of 13,000 franchise applications from all around the globe sitting in his office. Just 35 years old, Rodriguez is living proof that high-speed innovation is indeed the entrepreneurs secret weapon—and that you can still change the world with a good idea.

I recently had the pleasure of meeting and interviewing Rodriguez in São Paulo, Brazil. We met at one of his 230 DryWash locations so I could actually see the magic in action. Heraldo Tino, my company's long-term affiliate for Brazil, set this all up and even acted as the interpreter for the interview. After watching a couple of spectacular demonstrations of DryWash personnel cleaning and polishing cars without water, I was dying to know how Lito got into such a business. His answer, translated from Portuguese, was disarmingly down-to-earth: "As a car owner I saw the need for a professional approach to car washing. At all the places I used to go to wash my car I found dirty, ugly, and unfriendly people—in an unfriendly setting. I imagined that a chain of car washes with precise standards for the setting, the procedures, and the right way to treat consumers would be successful. It would especially be a more appealing place for women to get their cars washed. With standards, you could measure the results and with a chain you could get your brand name in the head of the clients. Two ideas could summarize my initial plan for the car wash business: high, consistent standards and a chain of locations.

I asked him how he actually started up the business. "I didn't start with the DryWash business at first. What I started was a traditional car wash, with water. I made it very plush, with good standards, a nice waiting room with magazines and coffee and all the amenities possible. That was my idea of a good car wash. We invested about $50,000 to get it started. Now that wasn't the amount we invested in the dry wash process. It was much less but I can't say exactly how much since it was money out of my pocket in the course of washing cars the traditional way. By the way, I forgot to tell you that in the beginning I had a partner. The first time the business required more money, he left. At that moment, I had to sell my car, the telephone lines, my wife's car, everything just to keep the first business running."

How Rodriguez got from the traditional car wash business to Dry-Wash is the heart of his story. "Originally, as a customer, I was not satisfied with what I was getting for my money in all the car wash shops I had been. As I said earlier, at first my considerations were simply two: standards and creating a chain. However, after getting into the business and studying the problem more closely—and I spent a small fortune getting my car washed over and over at other stations for months—I realized that a car washed by hand or by machinery generates a tremendous waste of water and electricity. We all know how precious water is nowadays and in Brazil we also suffer from high energy costs and sometimes have electricity rationing by the government. So I realized that it is almost impossible to have a clean place where so much water is being jettisoned at high speed against cars, spilling all over the place, and taking a large amount of dirty, greasy water down through the drainage systems. It couldn't be a clean place and it was terrible for the ecology. Anyway, the first thing a successful entrepreneur has to do is to know his product. He must be above everybody in his field on product knowledge. In my case, I really wanted to have the best car wash chain in the world. I started a car wash of my own, washing cars the traditional way, using a lot of water and electricity. But if you apply your intelligence, if you feel the need to improve, and you work in the field 16 hours a day, 7 days a week, you will eventually come up with a better way!

"In any event, the dry wash process was invented because I was unhappy with the wasted water I saw going down the drain everyday. I actually felt guilty wasting that much water. To give you an idea, washing just one car requires about 316 liters of water. If you multiply that over a million cars per year, you can see that DryWash is saving the country a tremendous amout of fresh water. Our process also reduces the amount of electricity used per vehicle by 99.5 percent! These are important things and that's why we began to experiment to find a better way. When I started the research, I found out I didn't really have to be a chemist to create this product. That was lucky since I failed chemistry in school! But I started asking questions to people who were chemists. And I read a lot about the cleaning process. So I didn't pay anyone to invent the product for me. After gathering all the information I could, I started trying components, materials, mixing this and that. I actually started by using my mother's cake mixer to do the mixing—much against her will I should add. I do have to admit however, we did pay a chemist to sign off on the final formula, because we legally needed a chemist to endorse and verify the product.

"I can't pinpoint exactly the moment when we finally invented the dry wash process. We were experimenting, experimenting, experimenting, and the formula was getting better and better until we could finally say: 'This is it.' In reality, all our research was based on a simple principle: Water does not wash anything. Friction cleans things, not water. You can stand for hours under a shower and your hair will not be cleaned. It's the friction of the soap and your fingers on the hair that actually cleans your hair."

In just six years DryWash has established a chain of 230 auto wash units, cleaning 90,000 cars a month, and employing close to 2,000 employees. The company also created a chemical manufacturing division, which produces all the products to supply the franchisees. This division also manufactures noncompeting DryWash products to sell through retail chains as do-it-yourself cleaning supplies for homes and offices.

The concept behind its main chemical product, called DryWash Neutro, is the transformation of heavy particles of dirt into light particles through a process of crystallization and fragmentation. This cleans the automobile and leaves a fine impermeable protective film that produces more shine and protects the paint against rain, pollution, and ultraviolet rays. This treatment greatly reduces oxidation and premature wear and maintains the original look of the car a lot longer. The application is simple and efficient, using on average only 220 milliliters of the product which is applied and removed by small washcloths.

The driving force of the company is the franchise system, which is growing by leaps and bounds. DryWash has some large, multiple site franchises, a lot of mid-sized sites which they call Express franchises, and has recently introduced the one-person franchise which has become the fastest growing part of the business. These individual, highly mobile franchisees handle between 10 and 50 vehicles per day at locations such as automobile dealerships, small parking facilities, autobody repair shops, and even upscale private residences. Rodriguez believes it's the individual franchisee segment that will continue to give the network its explosive growth in the future. And there's plenty of room to grow. The potential Brazilian market is roughly 40 million car washes a month. DryWash is aiming for a ten-fold increase in volume over the next decade from the current 90,000 car washes per month to one million. And that will still be only 2.5 percent of the domestic market.

Despite the cynicism of most marketing experts, DryWash has succeeded in developing a franchise network that ensures consistent quality and high standards of service in what has always been a low quality, haphazard industry. The DryWash method, with its strong environmental-friendly characteristics, has drawn a lot of favorable press which has also contributed to the company's rapid growth. Rodriguez has patented DryWash's products and its washing process. This is an important differential in a market which is still very informal, operates with virtually no quality standards, and shows little concern for the environment. Rodriguez's knack for innovation has actually given DryWash a tremendous cost advantage over its competitors. Since it uses no water, consumes 99.5 percent less energy than its competitors, and does not require expensive equipment or facilities, DryWash is able to keep the costs of its franchises very low, providing a healthy profit margin of 20 percent in a very price sensitive marketplace.

All these factors are creating a bevy of new growth opportunities for DryWash. Rodriquez's eyes sparkle when he talks about all the interest he's getting from other possible markets such as the cleaning of aircraft, cruise ships, public transport, and all manner of public facilities. And with such an innovative technology, it's not surprising that the Brazilian entrepreneur has also been showered with franchise applications from Japan, the Middle East, Europe, Australia, and of course the United

States. In fact, when we met, Rodriguez was up on the latest news from the U.S. pointing out that many states were suffering droughts at that time. He even named several states that were restricting the washing of vehicles. With a smile, he said to be sure and tell the readers of this book that he is ready to sign up new franchises anywhere in the world!

So Rodriguez has invented a great product and has already built a successful company. Where is he headed today? What's the future mission of DryWash? His answer came with an innovative twist, "The future of DryWash is all about creating self-employed entrepreneurs. We have now started selling a one-man franchise. For as little as $1,000 a franchisee can be trained by our company to apply the DryWash product as a mobile independent. He can do this with house calls, in public parking lots, at apartment buildings, at company parking lots—wherever there's a lot of cars parked. And remember, because of the DryWash process, he can do it without the use of water so our system does not make a mess in the parking lot. I am making an uneducated citizen the owner of his own business. He can make a decent living and raise a family all by himself. All the young people you see at the red lights cleaning windshields— they can become legitimate self-employed entrepreneurs using our product. We've just started this approach and we already have close to one hundred people working in this system. Since we introduced this concept, it's become so popular that our biggest problem is handling all the applications. We have more than 13,000 people applying to be a franchisee—with most of them in the one-man-shop category.

"The exciting thing is, we can actually create entrepreneurs. We can create entrepreneurs inside the company—so to speak. Even big companies need entrepreneurs. Of course you have to find a way to keep entrepreneurship alive in any business. I'm trying to do that by keeping DryWash small —in a way. I mean I do not want to see DryWash itself become a giant company. What I do want to see are thousands of small entrepreneurs like myself, owning their own franchised car wash, being face-to-face with their clients everyday. I think that's the best route for DryWash in the future."

DryWash's rapid growth and great success is clearly based on Rodriguez's abundant supply of high-speed innovation. I was curious to learn how he prepared himself to create such a radically different vision for such a fragmented and mundane market. This could be very important as there must be hundreds of similar, old-line industries just waiting for an entrepreneur to come along and create a revolution as Lito Rodriguez did. "First, my background is completely devoid of any technical education. As I said, I did not know anything about chemistry. In fact, I could not get into the University of São Paulo because I flunked the chemistry examination. I did graduate from another university with a degree in advertising. And I never really studied business administration. I guess the closest I came to studying business was taking two years of economics in college. But if I had to pick just one word it would be *creativity*. We should do our best to teach young people to be creative. I do not claim to know exactly how this can be done, but creativity is absolutely necessary if you hope to be a successful entrepreneur. I have learned, however, that the first step in coming up with a new and better way to do a business is to really identify with what you do. You have to like what you do. If you do not like it, the chances of success are very slim. At first, you may not be sure of what you want. I tried three businesses before DryWash. I did not succeed in any of them because I did not personally identify myself with them. In my view, most people become entrepreneurs because they feel a need. They feel the necessity to create. It's not an economic need. In fact, if you start a company just to make money, probably you will not succeed. I'm talking about the necessity to find better ways of doing the same thing. It's the necessity to create something. I think this need to create is actually what starts most companies."

Lito Rodriguez, modern Brazilian entrepreneur, typifies the principles of entrepreneurship just as faithfully as earlier legends like Walt Disney, Akio Morita, and William Lever. He obviously has a powerful sense of mission about his work. He is absolutely focused on customers and products. He is clearly self-inspired to do what he does. And he is just brimming over with innovative action. It's nice to know that a good idea can still change the world even if it starts in a single car wash in Brazil!

APPLICATION 7
Creating High-Speed Innovation

High-speed innovation is the fastest, cheapest, and surest way to gain competitive advantage in the marketplace. It truly is the entrepreneur's secret weapon. So it is critical that you have a plan of action, for yourself and your employees, to make this happen. Now is the time to think through the actions that you should take to make high-speed innovation a major thrust in your new business. Here are some suggestions and questions to help you get started.

- Review the three key practices discussed in The Necessity to Invent section of this chapter.
- Review the three key practices discussed in The Freedom to Act section of this chapter.
- How high a priority is it to you, and to the bulk of your employees, to improve something, anything, everyday?
- How much sense of urgency exists throughout your company? Are you leading by example in this area?
- Are you in danger of becoming a bureaucracy? Who's responsibility is it to prevent this?
- Where should you be directing your innovative action? Product development? Customer service? Improving internal processes such as hiring, purchasing, product quality, sales support? Which areas will give you the most payoff?
- Which of the deadly sins against high-speed innovation are most likely to affect your business? How will you guard against them?

APPLICATION 7-A
Creating High-Speed Innovation

What would you do if your "life depended on it?" It's an important question because the "life" of your entrepreneurial venture *will* depend on it. For each of the following practices, what are the most important action steps you can take, and when will you take them?

To Encourage Innovation: Improve something, anything, everyday.   **When**

1.

2.

3.

To Speed Up Action: Create a sense of urgency.   **When**

1.

2.

3.

To Wipe out Bureaucracy: Growing big by staying small.   **When**

1.

2.

3.

CHAPTER

4

Self-Inspired Behavior

Love What You Do and Get Very Good at Doing It

Inspiring Yourself

> I promoted myself.
> —Sarah Breedlove Walker, Founder,
> Walker Manufacturing Company

Feeling disadvantaged? Try being poor, uneducated, African American, and a single mother in 19th Century America. You can be sure that Sarah Walker never had an affirmative action promotion, a seminar on motivation, or a stock option, yet, somehow she managed to become America's first self-made millionairess. And back in 1900, a million bucks was still a million bucks.

Born in 1867, the daughter of former slaves and orphaned at seven, Sarah Breedlove never saw the inside of a school room. She was married off at 14, widowed with children by 20, and earned her keep as a washerwoman. In your great-grandmother's America, you couldn't get more disadvantaged than Sarah. Yet this ebony dynamo invented and manufactured health and beauty products for African American women, created a 5000 strong sales agent network, and became the most successful (and richest) woman entrepreneur in the country.

Madame Walker, as she liked to be called, set a whole new standard for self-inspired behavior, "I am a woman who came from the cotton fields of the South. I was promoted from there to the washtub and then to the kitchen. From there I promoted *myself* into the business of manufacturing hair goods, and I built my own factory on my own ground." And promote herself she did. By the time she died in 1919, annual sales were close to $1 million a year, and Madame Walker had etched herself a place in business history. How do such impossible dreams happen?

Why do some people appear so self-inspired, while others spend their lives waiting for something to happen? Dig a little deeper into Sarah Walker's history and some of her answers begin to emerge. Like many African American women of her time, Walker's hair began falling out at an early age. Whether due to poor diet, disease, or other reasons, there were certainly no special products to treat such maladies. Indeed, no manufacturers produced any products to meet the hygiene or beauty needs of African American women. In desperation, she began concocting her own shampoo and hair conditioner to save her hair. Once successful, the word spread throughout her community and she couldn't make enough to satisfy the needs of other African American women. She began selling door to door, with many of her customers becoming sales agents themselves. She attracted an army of other self-inspired African American women, eager to move up from $2.00 a week as a domestic, to the $20.00 plus per week Walker agents could earn. Sold as the Walker System, she soon had factories and hair salons across the country.

Driven by her self-inspired entrepreneurial spirit, Walker became an important figure in American business history. She single-handedly exposed the huge economic potential of creating special products for the African American market. In the process, she literally wrote the book on franchising and multilevel marketing on a national basis. And her indominable spirit carried over into her personal life. She was the country's first African American, woman philanthropist. She was tireless in supporting social issues of the day. She was especially generous with financial contributions to educational institutions for African American women. Through Walker's generosity and personal example, tens of thousands of similarily disadvantaged women have found the inspiration and knowledge to rise above their presumed place in society. They are all standing on Walker's shoulders today. Yes, Sarah Breedlove Walker's story is about self-inspired behavior at its finest.

It doesn't do much good if the founder of the company is the only one around feeling self-inspired. To successfully grow beyond the proverbial one-man shop, some enterprising, self-inspired behavior needs to be instilled in the employees. Inspiring yourself is laudable—that's where it has to start—but inspiring ten, or a hundred, or even thousands of work-ers is the real trick. The business world's all-time leader for inspiring his employees has to be that feisty, fast talking entrepreneur from Texas, H. Ross Perot, who believed that winning was all about loving what you do and being darn good at doing it. He called it soaring with the eagles, and we call it creating high commitment and high performance.

On Wings of Eagles

I'm looking for people who love to win. If I run out of those, I want people who hate to lose.

—H. Ross Perot, Founder, Electronic
Data Systems, Perot Systems

Finding people who love to win is easier said than done unless you're a be-liever like Ross Perot. This Texas billionaire, the quintessential American entrepreneur, is a big believer in winning—for himself and for his troops. I first became intrigued by Ross Perot back in 1979. It wasn't because of this Texas entrepreneur's business exploits, even though he had already made a name for himself as the founder of Electronic Data Systems (EDS). I had a more personal reason. Like many other Americans working in Iran around that time, I had gotten trapped in the wild and wooley Iranian revolution. Yes, that would be the same revolution that brought down America's pal, the Shah of Iran, and declared America the Great Satan.

I was in Teheran to close down an office I had myself opened just three years earlier. On my arrival I saw a very different Teheran from the one I thought I knew. The ride in from Mehrabad Airport had been an eye-opener. It looked like a war zone. We were stopped and searched every few blocks. Tanks, nervous soldiers, and sandbags clogged the streets while a million demonstrators screamed anti-Shah and anti-American slogans. It was an angry and eerie sight in a country where such behavior had been unthinkable for decades. Everyone in the coun-try seemed on strike save the troops loyal to the Shah and of course the Ayatollah's demonstrators. At the Sheraton Hotel where I stayed the windows were all broken, the staff was gone, and we few remaining "guests" helped ourselves to what food was in the kitchen.

Over the next week, the situation went from bad to worse. I won't bore you with the details but it evolved into a surreal mixture of "volun-tary" house arrest in the Sheraton lobby and being glared at by a lot of wild-eyed Iranians, all swept up in the revolutionary fervor. One thing seemed certain—there was no way to get out. That is, until a young Frenchman, an employee of Air France, came to my rescue. Because Ayatollah Khomeni had been given political refuge in France for many years, the French were still free to come and go as they liked. This brave young man offered to help me escape if I was game to try. I was—and he did. I'll never forget our backstreet ride to the airport, trying to avoid both the nervous soldiers and the frenzied demonstrators. What was normally a 30 minute drive took about 5 hours. It didn't really make much difference as the airport was closed and everyone was on strike. No planes were allowed to land or take off. I did have lots of company, however. There must have been 10,000 Iranians and all sorts of foreigners at the airport trying to leave the country.

Once inside the airport my French host and helper seemed particularly encouraged with my chances when I told him I had no preferred destination. "This means you will go any direction?" he asked. "Yes, any direction, any country," I responded. "This is good. Just sit or sleep on the floor near the Air France counter, and I will find you when the right time comes." So I took up my spot on the floor just like any other refugee. Over the next 36 hours, I waited.

In the middle of my second night on the floor, like a shining knight in blue, the Air France agent leaned over and whispered, "Come with me. There's an Air France 747 out at the end of the runway. She's been allowed to refuel but cannot discharge or take on any passengers. But I think I can get one person on." He shoved an Air France jacket toward me, "Put this on, it's safer." In a bit of a daze I followed him behind the counter, through the office area, down several corridors and presto, we were on the tarmac. There was no ticketing, no passport control, no customs, nothing. We got in an Air France jeep and shot across the runway heading for a beautiful, blue and white bird with Air France emblazoned across its side. The agent was yelling as we drove, "I can give you no ticket. Everything is broken. I will tell the Purser you have to buy your ticket when you arrive." Just then it dawned on me that I didn't even have the foggiest idea where I would be arriving!

At the plane, the agent directed the mechanic's ramp ladder to the front cabin door. Up we went, the door opened, and a rapid fire exchange in French took place between the agent and the purser. The agent turned to me, stuck out his hand and said those wonderful words in French that even I could understand, "Bon voyage." The purser led me to a seat and asked, "Monsieur, where do you want to go?" I replied: "I want to go wherever you're going" "We're going to Bangkok, is that okay?" was the polite response. Without thinking I sputtered, "That's wonderful. I've never seen Bangkok before. Let's go to Bangkok."

After I returned home, one evening I happened to be watching the news on TV when Perot's face popped up on the screen with the incredible story of how he had rescued two EDS executives from Evin Prison in Teheran. The news story, which was later turned into a book and movie titled *On Wings Of Eagles*, reported how Perot had organized and paid for a commando team of ex-Green Berets, a couple of planes and helicopters, and plenty of guns to bring his two employees home. It seems that when Perot became convinced that President Carter couldn't or wouldn't rescue his people, he decided to do it himself. I was of course fascinated by this daring exploit in a place I had just escaped from on my own. And I was stunned that a company CEO would put so much on the line to save a couple of employees. I remember turning to my wife, Julie, and musing: "Do you think my company was going to send commandos to rescue me?" We both knew the answer of course. Perot's heroic mission seared into my consciousness a question I still ponder, which you might want to ponder also—*if you ever get thrown into a foreign prison, who do you want to be working for?*

All of this made great headlines and even a great book and movie. Perot has in fact become a bigger-than-life character with his brand of example setting. Over 25 years ago he personally went into Laos trying to get supplies to American POWs in North Vietnam. He bought the Magna Carta for $1.5 million and promptly gave it to the U.S. National Archives to be a national reminder that individual liberties only come from individual action. Amid great controversy, he headed a commission to get Texas education out of last place in the country; his thanks was the eternal resentment of the education establishment. And no matter what your politics, his 1992 run at the Presidency produced one amazing result. He forced Republicans and Democrats alike to take the out-of-control U.S. budget deficit seriously, something neither party had done for decades.

Like most people willing to take strong stands on controversial issues, Perot has ended up in the love-him-or-hate-him category of opinion polls. But in the opinion poll that counts most with Perot, there's no ambivalence. There's no CEO in the world who has had more respect and loyalty from employees that Perot enjoys. The commitment of some of his people borders on the unbelievable. It's out of step with the modern world. One executive gave up $900,000 in GM stock to go back and work for Perot Systems. Perot has been out of EDS since 1986, but the admiration lives on even there. Recently in Brazil, two EDS employees choked up in describing to me how Perot had inspired them early in their careers. The corporate motto at Perot Systems is "One for All and All for One." It may sound corny to some, but if history is any guide, this slogan really means something when you work for Ross Perot.

Yes, Perot's style makes great headlines. It also makes for great people management, if you're looking for extreme commitment and performance from your people. His personal history as a high performer is well documented. In his first job as an IBM salesman, he met his annual sales quota by the end of January. When he found out he had maxed out on the commission system and would receive no additional sales commissions for the next 11 months, he quit and started up EDS with $1,000 he borrowed from his wife's saving account. On the commitment side, his deeds are legendary. Imagine what would it be like to work for a CEO who built a company worth billions, but set his salary at $68,000 in 1965 and never gave himself a raise? Having a boss like that would be a unique experience for anyone. Or, if you were a GM "rivethead" working the assembly line, how would you feel when the largest shareholder went public with the very things you'd been saying all your life? Odds are you'd be cheering when Perot unleashed his public, take-no-prisoners attack on the entire GM Board: "Get rid of the committees and consultants and MBAs. Stop showing contempt for your dealers, your employees, and your customers. Give up the corporate dining room, the chauffeured limousines, the hefty bonuses in hard times. Get back to the trenches. Listen to the troops. Take care of them first, and they'll take care of you." Of course, GM eventually paid him another $750 million to get him off the board and shut up about their "contempt" for customers and employees. And perhaps most dramatically of all, what would you do in return for the CEO who hires commandos to rescue you from a foreign prison?

Ross Perot isn't finished yet. He may never become President of the United States, but his entrepreneuring days are hardly over. Just 2 years ago, 35 years after starting EDS, he took Perot Systems public and added another cool billion dollars to his personal war chest. So there's another billion for whatever crazy, self-inspired idea he comes up with next.

Now, you'll probably never have to rescue employees from a foreign prison. And you're probably not going to run for President. And you may never accumulate several billion dollars to throw around the world at various causes. But, the underlying Perot message is one every entrepreneur can and should embrace—instilling high commitment and high performance in your employees is the tried and true way to keep an enterprising spirit alive and well in your buisness.

High Commitment and High Performance

If entrepreneurs like Sarah Walker and Ross Perot are self-inspired, what exactly are they self-inspired to do? Do quite different entrepreneurial personalities such as Bill Gates, Soichiro Honda, and Anita Roddick share any common practices as workers? Yes they do, but it is a surprisingly short list. One characteristic of all entrepreneurs I've met is they like what they do. They're highly committed to what they're doing. In addition to liking what they do, they're very determined to be good at doing it. At least as good, and hopefully better, than the competition. In personnel jargon, they're out to achieve high performance. So the self-inspired behavior of entrepreneurs rests on two pretty basic qualities: high commitment and high performance. In plain English, entrepreneurs love what they do and they're very good at doing it.

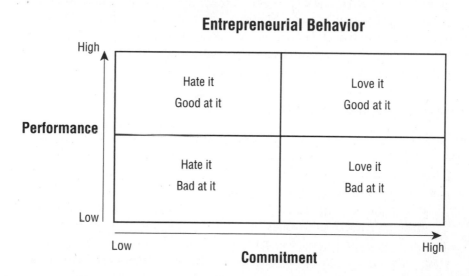

You can, or will, actually find employees occupying any of the locations on the illustration. You've probably worked with all of them at one time or another. Here's a quick definition of each.

High Commitment/High Performance

The upper right-hand corner is entrepreneurial territory. "I love what I do and I'm good at doing it" is the clarion call of all self-inspired entrepreneurs.

High Commitment/Low Performance

In the lower right-hand area are those people who love what they do but aren't so good at doing it. It's not unusual to find new employees here. They can be bursting with enthusiasm for their new job, but they just don't have enough knowledge or experience yet to do the job well. You can also find, unfortunately, long-term employees occupying this spot. They're loyal and they do love the company, but they stopped learning and improving a decade ago.

Low Commitment/High Performance

The upper left-hand area houses the exact opposite type of worker, and is much more common. This is home to those who may actually hate their job but are good at doing it. They're usually highly skilled people who don't like the environment in which they have to perform. Commercial airline pilots come to mind. Flying tourists to Orlando has to be pretty dull stuff compared to combat missions over Iraq. You can see this type of worker everywhere, especially in large bureaucracies that can drive the commitment out of even the highest skilled workers.

Low Commitment/Low Performance

What can we say about workers who hate what they do and are no good at doing it? If you make such a blunder and hire them for your business, don't compound the problem by wasting months or years trying to fix the person. Cut your losses and say sayonara.

Successful entrepreneurs, by definition, are squarely in the high commitment/high performance area of behavior. That's not the problem. Your big challenge will be to pass on and instill the same behaviors in your employees. High commitment and high performance are easy to describe, but they can be hard to achieve. How many people in a typical company really love what they do and are really good at doing it? What percentage work as hard as they can and as smart as they can, all the time? Certainly some, but probably not most. Yet high commitment and high performance are the fundamental employee behaviors required to produce a successful enterprise. Think about it—developing a team of people who absolutely love what they do and are very, very good at doing it—well, that's going to make you one tough competitor!

So how do you create and maintain these entrepreneurial qualities in your people? While carrying overlapping effects, the distinctions are important. Training, for instance, is an action to improve performance. It presumes a lack of knowledge or experience. If someone hates their job, training them again and again won't raise their commitment. The worst mistake you can make is to wait 10 years to get going on this. The time to start is now with your first employee. And the place to start is to make sure that you, as the founder, are personally demonstrating high commitment and high performance in whatever you do—just like Great Britain's greatest entrepreneur, William Hesketh Lever.

Creating Entrepreneurial Commitment: I Love What I Do

We had 18,000 employee shareholders by 1925!
—William Hesketh Lever, Founder,
Lever Brothers (Unilever)

To set the record straight, employee stock ownership wasn't invented in Silicon Valley in 1990. Way back in 1909, William Lever introduced the Lever Co-Partnership Trust, the world's first employee stock ownership program. By 1925, an amazing 18,000 employees were members of the Lever Trust. Was Lever a man ahead of his times? Probably. If nothing else, he put his money where his mouth was in urging workers to cast their lot with his company.

Lever was an early believer in entrepreneurial tough love— doubly inspired by entrepreneurial passion and the belief that workers should get their fair share of the pie. In 1900, Lever Brothers was the largest company in the world. Unilever* today ranks 43rd in global revenue and 32nd in profits. With $50 billion in sales and 267,000 employees, it is also widely recognized as a great place to work. This amazing 100 year performance gives Unilever the best record of any large 20th Century company in maintaining its global ranking. They must have been doing something right all these years!

---

*Unilever was formed in 1929 through the merger of Lever Brothers and several smaller Dutch companies. It operates today as a Dutch/UK group with headquarters in both countries.

When it came to business, Lever was a very tough competitor indeed. Aggressive and expansive, he literally overwhelmed traditional competitors. He traumatized the gentlemanly world of London commerce with massive and outlandish American-style advertising. He literally invented brand recognition, the concept of market niches, and the production of multiple brands to compete against each other. By 1888, he dominated the British market and, by 1910, Lever Brothers had 60,000 employees in 282 operating companies spread across 5 continents. He also demonstrated an autocratic model of leadership, demanding hard work and high morals from employees, insisting they were the root of all success in business and in life.

But we also find caring words and radical deeds in his commitment to employees. Creating the first employee stock and profit sharing program was truly revolutionary for the times. Taking this giant step toward the creation of mini entrepreneurs within the organization was among his proudest achievements. Beyond the Co-Partnership Trust, Lever instituted many employee benefit programs we all take for granted today. Unilever was the first company on record to provide company training, sick leave, annual paid holidays, and pension plans. These were all radical steps for the times.

The most famous example of Lever's commitment to employees is Port Sunlight, the model community Lever Brothers built for its employees in 1889. Working class Britain at that time endured living conditions equivalent to the worst, modern day slum. Port Sunlight eventually housed 3500 people and became a model of company-sponsored living unequalled to this day. A less famous example, but in some ways more telling, was Lever's battle with the trade unions over the length of the work day. No, management wasn't pushing for more and the union less. Quite the opposite. Lever proposed to reduce the standard work day to six hours and provide two hours of self-improvement classes for workers. His fellow industrialists thought he had lost his mind. But the real surprise came when the union leadership opposed the idea of compulsory education and that was that. Talk about being ahead of your time! Perhaps the capstone of Lever's efforts to honor the dignity of the common man came late in his life while serving in the House of Commons. In 1907, he was the author of Britain's first legislation to provide old age pensions for its working class citizens. Not exactly the act we'd expect from a soap tycoon.

So what are we to make of this self-inspired entrepreneur and his lifelong commitment to workers? The legacy of Lever's tough love approach to employees is clear: The company has enjoyed a high commitment/high performance workforce for over a century—and it is still overwhelming the competition.

Commitment comes from the *heart* and produces an abundance of pride, loyalty, and plain old hard work. And, like most things in life, it's a two-way street. The underpinnings of creating high commitment may seem obvious, but they are worth reciting. The following points are four of the most important.

✔ Love What You Do.

The number one rule in commitment remains, you gotta love what you do! Fortunately, 99 percent of all entrepreneurs really *do* love what they do. It comes with the territory. They're proud of their enterprise, and they see noble purpose in every mundane step they take. They love it so much that they'll work night and day to see it succeed. A little of this will go a long way in any growing company.

It will be your job as the founder to define that noble purpose and pass it on to your employees. Every job will have to be made important. Challenges will need to be built into even the most mundane tasks. Whether you're in landscaping or finding a cure for cancer, the long-term payoff for getting your people to like what they're doing, and be proud of it, is simply enormous.

So maybe everyone can't love every job they will ever have. I haven't and probably you haven't. But that doesn't change the principle. People will never be committed to jobs they hate or companies they're not proud of. But if you can make it happen in your business, you'll have attained an enormous advantage over all those competitors who haven't figured out how to do it. It starts with hiring people who are interested in what you do, trying hard to enrich the jobs that are not inherently exciting, and really letting people own their piece of the business. Rewarding those who are highly committed to the mission should be part of the mix also. Those rewards, monetary or otherwise, should be a great investment in your future. And in some cases, it may have to come down to saying goodbye to those who just aren't ever going to give a damn about their job or your company.

At the end of the day, why should people love what they do? We know it's good for the business. That's obvious. And a fair day's effort for a fair day's wage is still a fair obligation. But there may be an even more important reason. Think about it. If you have to work for a living, which virtually everyone does, you're going to spend more time in your life at work than with your family. You'll spend more time at work than with your friends, or enjoying a hobby, or just taking it easy. In fact you're going to spend more time at work than on any other activity in your entire life. This is why it's important to love what you do. It's your *life* we're talking about! And it's the *lives* of your employees. And God help you and your employees if you spend your lives doing something you hate. So taking a little extra effort to ensure that everyone loves what they're doing is a bargain you shouldn't pass up. Remember, it will be great for the business *and* great for you and your people.

✔ Give Autonomy, Demand Accountability.

One surefire way to build commitment is to give people some autonomy and freedom to do their jobs. But the entrepreneurial approach is a lot more sharply focused than run-of-the-mill empowerment programs at *Fortune 500* type companies. In an entrepreneurial environment, empowering people, or giving them autonomy, also means they're accountable for results. It's a two-way street. Employees not only understand this, they like it. For some it may be the first time they've ever been treated like a responsible adult at work. The results can truly be astounding. And once again, you'll have gained a huge competitive advantage over your larger competitors.

In the endless debate over control versus delegation, big business continues to control the wrong things. Imagine the production line supervisor who's responsible for 10 workers and $2 million worth of equipment, but can't spend $50 of company money to take his team out for a beer to celebrate a good week. This story gets replayed a thousand different ways for factory supervisors and any other employees who don't have the status to be trusted to do the right thing with a few bucks. The message they get is, you're responsible for the productivity of the 10 people and the $2 million worth of equipment, but we don't trust you to spend $50 to build your peoples' commitment. Perhaps this wouldn't be so awful if we didn't also realize that one unnecessary first class airfare by an executive can cost $10,000 and nobody thinks twice about it.

The point isn't the $50 or even the $10,000. It is that to get the commitment of people, a little freedom goes a very long way. And everyone understands with freedom comes the responsibility to perform. We call it giving a little autonomy, and getting a lot of accountability in return. That happens when you begin to treat people like minientrepreneurs, responsible for their piece of the business.

Ron McDougall, at Brinker International (Chili's Grill & Bar, Romano's Macaroni Grill, Big Bowl Asian Kitchen), has this down to a science. Going from zero to over 90,000 employees in two decades would be an HR nightmare for most companies. McDougall says the key is to get everyone, from Vice Presidents to the waitstaff, focused on customers and then cut them loose to run their own piece of the business. "All right, we're not a small company anymore," McDougall said, conceding the obvious. "But we really try to have every individual's job tied back to the customer somehow. Anything you're working on here in corporate for example, see if you can find a strand back to the customers. I don't want a corporate staff fighting against the field. That's not the battle— we're all on the same side trying to give the customer better service out there. If my MIS department can find a better way to schedule labor in the unit and save the manager time, that's something that's driven right into the manager's hands and helps him—at the restaurant level.

"We also stress that everyone is here to make the restaurant operator's job easier— give him the autonomy to run his own show, make him more efficient, take the paperwork off his back, get him out taking care of the customers and the employees—and at the end of the day produce some great results! If you're working on a project here in headquarters, it can't be simply to make your desk look neater. It's got to be something that impacts the operator and ultimately the customer."

And what about the field? McDougall continued, "They're highly decentralized and spread out into hundreds of little entrepreneurial style businesses. In a smaller company you know, you can have an open-door policy. But I can't handle 90,000 employees walking in with ideas. So as we decentralize, we have the regional directors and vice presidents take more and more of the corporation with them. It just focuses down. Everything can't come through my office here—we don't try and do that. We *really* try to delegate—to decentralize! And the field stays focused on what they're doing because it's in their self interest. Everyone's in profit sharing. Everyone. The waitstaff runs their own profit sharing with tips. All the managers in the units get bonuses based on what their restaurant itself does in profitability. So they're kind of self-contained little businesses out there. Each restaurant is like a little $2 to $3 million factory. And when they hit their goals, they all get their bonuses. So they're very focused within their four walls to make it happen."

Lest you think it's all positive consequences under Ron McDougall, be sure that he is absolutely sure that employees must produce improved performance and profits. He wants his people to succeed. And he wants them to enjoy succeeding. But there's a downside, and it's a big one. In this super-charged growth environment, there's just no room for what McDougall calls the *laggards*. The humor disappears from his face as he gives the bottom line on preserving the sonic pace of the business, "The laggards? They set bad examples for the people that are working for them and with them. Tough as it sounds—it's bad for morale to keep the laggards around. So you've got to be proactive. You've got to prune the tree. Dead branches just make the whole tree look brown."

Every company must find its own particular way to focus on employee autonomy and accountability. Brinker International's amazing record says it has found a pretty good way. It is energetic commitment from the top. A completely decentralized organization with self-managing, entrepreneurial units in the field. Both headquarters and field performance goals that are tied into satisfying customers. And the finishing touch—all 90,000 people in the company are on profit sharing. Is it all worth trying yourself? Of course it is, and please don't wait until you have 90,000 employees yourself. In fact, why not start off with your very first employee—giving a little autonomy and getting a lot of accountability in return?

✔ Share Fortune and Misfortune.

As an entrepreneur, you will have little choice but to pin your hopes and fears on the future of your company. You will have to share the fortunes as well as the misfortunes of the business. And so it should be for your employees. What's good for the company should be good for the workers. And if it's good for the workers, it should be good for the company. Conversely, if it's bad for the company, it's going to be bad for employees. This is the ultimate entrepreneurial mind-set about suffering fortune and misfortune. Handing out negative news is never easy, but sometimes it has to be done.

It's called having a shared destiny, and without it, you can forget about a committed workforce. How in the world could it be otherwise? Nowhere in the world will employees commit to a company that isn't committed to them. It's simple common sense. No one can have just a half loaf of commitment. Unless you and your employees truly get in the same boat, real commitment—accepting the good and the bad—will never exist.

Of course it's easier to share the good times than the bad. But for sure, no employee will be ready to share any company misfortune if they haven't experienced along the way a fair share of the company's good fortune. Unfortunately, at too many companies, large and small, the first real sharing employees are asked to participate in has been a cost reduction program, a downsizing, or some other equally unpleasant edict from headquarters. And in many other organizations, the government for example, neither fortune nor misfortune have ever been shared with employees.

All these examples illustrate why handing out million dollar executive bonuses while lowly employees are being downsized is guaranteed to destroy commitment. Such actions may not be immoral, but they're certainly stupid. These, and others too numerous to go into here, are all very bad managerial practices that destroy employee commitment. There can be no place for them in your entrepreneurial world. The one absolute, a priori, requirement for creating commitment to the cause is a full sharing of both the good and tough times with your people. So do yourself a huge favor and start developing your plan now for doing just that.

✔ Lead by Example, Never Compromise.

How can you expect your people to care about what they do if you don't seem to care about what you're doing? You don't have to be the best salesman or the greatest product developer in the company, but you cannot take a second seat to anyone in terms of commitment to the mission. Leading by example is a rule everyone agrees on, but few really practice. It's actually more critical that entrepreneurs do this than their managerial counterparts in larger companies. Everyone can accept having a cynical, uncommitted manager a few times in their career. It's the luck of the draw and you likely won't have to put up with him very long anyway. But if the creator of the company hates his work, or hates his customers, or whatever, who could blame the shipping clerk for some slippage in his commitment to the cause? Remember, your people are watching you like a hawk, so never forget to show them that you love what you do, even on a bad day. You owe it to your people and you owe it to yourself. There are hundreds of specific policies and programs you can initiate to foster high commitment. Whatever you do, from major steps like employee ownership to the most mundane of personnel practices, remember that leading by example should top your list.

Creating Entrepreneurial Performance: "I'm Good at Doing It"

If I can't sell better than anybody in the company, I don't deserve to be President.

—John Johnson, Founder,
Johnson Publishing

Would the Harvard Business School hire a professor who said he believed the most important management principle of all is hard work? You doubt it? Well, that means they wouldn't hire the entrepreneur who founded and ran for many years America's largest African American company. Meet John Johnson, whose grandmother hocked her furniture to loan him $400 to start a magazine in Chicago back in 1946. Against great odds he created *Jet* magazine, and then *Ebony*, and ultimately built the great empire we know today as Johnson Publishing. He also said he only had two important jobs in the company: First he wanted to know exactly what his employees thought of their jobs and the company. So he personally interviewed every new employee and every departing employee. Second, he had to sell a lot of advertising space which, he learned on day one, was the only way to stay alive in the magazine business. He actually believed presidents of companies are supposed to be able to sell their product. What a novel idea that would be to many young MBAs coming out of business schools. He took it even further with his motto that if he couldn't sell the product better than anyone else he didn't deserve to be president. This is performance aimed squarely at the heart of the enterprise—the only kind that interests entrepreneurs.

All kinds of managerial techniques and training programs have been invented to improve the performance of employees. Some of them may even be useful, if everyone first understands the entrepreneurial mandate that says moving the business forward is the goal—not writing long reports that nobody reads, or looking good at staff meetings, or going on another management seminar. In other words, you want your people to perform like entrepreneurs.

Entrepreneurs look at performance as a fight to the finish. It's a matter of survival, not scoring points for the next merit review. Their performance is also highly focused around making products and selling customers. In this arena, typical big company job descriptions and performance reviews are probably useless. They rarely focus on customers and products and almost never help you get better at what you do. Here are four key practices that will actually define and deliver entrepreneurial performance in your company.

✔ Get Better At What You Do.

It was quite chic a while back to go around saying "work smarter not harder." That turned out to be bad advice. The people and the companies who get to the top do both. Working smarter *and* harder is what it takes to be a high performer. When people can outthink *and* outwork their competition, they're simply unbeatable. Ask anyone who's come up against our friends at Chiron—a certified champion in the smarter and harder league.

Ed Penhoet and his two co-founders, William Rutter and Pablo Valenzuela, scratched out their first business plan on Easter Sunday, 1981, in Penhoet's living room. They were far ahead of the curve. There weren't yet any markets to analyze or competitors to emulate. Indeed, there was no biotech industry at all. It had only been a few short months since the historic Supreme Court ruling (allowing genetically produced hormones to be patented) that would ultimately turn thousands of scientists into entrepreneurs. Since that day, these three scientists-turned-entrepreneurs have turned an abundance of self-inspiration into both a medical and business miracle.

Penhoet recounted the start-up during our interview at Chiron headquarters in California. "So why would anyone move from the academic world to a business environment? In our case there were two main reasons. First of all, the scope of the science was dramatically increasing. It became clear by the end of the seventies that very large sums of investment money were going to be devoted to the practical application of this technololgy. So if you wanted to stay competitive in the science, it was important to participate in this growth phase. Second, and somewhat related, we had as a group, a strong interest in doing something practical with the technology. I mean, in one sense, it was almost an explosion about to occur because all of this technology had been building up and building up in the academic world, and not much of it had gotten transferred to the traditional drug world. For us the technology was maturing, but people weren't using it as aggressively as it could be used to solve real important medical problems. So it really was a drive not only to remain competitive in the field, but expand our competitive base and apply that to doing something really meaningful on the practical side. That's the underlying dynamic of why we started Chiron.

"So, naively, off we went into the wild blue yonder. I mean, there is no way to do this except naively, because in one sense, if you had experience in doing it, you would probably do it differently. So by definition, almost all entrepreneurs are naive. I guess that's both the strength and the weakness. You are not colored enough by experience so that you are not willing to try some completely new things, and at the same time, it's a weakness because you undoubtedly make a lot of mistakes as you go along."

At this point, Penhoet began describing the kind of performance behaviors needed to succeed in biotech. "What's important to understand was that this was a horse race. It was in fact a race between Bill Rutter at the University of California at San Francisco, the co-founder of Chiron, and Wally Gilbert at Harvard who was associated with Biogen and Genentech. They were competing to do the first cloning of a human gene, which happened to be the insulin gene. It's important to understand the essence of the competition between these groups. You see, in order to understand the dynamic of the industry, you also have to understand the dynamic of the academic schools which founded this industry. I think probably the biggest misconception that the American public has about science and scientists is that it is an occupation which is somehow fundamentally different from any others. Different in the sense that most scientists are not viewed as highly competitive people. The typical American view of scientists comes from Saturday morning cartoons with crazy guys in white coats working in a lab, and being isolated from each other off in a corner doing their little bizarre things." At that moment in the discussion, I have to admit that my mind was reeling back to high school biology class where my teacher was always cutting up toads and did seem a little crazy. A lot had obviously changed since the fifties.

Penhoet continued. "So Larry, before all these biotech companies were started, the scientific enterprise around molecular biology and biochemistry was already tremendously competitive. So the field was, and is, populated by a lot of hard-charging, aggressive, very hard working people. San Francisco was probably the epitome of that. The biochemistry lab at UC San Francisco during the seventies was a place where you could find people at work 7 days a week, 24 hours a day. Anytime that you went there, there were people working, competing, and moving the science along. It wasn't entrepreneurial in the classic sense we normally think about because the end result was not profit—but the behavior was there. So for most of the biotech companies, the behavior of the people who were critical to the enterprise didn't change that much when they moved from the university environment to a commercial environment. They competed aggressively, worked very hard, had a strong drive for success, and basically continued to work in the same style as they had before.

"What distinguishes biotech groups today is the dynamic they established before they started a company, as much as what they have established in the company itself. For example, of all the people I know, Bill Rutter is one of the most hard working. He is a guy that enjoys working 7 days a week, 16 hours a day—and he always has. His style of working permeated UC San Francisco because he was head of the department. So many of us in Chiron had worked for Bill at some earlier point in our career. I got my Ph.D. in his laboratory. Pablo Valenzuela, the third founder and our research director here, was a post-doc in Bill's lab. Pablo's another guy with no energy barrier. You can discuss a new line of research one afternoon, and the next morning he's already got experiments going. So in many ways, Chiron is an extension of Rutter's lab at UC San Francisco. It certainly is in terms of people's work ethic and people's competitiveness."

Near the end of our conversation, I asked Penhoet what he thought accounted for Chiron's great success compared to most of the other thousand or so companies. Many of them haven't yet produced a commercial product and are going through their venture capital money hand over fist. His full answers are summarized into what I think were his three major points.

- **High Speed Is *the* Competitive Advantage.** As noted earlier in Chapter 3 I had assumed Chiron was so successful because they were smarter than their competitors. But Penhoet's surprising answer was that just being smart isn't enough to win in biotech. "We're all smart. In this industry there are very few people who are really very much smarter than the rest, damn few. The reality is, since the beginning this industry has been just a race. We all knew what had to be done. We had to hit the ground running and stick with it. The value only comes if you get products to the marketplace. The winners in biotech are the ones that get to the finish line first!"

- **Stay Close to Sources of Innovation.** Penhoet continues, "We wanted to stay plugged in to the university. We were quite sure that the academic world was going to continue to create new knowledge that would have practical applications. But historically, there was always this big schism between business and academia. And, in our particular field, there was very little need for each other because the traditional pharmaceutical companies were developing drugs based more on serendipity than on knowledge. They screened thousands of chemicals to find ones that would do a certain thing and many drugs got to market, still do in fact, without a deep understanding of how they worked. Therefore, the pharmaceutical companies themselves, did not have a great need for the knowledge that was being built up in the universities. Anyway, back in 1981, we thought we could bridge this gap. We had good reputations scientifically and, at the same time, we had personal skills which allowed us to be seen as acceptable partners for commercial organizations."

- **There's No Substitute for Hard Work.**   Penhoet comments, "What distinguishes successful biotech entrepreneurs is really the degree to which they focus their energies and apply themselves to their tasks. So it's really hard work that in the end is the absolutely critical factor. Hard work is in fact the difference between success and failure. As I look around at who has been successful in our field and who hasn't, there is no question in my mind, for example, that the UC San Francisco work ethic was a significant factor in Genentech's success and in our success. And I think the difference is bigger than it seems between people who work extremely hard and people who just put in an average week. The productivity may go up by a higher order factor, not a linear extrapolation. That is, somebody who works 60 hours, probably gets more than twice as much done as somebody that works 30. They may get four times as much done, because it's a matter of total focus on what they're doing. In any event, I can tell you this for sure. We got the hepatitis B vaccine for only one reason—we started working very hard on it way back in 1981, and we never stopped until we got it. I mean it wasn't an accident. It didn't just fall out of the sky one afternoon."

✔ **Winning at Quality, Quantity, Speed, and Cost.**

Quality, quantity, speed, and cost are the entrepreneur's four fundamental parameters of high performance. How good can I work? How much can I do? How fast can I do it? And how efficiently? The answers to these four commonsense questions will define the competitiveness of your employees and your company.

Your challenge, therefore, will be to make sure your people are better than the competition at these four fundamentals of performance. Instilling these fundamentals in your people, constantly getting better at them, and measuring every employee by them will give you the employee performance standards you'll need to end up in the winner's circle. This may not have the cachet of some new-age human resource management system, but it does have the redeeming value of helping you beat the competition in the market place.

To help make these fundamentals easier to remember, the following is an entrepreneurial dream team that illustrates extreme achievement in each of the four parameters of high performance.

1. **Quality—How Good.**   Gottlieb Daimler and Karl Benz set out to make the highest quality car in the world every year. One hundred years later, their great company is still doing it.

2. **Quantity—How Much.**   Ray Kroc started a hamburger empire that has grown to 30,000 locations around the world and each day sells enough food to feed 50 million people. How much did he accomplish? A lot!

3. **Speed—How Fast.**   Think about Larry Hillblom and DHL's expansion to 120 countries in a decade—still an all-time record.

4. **Cost—How Efficient.**   Lito Rodriguez' DryWash technology in Brazil uses not a drop of water, saving 316 liters of fresh water per car, and 99.5 percent less electricity per car than its competitors. Now that's efficient!

Such a list could go on and on, but I think you get the point. Such incredible achievements are simply a reminder that the greatest danger in trying to create high performance may be setting your sights too low. So why not aim to instill the various talents of Daimler and Benz, Ray Kroc, Larry Hillblom, and Lito Rodriguez across your future workforce? If you even come close, you will simply be unstoppable. So try it. I'm sure you'll like the results.

✔ **Save Your Best for Customers and Products.**

Entrepreneurs save their best efforts for making great products and selling real customers. It's called focus. As an entrepreneur, you should have this kind of focus in spades. It's absolutely essential to getting a new enterprise up and running. As always, the trick will be to pass this on to your employees. Time after time, we've seen promising start-ups lose their focus and blow their opportunity to become a great company. This often happens through the good intentions of employees who just don't share the entrepreneur's laser-point focus around customers and products. You begin to see time, energy, and money being spent on all manner of marginal activities and internal battles. The result? Your company gets diverted from its mission and becomes a candidate for early demise. You can avoid this by making sure you and your employees focus your performance on the things that matter, like saving your best efforts for making great products and serving great customers.

To really drive home the point, let's briefly revisit a company that can only be described as obsessive in its focus on customers and products. Of course we're talking about the company Walt Disney founded, and specifically their theme parks in Anaheim, Orlando, Tokyo, and outside Paris. I reviewed the Disney training manual for hosts and hostesses working in the theme parks. The section titled the *The Disney Look* is fascinating. There are separate sections for hosts and hostesses with instructions on everything from costumes and hair styling to deodorants and fingernails. The paragraph on deodorants for hosts sets the tone and pulls no punches, "Due to close contact with guests and fellow cast members, the use of a deodorant or antiperspirant is required. The use of heavy colognes is discouraged. A light aftershave or cologne is acceptable." *The Disney Look* guidelines for a hostess' fingernails seems to cover everything that could ever possibly happen to your nails, "Fingernails should be kept clean and if polish is used, it should be clear or in flesh tones in cream enamels. Polishes that are dark red, frosted, gold or silver toned are not considered part of the 'Disney Look.' Fingernails should not exceed one-fourth of an inch beyond the fingertip." The introduction to *The Disney Look* says that strict adherence to these guidelines is a condition of employment whether you're a ticket taker, a street sweeper, performing as Captain Hook, or strolling down Main Street as Sleeping Beauty. At first glance, some of Disney's rules and expectations of employees may appear strict and even unrealistic in today's world. But creating the best products in the world and the best customer service in the world doesn't come easy. Disney's attention to detail is, of course, legendary. Extremely high performance standards are set and expected of all employees. Every inch of the park has to be picture perfect. Not just the streets and the attractions, but right down to the details of every cast member's appearance.

In contrast to Disney hosts and hostesses delivering their best performances around customers and products, some employees in other organizations, and not just giant ones, seem to save their best shots for internal turf wars and impressing the brass. Enormous effort and expense can go into these side issues. Of course this kind of behavior can only happen if the brass (you in this case!) allows it to happen. If employees believe that making a great board presentation will get them more kudos than coming in on Saturday to make sure the right product was shipped to their customer, you've already got a huge performance problem as well as a dangerous lack of focus on what's important to your enterprise. If you really want to transform your employees into high performers, you simply must keep them focused on the important things in the business—especially anything to do with customers and products. There is no better way to do that than being focused yourself—which takes us to the final practice, leading by example.

✔ **Lead by Example, Never Compromise.**

If leading by example is the way to foster entrepreneurial commitment, the same message applies here—in spades. As the creator of the company, you have to personally set the standards of performance for your people. You can't avoid it. It comes with the territory. This doesn't mean that you have to be, or even should be, the top performer in your company. It does mean you have to be ready, willing, and able to roll up your sleeves and give it your all—side by side with your employees.

The best example I've ever seen of doing just that is my old friend Po Chung, the very first entrepreneur/partner signed up by Dalsey, Hillblom, and Lynn, the three young law students who founded DHL. Po did it in the hardest working and fastest moving business environment in the world—that beehive of energetic entrepreneurship, Hong Kong. Po founded DHL Hong Kong way back in 1972. At that early stage, no one had ever heard of DHL. There were no manuals to read or training classes to attend to learn how to run the world's first international courier business. He learned it by doing it all himself. His five step program provides a powerful, personal prescription for creating and maintaining the highest performance standards:

Step One.   Personally feel the need for the product.
Step Two.   Personally deliver the product to customers.
Step Three.   Stick to the basics and don't get side-tracked by management theories.
Step Four.   Personally demonstrate belief in and commitment to the company mission.
Step Five.   Continuously pass steps one through four on to your people.

High Commitment and High Performance in the Rust Belt

People are amazed when I tell them that some Lincoln factory workers earn in excess of $100,000 a year.
> —Fred Mackenbach, Retired President,
> Lincoln Electric

Talk about high commitment and high performance! How many companies do you know that have to keep their gates locked before the morning shift to keep employees from starting to work too early? Welcome to Lincoln Electric, an old economy company, manufacturing heavy industrial equipment in the rust belt of America. They're also the world's largest maker of welding equipment and a company that stands conventional wisdom on its head. When I first saw the story on CBS TV's 60 Minutes, I couldn't believe it. So I checked it out personally with President Fred Mackenbach in Cleveland, Ohio—ground zero of the rust belt. Along with the locked gates to keep workers out, Lincoln Electric also has some very strange ideas about compensating employees. Mackenbach says, "The company only gets paid by making good welding equipment, and we don't see any reason for paying employees for anything other than making that welding equipment." And they don't. They don't pay anyone for holidays, sick leave, lunch time, coffee breaks, trips to the toilet, or for poor quality products that no one will buy.

Then, with a twinkle in his eye, Mackenbach let slip that the employees don't really seem to mind since they are all earning from $60,000 to over $100,000 per year, making them the highest paid factory workers in the world. Mackenbach said they had built the entire company on the notion that "Lincoln can pay the highest factory salaries in the world because our people know that, like entrepreneurs, the more good welding equipment they produce the more money they will make. And second, also like entrepreneurs, they know they don't get paid for downtime or rejects—so they've all become self-managing which means we don't need to hire 500 supervisors to stand around and watch them work. Anyway, they all work damn hard and there's a lot of profit to be shared in that welding equipment." It's a modern version of 19th Century piecework pay, with two huge differences. First, all those savings go back to the workers in profit bonuses. In a good year, they average more than $20,000 per worker—an unheard of figure in American factories. Second, the company guarantees continuous employment to its workers, and hasn't had a layoff since it was founded in 1895. Over the years, all Lincoln employees have been asked to temporarily cut their time as much as 25 percent, but everyone in the company agrees this is preferable to the standard industrial practice of layoffs and outright terminations.

Other unusual things happen when extreme employee performance and commitment takes hold. Mackenbach explains, "Large organizations are usually devoted to minimizing risks, not seeking them out. We're fortunate at Lincoln because our strong pay-for-performance system forces us to take risks on a daily basis. We take a risk every time we make a new hire. We look for a strong work ethic and a burning desire to succeed. Evidence of that desire is the best predictor of success in the Lincoln culture. If we are wrong about a new hire, that person's substandard performance will adversely affect the productivity of everyone in that department. Since we are exactly staffed, the other employees will have to pick up the slack. So at Lincoln, we consider each new hire to be a risky business decision.

"We also take many risks by encouraging our employees to be self-managing. This means that we are willing to relinquish a high degree of control, in exchange for the tremendous energy and intiative highly motivated people bring to our enterprise. Of course the big benefit of having 6400 self-managing employees is that we don't have to pay people to watch other people. Our customers couldn't care less about how much time and money we spend micromanaging our workforce. But the non-productive cost of supervision could have a devastating impact on the prices we charge our customers—and *that*, they care about!

"And of course our formal policy of guaranteed continuous employment entails an almost unheard-of risk. It is a risk we have continued to take, day by day, month by month, year by year, through recessions and very hard times in our industry. But we believe the upside in all this is worth it. An example is the remarkable performance of our people last summer, when a sudden spike in demand for our products forced us to sharply increase production. Lincoln employees voluntarily deferred 614 weeks of vacation in order to meet that challenge. Their efforts broke all of our production and sales records. And I must tell you, our records were already high."

The most current financial results say Lincoln Electric's entrepreneurial approach is still working. On this year's *Fortune 1000* list, they are once again a star within their industrial grouping. You'll find them listed in the "Industrial and Farm Equipment" category—about as old economy as it gets. In this most basic of basic industries, stalwarts like Caterpillar, Detroit Diesel, and Timkin are bigger and better known—but the Ohio manufacturer of welding equipment really shines when it comes to the key financial ratios. With $1.2 billion in revenue, it ranks only 36th of the 37 companies in size. But here's the high commitment payoff: As percentages of revenue, it ranks number *two* in profitability and number *three* in total return to investors!

As Fred Mackenbach concluded, "People are amazed when I tell them that some Lincoln factory workers earn in excess of $100,000 a year. Well, it's not very complicated. The first point is that to get a commitment *out of people*, management must first make a commitment *to those people*. And secondly, when workers are treated like entrepreneurs, they behave like entrepreneurs. Lincoln Electric employees will do anything it takes to produce more welding equipment. It's just amazing." Then he chuckled, " That's why we have to lock the gates sometimes!"

I recently called Don Hastings, the retired CEO of Lincoln Electric, to thank him for sending me a copy of his *60 Minutes* interview. He's an incredibly nice guy and said sending the tape was the least he could do given my interest in Lincoln Electric. During our conversation, I asked him if he had any current words of wisdom to offer on creating high commitment/high performance employees in light of all the corporate scandals swirling about. His answer, "It's very simple really. Most companies talk about people as their most important asset. They always say it and you see it in their mission statements. But they don't really walk the talk. They say people are the most important, then the next day they lay off a thousand of them. At Lincoln, the customers and the employees always come before the shareholders. Of course by doing this we've made our shareholders wealthy in the long term. Today Lincoln has a hundred year plus tradition of doing this: of valuing customers and employees ahead of the shareholder. It's so deeply embedded I don't think it will ever change. So that's the message Larry—and it's pretty simple."

If it's so simple to create high commitment and high performance across an entire workforce, why aren't more companies doing it? Could it be that it would require the top executives to lead by example—and most of them are simply not willing to do that? As hard evidence, the Lincoln CEO's compensation is a modest five to six times that of the average Lincoln worker—compared to an incredible 531 times at *Fortune 500* companies! As a brand new entrepreneur, you can't afford to *not* lead by example. The best part of the Lincoln Electric story is that you could do most of the same things at your start-up venture from day one! There's nothing holding you back. And to give you a head-start, the following is a handy list covering the key points of Lincoln Electric's amazing approach to creating employee commitment and performance.

- Customers and employees always come before shareholders.
- Lincoln has the highest paid industrial workforce in the world, which ends up being very good for their bottom line.
- Like entrepreneurs, the more good product employees produce, the more money they make.
- Like entrepreneurs, employees don't get paid for downtime (vacations, holidays, sick days, coffee breaks, and so on.) or for making poor quality product.

- Employees are self-managing so the company needs no supervisory staff. The savings allow Lincoln to pay best-in-the-world salaries to workers.

- Lincoln offers guaranteed continuous employment. There have been temporary reductions in work up to 25 percent, but there's never been a layoff.

- The Lincoln CEO makes five to six times the average salary of employees. Compare this, one more time, to the outrageous 531 times at *Fortune 500* companies.

Inspiring Others

The genius of the Honda Motor Company is in the average worker.
—Soichiro Honda, Founder,
Honda Motor Company

Most of us can figure out how to inspire ourselves. But can we inspire others? The successful entrepreneur, as well as the successful manager, has to be able to do it. But it's a lot easier said than done. Both entrepreneurs and professional managers have a spotty track record on fostering commitment and performance in others.

The good news is, as an entrepreneur, you will have a real leg up in this area against most of your competition. For company managers, it can be next to impossible to inspire their troops. Not only do they have to operate in a numbing Dilbertesque environment, complete with outrageous CEO pay and neverending downsizing, there's a whole world of professional HR people, in and out of the company, giving them a lot of really bad advice. On the inside, the HR folks have usurped large chunks of the line manager's relationship with his workers, often leaving him with little responsibility and even less authority for doing much of anything about worker commitment or performance. And while slowly changing, it's still the personnel function that attracts the most antibusiness minded people in all business. Remember, HR is still the place in the company where a sheepskin in psychology carries more weight than the last 30 years of common sense learned on the factory floor. On the outside, there's no other area of management consulting or training that is so riddled with charlatans, incompetents, and just plain crazies as the how-tomotivate-people crowd. The nonsense that goes on would fill another book, but I'm sure you get the point.

In any event, this is not your problem—at least not for another 10 years when you can afford to have your own wonderful HR department. Your only potential problem today is that like a lot of great athletes who make terrible coaches, you may have trouble passing on your own entrepreneurial self-inspiration to your employees. The reason for this is clear: Even great entrepreneurs are often unaware of what they actually do and the special ways they go about doing it. They don't analyze it or even think about it much. Consequently, they sometimes have a hard time teaching or instilling their natural ability at enterprise in their people.

But don't worry. Fortunately, you are reading the right book to overcome this small hurdle. The best way—maybe the only way—to inspire others is to get them to inspire themselves. One of the all-time masters at doing this was the legendary Japanese entrepreneur, Soichiro Honda. His story provides the first lesson on how you can inspire your own future employees.

Honda was, hands down, the most interesting Japanese entrepreneur of the twentieth century. His death in 1991 produced the greatest outpouring of grief and respect by employees ever accorded a Japanese corporate leader. Interestingly, Honda was an outsider to Japan's industrial establishment. He was the son of a blacksmith, who at 16 began his working career as a mechanic. He moved on to auto racing, but after a near fatal accident, he decided to try producing scooters and eventually cars. With only a third grade education, he was the working man's man.

He was also a master of the carrot and stick, and never hesitated to use them. He understood that inspiring others fundamentally boiled down to answering the what's-in-it-for-me question. Honda answered by showering attention on good performers, always promoting fairly (Honda's relatives were not even allowed to work in the company), and putting his money behind his compassion (such as building entire factories just for handicapped workers). He also carried a big stick. He demanded top performance from Honda's engineers as well as from the engines they made. His temper flared when they missed. In one crushing outburst he could devastate a misperforming engineer or production team. The next morning however, he was back, sleeves rolled up, working together until they solved the problem.

"The young people just idolized him," remembers Tetsuo Chino. He grew up with him in the car business and knew him well. Chino was President of Honda USA from its startup in Marysville, Ohio, in the late seventies all the way through their record breaking decade of the eighties. He was in fact the first man to produce Japanese cars with American workers. And he was also the man who pushed the Accord to become the number one selling car in the United States. I met with Chino at Honda Headquarters in Tokyo. He had recently entered semiretirement, a phase in Honda known as *soft running*. He had enthusiastically agreed to meet me to tell the inside story of the real genius of Soichiro Honda.

"The Honda Company is probably most famous for its attention to customers. It also has a reputation of being the automobile company run by real automobile lovers. But maybe the untold story of Honda is how the founder inspired his people—even those American auto workers who everyone said couldn't make a competitive car anymore. Everyone, that is, except Mr. Honda."

So what kind of man was he? "On the one hand, Soichiro Honda was tough. He was a self-made man and he didn't like to be guided by anybody else. You know our MITI (the powerful Ministry of International Trade and Industry) which is full of Japanese bureaucrats? When Mr. Honda tried to enter the auto business from just making scooters, MITI said no. They told him, 'Japan has enough auto makers already. You keep making scooters.' So Soichiro Honda fought the government. He told them, 'MITI is not our shareholder. You cannot decide my destiny. I want to make automobiles and certainly you cannot make that decision for me.' This was a famous fight in Tokyo. So he entered the auto business in spite of MITI. This was not done in Japan. Soichiro Honda was a very unique Japanese, and the employees admired that.

"On the other hand, he was a humanistic person. He always said the technology is just a means to make people happy. The company was founded as a people oriented company. And even though he was the founder, he didn't allow his heirs in the company and none of the top executives were allowed to have their heirs in the company either. This was greatly appreciated by the employees and is very unusual in famous Japanese companies. He was interested in the people in the community also, like the handicapped. Do you know he founded two plants in Japan specially designed to employ only handicapped people? Anyway he was very people oriented himself. Very easy to talk to. He was kind of an entertainer actually. He played music for people and entertained them. When you met him, he tried to have you enjoy the time. He tried to make everybody happy. When he was inducted into the American Automotive Hall of Fame, all the U.S. Honda dealers came. They said they appreciated his efforts and his products. But Mr. Honda said, 'It's not me, all the merit has to go to you, the dealers.' Then he disappeared from the headtable. He asked for a wine waiter's uniform. He dressed in the uniform and reappeared. He served wine to every dealer. He was saying to each, 'Thank you, thank you. It is only because of you I'm even in this Hall of Fame.' I know that no other Japanese CEO would behave this way. And I doubt that any of the American CEOs in Detroit would either. But that was the type of man Soichiro Honda was.

"Mr. Honda truly thought the genius of the company was in the workers. And they knew that he trusted them. He always liked the workshops and the plants best. He went there a lot himself and discussed things with the workers and the technicians and the engineers. He discussed things in great detail. He would make his comments and he listened to their ideas. He strongly inspired employees about the product. Of course when he was young, he raced cars. He had a very bad accident and quit, but he was always keen to develop race cars. This is an important thing at Honda. It's not just for promotion purposes. It's very good for the engineers in developing new ideas and new technologies. Working on racing engines is a very serious business and is also very good for speeding up the learning. He always said, 'Beating the clock is the most important factor to becoming number one.' That kind of spirit about high performance cars was very inspiring to the engineers and even the production workers. You can foster a good spirit in the automobile business through racing. Honda people in Japan, in the States, everywhere, are very proud of our Formula One championships. You see, Mr. Honda believed technology has no end. You can always improve it. For example, that's why we produced the all aluminum body car and we're now testing the 100 mpg engine. It's also why Honda was the first company to meet the tough U.S. emission standards. There are many difficulties in doing these things but our engineers are always encouraged to challenge limits. Automobile employees are very motivated by making machines no one else can make!

"Of course I must also say he was a very serious minded person. If you made a mistake in the business, he could get so mad. His anger was not just emotional. He used it as a kind of teacher, too. He really wanted all of us to learn to do better. The next day he would recover and come back to us and ask how we could all improve the situation. He always did this. He was aggressive about the business but he would always try to help us. He did this especially with the young people. They knew he was serious but also there to help them. As I said, he was a very unique Japanese."

Call it what you want, Soichiro Honda clearly understood the power of positive and negative consequences. Using his own version of the carrot

and stick, he inspired Honda employees to extraordinary levels of commitment and performance: extraordinary commitment to the company's mission and extraordinary performance in building the best and fastest
machines in the world. This is exactly what entrepreneurial leaders have
to be able to do whether in a factory in Tokyo, Japan or Marysville, Ohio.

The Almighty Power of Consequences

*Our folks don't expect something for nothing . . . they want to win so
badly, they just go out there and do it!*
                                        —Sam Walton, Founder,
                                        Wal-Mart Stores

Even a charasmatic, entrepreneurial leader like Sam Walton, arriving at
each store in his old Chevy pick-up and leading the troops in the Wal-
Mart fight song, found that hoopla can only take you so far in the business of inspiring employees. Walton got more mileage out of company
hoopla than most, probably because he was so darn good at doing it. But
even Wal-Mart, the fastest growing, and now biggest, company in history
uses carefully thought out policies to help answer the what's-in-it-for-me
question. Their most ambitious effort is an across the board employee
stock ownership program for their 1,383,000 employees. The program is
reenforced by making subordinate employee participation a part of every
manager's annual goals. Of course the one-two punch of having a charis-
matic leader like Perot, Lever, Johnson, Honda, or Sam Walton—combined with solid, ongoing policies that foster a spirit of enterprise in
workers—is a tough combo to beat.

And of course, implementing your own version of this one-two
punch is exactly what you can and should do in your new business.
Which brings us face-to-face with the challenge of exactly how to create
more self-inspired employees. In our experience, the only way to do that
is to figure out how to instill entrepreneurial style consequences
throughout the organization.

There's really no mystery to why people do the things they do in
life—and perform the way they perform at work. The platinum rule
of human behavior is that people behave in their own self-interest.
They do things where they perceive the personal consequences will be
positive. And they avoid doing things where they perceive the personal consequences will be negative. Of course, this bone-deep law of

behavior depends on the positive and negative consequences being accurate, timely, and powerful. The more the consequences fit this bill, the more self-inspired a person's behavior, or performance, will be. This also happens to be the classic model of entrepreneurial performance, which is squarely based on the power of consequences.

Entrepreneurial Performance

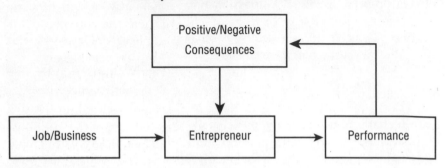

If you're looking for the number one difference between entrepreneurs and bureaucrats, here it is. Entrepreneurs feel the consequences of their performance every Friday night when they count the money in the cash box. If it's full, they feel on top of the world. If it's empty, their kids don't eat. These are accurate, timely, and powerful consequences which would affect anyone's behavior. In a true entrepreneurial environment, there is no place to hide. There are no six month probation periods. There will be no second chances to try it again next year. And most of the time, everything you have is on the line.

Bureaucrats, on the other hand, rarely feel any consequences, positive or negative. I learned how this works in my very first job many years ago at American Express Company in New York. My salary was $1,250 a month, a princely sum to me at the time, and I was excited to be working in the Big Apple. American Express was and is a decent company, but they taught me a very important (and frustrating) lesson about consequences, or the lack thereof. Here's what I learned in the first six months working for a *Fortune 500* company. If I worked very, very hard for a month and brought in several big, new clients, a pretty spectacular performance really, at the end of the month I got exactly $1,250 in my pay envelope. Then during the next month, if I took it a little easier, did nothing special, a fairly humdrum, average month, once again, at the end of the month, I found exactly $1,250 in my pay envelope. And finally for the third month, if I decided to do absolutely nothing at all, and basically just showed up and managed to stay awake at meetings, at the end of the month I got—you guessed it—exactly $1,250! The message was loud and clear. The company was practically screaming at the employees, "It really doesn't matter what you do!" If this seems a far-fetched example to you, good. Hopefully that means you'll never tolerate such a crazy system in your own company.

Your options are clear. You can manage people in your start-up company the *Fortune 500* way, or you can manage them the entrepreneurial way. Obviously, we recommend the latter. And please don't assume this is a problem you can tackle later when your company gets bigger. If you don't focus on inspiring your people from day one, you may find yourself leading an entrepreneurial mission that no one is following. That's a pretty good sign it may be too late; that you're fast-forwarding through your life cycle and careening down the managerial side of the curve. At that point, all the consultants and HR gurus will be telling you that what you really need is a super-duper personnel department to figure out how to remotivate the troops. You'll then reach into the bottomless pit of available HR professionals, and it will go downhill from there. The power of consequences will get lost in a sea of personnel mumbo-jumbo.

Do not let this happen to your company! There are things you can do to ensure you have self-inspired, enterprising employees from day one. All you have to do is make sure you've got some entrepreneurial-style consequences working from the day of your very first hire. Fortunately, there are at least three proven ways to instill consequences in the company. Employees can become owners or shareholders in your company. You can create new, little pieces of the business that some of your best employees can run as *intrapreneurs*. Or, you can create a company-wide Entrepreneurial Performance System whereby every worker will perform their job in a more entrepreneurial way.

✔ Workers as Owners.

Many companies in recent years have become employee-owned, often with incredible results. There are examples every year of workers buying their company and miraculously saving it from bankruptcy. They do it with the same products, the same customers, and the same people. How can it be? It's not because they get smarter or more skilled. It's because they have, for the first time, a personal stake in the success and failure of their company.

There is an older, more common form of employee entrepreneur-ship—the partnership. There's no question that the partnership form of organization has always produced incredible levels of commitment and performance. Regardless of what one thinks about lawyers, auditors, and consultants, we have to admit that the senior partners, the junior part-ners, and the wanna-be partners usually work circles around their own clients, which are mostly large, public corporations.

Less radical forms of employee ownership have been around for years. These would include all the various types of employee stock ownership programs. Even these efforts, where employees may only own a small number of shares, have a positive impact on results. All the studies in the United States clearly show that companies with employee shareholders outperform competitors with no such employee involvement. The exam-ple of Wal-Mart is a good one. They believe so strongly that employees should be shareholders, they've made the level of participation by workers a part of every managers annual performance review and bonus.

Whether it's Wal-Mart in North America, or Unilever in Europe, or former state industries in China now owned by the employees, the result is the same. Any form of employee ownership simply has to have some posi-tive effect on the behavior of employees. There's no mystery to it. The only mystery is why 80 percent of companies around the world still don't do it.

✔ **Intrapreneurship.**

This is an old idea with a new name. Give a small group of highly commit-ted, top performing managers a little seed money, a lot of autonomy, partic-ipation in the financial results, and ask them to create a new business for the corporation—but outside the corporation. For some big companies such as Xerox and Levi Strauss, this method is providing the chance to create new entrepreneurial businesses and not lose the entrepreneurs. Like true-blue entrepreneurial start-ups, these small spin-offs can move quickly to capture changing markets and niche markets that their parent companies could never hope to do. The only downside of intrapreneuring is that only a few can play. The other 99 percent of your people will not be involved.

✔ **The Entrepreneurial Performance System.**

If making workers the owners isn't for you, and if intrapreneurship affects too few people, what can you do? How can you get your employees to be-have more entrepreneurially right now in their current jobs? Here's the answer! I call it the Entrepreneurial Performance System, the third proven way to foster self-inspired commitment and performance in your people. This is a practical step you can implement with your very first hire. The next section details how to create and make this system work for your business.

Creating an Entrepreneurial Performance System

Remember Lincoln Electric? Produce a lot of good welding equipment and you'll be the highest paid workers in the world. Produce poor quality

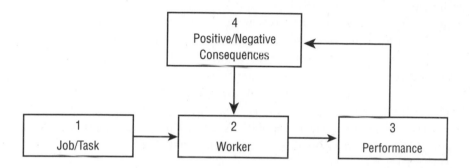

1. The Job or Task at Hand. This is the stimulus or input to the worker. It could be anything from the key points in a job description, to the ever-changing daily requirements of the job, to even a department's annual plan and budget.

2. The Worker. Whether it's a senior manager or a shipping clerk, the worker acts as the central processing unit of the human performance system.

3. Performance. This is the response or output of the worker. Whether measuring hard items like annual sales achieved, or soft areas such as customer courtesy, the worker's output is the key factor we are trying to improve. For positive performance, you want to make sure there is a positive consequence back to the worker. Likewise, for poor performance, you want to make sure there is a negative consequence to the worker. When this doesn't happen, we say the consequences are out of balance with the performance.

4. Positive or Negative Consequences. The important consequences come from customers—the true external customer or even the internal customer/user. The job of the manager is to make sure those consequences are fed back to the worker in an accurate, timely, and impactful way. Whether it's a sincere thank you for a job well done, a $1,000 award for a good suggestion, or when necessary, the delivery of a negative performance review, the feedback loop has to be completed by the manager.

or no welding equipment and you'll get nothing. That's the deal at Lincoln. And that is how an Entrepreneurial Performance System (EPS) is supposed to work. It's certainly working for Lincoln Electric in Cleveland, Ohio, and it can work for you.

The EPS focuses on consequences as the primary people management tool. The point is to duplicate for your people, to the extent possible, the real-world performance environment of entrepreneurs. The EPS's fundamental assumption is that 99 percent of all human behavior can be explained in two words: *stimulus* and *response*. The salesperson sees a customer enter the store and responds with courteous service. Or the shipping clerk gets a customer order and responds by shipping the product. The diagram on p. 183 depicts the complete human performance environment in which we all work. The underlying principles never change and they apply to entrepreneurs, bureaucrats, and everyone in between.

While the principles of the system never change, individual responses (performance) to a particular stimulus (job or task at hand), can be quite different. Some salespeople are courteous to customers, and others aren't. One clerk may ship the product the same day while another will ship it three days late. Why the different responses? Read on! The following illustrates the possible causes and the frequency of their occurrence.

Component	Cause	Causal %
1. Job	Job not clear.	10%
2. Worker	Lack of knowledge.	15%
3. Performance	Lack of resources.	10%
4. Consequences	Out of balance. Poor feedback.	65%

A breakdown in any of the major components of the system can cause performance, or commitment, problems. And this leads to the EPS' second fundamental assumption: The greatest influencer of behavior is the workers' perception of the consequences, positive or negative, to his performance. That's why we call it the almighty power of consequences.

Consequences is number one by a wide margin. And it makes sense. Think about it, how many jobs have you had where the consequences were totally out of whack? They were either nonexistent, or the reverse of what they should have been, and/or your boss never got around to feeding back the consequences, in any meaningful way, to you. The three other possible causes—the job is not clear or well defined, the worker doesn't know how to do the job, and there is a lack of resources to do the job—are breakdowns that occur less frequently. The small causal percentages in these categories also makes sense if you think about it. Most workers know *what* their job is, and most workers know *how* to do their job, and most workers have adequate resources to do the job.

This is why we say consequences represent the biggest single difference between entrepreneurial and bureaucratic behavior. Entrepreneurs live and die on the direct feedback of consequences. The consequences are powerful and immediate. In bureaucracies, it's exactly the opposite. The consequences are out of balance, they rarely come from customers, and you only hear about them during an annual performance review. This can't be the way you operate your own business if you hope to grow and prosper. As the leader of your company, it will be your job to manage the performance system of your workers. The trick will be to make sure all your employees feel the consequences of their performance, positive or negative, in an accurate, powerful, and timely manner—just like an entrepreneur.

If you're ready to begin bringing on employees to help you grow your business, and you want them all to have the same self-inspired commitment and performance that you have, you've come to the right place. Step one will be to set in place strong positive/negative consequences—and make absolutely certain those consequences are fed back to every performer, every week. This is the surefire way to inspire your people and instill the entrepreneurial spirit throughout your company.

For a current, real-life example of practicing everything we've covered in this chapter, we'll close with an interview from the rough and tumble Asian retail industry. Meet Jannie Tay, entrepreneurial superwoman and Chinese mamacita to a sprawling watch and jewelry empire stretching from Monte Carlo to Tokyo to Sydney.

It's All in the Family

They become your corporate family and you have unconditional love for each other—you forgive and forget and you share the good and the bad.

—Jannie Tay, Founder, The Hour Glass

Jannie Tay was named one of the Fifty Leading Women Entrepreneurs Of The World.* In the tough, discount crazy Asian retail market for watches and jewelry, you have to be doing a lot right to hit $300 million in revenues after just 20 years in business. Today, The Hour Glass has some 15 retail outlets spread over Singapore, Australia, Malaysia, Indonesia, and Hong Kong. Their carry the world's top brands such as Cartier, Rolex, Christian Dior, Patek Phillippe, and Mondial Jewelery. They have also integrated backward with two joint-venture watch factories in Switzerland, as well as wholesale operations in Tokyo, Singapore, Hong Kong, Geneva, and Monte Carlo.

The Hour Glass has a strong public reputation based on two things: high quality products and exquisite, upscale service. This reputation is backed up by the fact that they were the first watch and jewelry retailer in the world to be awarded the ISO 9000 Quality Certificate. What the outside world doesn't know, however, is that both the high quality and the great service are, in truth, driven by Jannie Tay's greatest personal asset: her amazing instincts for inspiring her people. It's her secret formula for making sure all 300 of her employees truly have that all-in-the-family spirit.

Jannie Tay, always in a hurry, was several sentences into her story before I had even turned the tape recorder on: " . . . so yes, my father was a very big influence on me. He was a physician by hobby and produced medicated oils as a small business. As a young girl I used to go to trade shows with my father to sell this medicated oil and on the trips I remember stopping in all these little towns where we would visit his customers and have a cup of tea—so maybe early on I got the idea that business could be like a family activity. But you know, back in the 1950s girls didn't have to work. All I really wanted to do was get married, have children, and have a good time, like all the girls in Singapore. But at 16 I went to Melbourne, Australia, to study. The day I entered the university my dad died. It was very sad. In those days young Chinese ladies certainly didn't go off to foreign universities, and I always thank my father for sending me. My basic degree was in physiology and I got a masters in pharmacology. I also met my future husband in Australia. Henry was a Singaporean medical student.

---

*Tay was recognized as one of the "Fifty Leading Women Entrepreneurs" by The National Foundation for Women Business Owners as part of a global research project, funded by IBM.

"In 1971, we came back to Singapore. I taught at the University of Singapore in the Physiology Department for two years, but I was very bored by academia. After every lecture I'd say 'What am I doing here?' On the other hand, my husband's family had a small retail watch business. Henry said if I wanted to leave the University, why not work at his family's shop? So I became a sales girl in my in-law's shop selling watches. I loved it. I was very happy behind the counter, working with the customers. A lot of people said: 'You're a university lecturer, why do you want to be a lowly sales girl?' But I was happy meeting customers, and I really liked selling watches to people.

"At that time in Singapore, the big stores began moving out of our traditional retail areas and started opening on the more up-scale and beautiful Orchard Road. I observed that those stores had a very good turn of business and all the tourists wanted to go to Orchard Road. The tourist market in Singapore was beginning to grow rapidly and our little shops in the more traditional Chinese areas were static and not growing. But when I told my mother-in-law we should move to Orchard Road, she didn't want to. So my husband and I decided to sell out of the family business. But it took a lot of money to go to Orchard Road and compete with the big stores. I went to Metro which was the only retailer in town listed on the stock exchange and proposed a joint venture with them. If they would provide the financial backing, we would provide the management for an upscale retail watch business. We were completely surprised when they said okay. It taught me a valuable lesson: You never get anything if you don't ask for it. Anyway, they took 51 percent and we had 49 percent and we started The Hour Glass in October, 1979. We opened with just one shop in Lucky Plaza, a new, fancy shopping area. After a few years, we bought out our financial partners, and owned the entire company—until we went public on the Singapore stock exchange in 1992."

The thing that people remember most after hearing Jannie Tay talk is her passion for The Hour Glass front-line employees. See if you agree. "The number one lesson I have learned is that the value of The Hour Glass or any company is in its human resources. Everyone today talks about customer service, and it's true that customers demand good service from the people that work for the retailer. The truth is, if you develop and treat your human resources with respect, and I mean the front-line people as well as the management, you will win the customer's heart. I like the upside down triangle and initially some of my corporate staff were upset because they said I only think of the front-line people. But we have to remember, in a hierarchical situation, the people who are up here in the so-called head office are like gods. They are the ones who tell you what to do. They are the ones who pick up your mistakes. And they usually are the ones who get the most benefit from the company. In The Hour Glass, this is reversed. The front-line people who are closest to the customers are the ones who will benefit most and I support that. It's a complete culture reversal from most retail companies.

"Managers in a hierarchical system feel they have gone through the doghouse so to speak to get to the top, and now deserve to enjoy their position and their power. In my philosophy, I may have the title of Managing Director, but I'm still that sales girl first, and then I'm the MD. Some of my early managers could not buy this philosophy and they left. They even said it was 'morally demotivating' to them. I told them that without the front-line people we wouldn't even have jobs. We wouldn't be sitting here. But some people just can't accept that so they have to leave.

"I dont want any antientrepreneurial managers because that's the same as antigrowth in my opinion." This is Tay at full stride, describing exactly why and how The Hour Glass has become one of the most entrepreneurial companies in Asia—and I'm sure why she keeps picking up kudos like the Fifty Leading Women award. "Entrepreneurship is all about being challenged and wanting to do innovative things to keep growing—but a manager typically wants to play it safe. You tell them what to do, they do exactly what you tell them, and they deliver the result—but no more. That's managing.

"I think The Hour Glass is a very entrepreneurial company because we have developed as an entrepreneurial society in the company. I really believe you can help people change, you can develop them and you can support them. You can do this by letting them make mistakes, by nurturing them along, and giving them a second or third chance. And of course you do push them, you try to break their mind-set, all their limiting beliefs about themselves, and you keep pushing them. At the end of the day, if you do all this, you can bring out the entrepreneurship in anybody. But you have to do it all. People in their forties and fifties who join The Hour Glass, do find it more difficult to be entrepreneurial because for so many years they were so set and structured in their mind. But I've found that they can be very entrepreneurial once they get rid of their limiting habits. Even the accountants, who have been taught a certain way to do things, to be very responsible, to be careful—even they can be more entrepreneurial in their job.

"You see, when I say entrepreneurship, I mean allowing people to be creative, to be open minded, to test new ground, to be more motivated. Of course you also want them to work as a team, to think first of the customer, to push for sales, but at the end of the day they should enjoy what they are doing, and be very committed to it. If you do all that you will have more entrepreneurial people and you will be a more entrepreneurial and successful company."

The Hour Glass has the highest retention rate of employees of any Asian retail company. It is truly an amazing record. I was hoping to get from Tay some of the specifics on how this has been achieved. She didn't disappoint, "I realized that if I wanted the 10 people who started with me to stay with me, I had to let them be their own bosses and be my business partners. I had to let them run their own businesses or else they would leave me for someone else who would take them away with a higher salary. So today those 10 people, plus many after them, have been with me a long time. Now how did we do that?

"First, we develop them. Every Monday we still do training in the offices, particularly personal growth type training. I know these things can help. When I first started I went to a lot of courses on building up my own self-confidence. I even went to an Anthony Robbins course once.

"We all share our information completely. We share our experiences and how we tackle problems, and we discuss these things like owners of the business, not employees. I tell you, even though many of them haven't gone beyond high school, they have become more knowledgeable than MBAs.

"All decision making is done by them in their stores and their departments. We support them, even advise them if they need help, but they make the decisions for their own areas of the company.

"In our culture, we want employees to feel like owners, and we do something very important about this. Everyone knows what the profits are and we share 10 percent of the company profit with all the employees—*every month without fail*. This monthly distribution is on top of their salary and commission. And at the end of the year, they are also eligible for a one to six month bonus based on their individual performance.

"All these approaches go right down to our front-line people—sales girls and boys just like I used to be. I know what motivates them because I did the same work. You know that more than 70 percent of our people have been with us more than five years which is unheard of in retail in

Asia. And 40 percent of our people have been here more than 10 years. I truly believe this is because they are their own bosses and feel like part owners. At the retail level, we hardly ever have anyone leaving The Hour Glass. I guess if someone would offer to double their salary they would leave. But really we have no one leaving us which is very unusual for front-line people in retail."

And then we reached the concept that Jannie Tay is most famous for: an approach to employees that puts her somewhere between Mother Theresa and a Mother Hen, and never ceases to amaze outside observers. I think our own title of Chinese Mamacita may best describe the flavor of it all. "The key to everything we do is treating ourselves like a family. The employees all know my philosophy—that within a genetic family we love each other unconditionally and we share things with each other. If a member of our family upsets us, we're not political about it. We forgive them and we go on. But when you come to work, if your colleague does something to you, you become political and want to get him out of the company. So I say to our employees, 'Think a minute, and close your eyes. You know we spend more of our waking hours at work than at home. So what would happen if we feel everyone here is part of our family—our corporate family? Keep your eyes closed and imagine yourself in your home environment, but surrounded by the people you work with. They become your family and you have unconditional love for each other—you forgive and forget and you share the good and the bad.' It's an amazing exercise to go through with your staff.

"I'll tell you one thing that is happening just now, which so touched me. It's about one of our junior staff, a very nice young man really, at one of the outlets. I just found out yesterday morning that he took more than $100,000 of our stocks, pawned them, and lost the money gambling. He obviously has a serious problem. He was confronted and he voluntarily went to the police and confessed. Now it turns out his wife also works for us and is expecting their first baby. If we could have found this sooner I'm sure we could have stopped him. We could have minimized the loss and counseled him. Of course now this young boy has to go to jail in Singapore. Well today, I was so touched because a movement has started among our employees. They are saying we do not want him to go to jail because he is so young. We will all chip in and try to cover this loss, and hope the courts will not send him to jail and send him back to his wife with some kind of treatment for gambling. His manager even recommended that we hire him back, counsel him, and help him. You see, this is how a family would try to deal with a serious problem. Of course this is a difficult example, but my point is that even in such a sad case, we can still try to be a corporate family and not turn our backs on each other.

"At The Hour Glass we do a lot of 'internal charity' work, and I insist that every employee must be involved somehow. We have cases where an employee has died or maybe gotten badly injured in an auto accident, and we keep helping the family. It sets a good standard for the employees, and they see that a company can treat its employees like a caring family."

And finally we got to the bottom-line businesswoman in Tay: where the power of consequences always hangs in the air. "Of course employees must understand that in a very dynamic industry like high-end retail, doing business also means cutting expenses, being more productive, and always trying for a better response to customers. From all this effort the profit or loss will come. Our people understand consequences. It's not a difficult concept. They understand that unless everyone in the company focuses on performance, on being a team, on sharing the ups and downs, we all lose. It's that simple."

Then in an almost automatic return to focusing on the positive side of human nature, she ended the interview with these powerful words, "You know, just a few years ago, entrepreneurship was not recognized as something to be proud of. Entrepreneurs were wheelers-dealers. They were people who did not succeed in a job in a company. And they all had to be a little crooked. That was the image in Singapore. After all these years, I now know that being an entrepreneur is about integrity, honesty, truth, and credibility. And at the end of the day, it's your relationship with people that counts the most. It's all about people. It's how you deal with people. How you relate. It's a gut feeling I guess—a common sense feel I have about what's important in my company."

Taking the cue from Jannie Tay's "common sense feel," what are some common sense rules you can depend on to inspire others in your new business? Can you really instill entrepreneurial commitment and performance in your future employees? Of course you can. Tay cloaks her approach in her all-in-the-family idea, and others have equally successful ways to get at it. But whatever the slogans or cosmetics, a few central principles run through every successful effort to create mini entrepreneurs in a company. You'll recognize each of them from Tay's own story: Individuals must run their piece of your company as their own business; satisfying customers is the bottom-line always; we're all in this together; and the most basic rule of all—making sure that all employees feel the consequences of their behavior. The last one means you have to have rock-solid answers to the eternal question of every employee: "What's in it for me if I do, and what will happen to me if I don't?" You have to put *powerful*, *timely*, and *accurate* consequences into the work life of all employees. They have to know there will be positive consequences for good performance and negative consequences for bad performance. Do these things and you'll be well on your way to creating an entrepreneurial performance system in the company—using the full power of consequences.

Try these common sense principles and you can forget most of the personnel jargon you ever learned and all those made-in-hell performance evaluation systems dreamed up by consultants. You can trust these basic entrepreneurial ideas, and you can trust Jannie Tay when she says, "If you do all this, you can bring out the entrepreneurship in anybody."

APPLICATION 8
Raising Commitment and Performance

Commitment

• Working harder
• Respect for customers
• Pride in products
• Belief in the mission

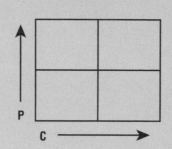

Performance

• Working smarter
• Innovation
• Market knowledge
• Product knowledge

What are the most important actions you can take to raise employee commitment and performance in your company? Here are a few starter questions to assist you in coming up with your answers.

• Review the four key practices discussed in the Creating Entrepreneurial Commitment section in this chapter.

• If you significantly raise employee commitment, what would the major effects be?

• Review the four key practices discussed in the Creating Entrepreneurial Performance section in this chapter.

• If you significantly raise employee performance, what would the major effects be?

• What about consequences? Are they in place for everyone?

• If you're already in business, how does your company rate (1–low, 10–high) on employee commitment and performance against your best competitors? Circle the low and high ratings for individuals, and the average for the entire company? What do the ratings suggest in terms of areas to improve?

	1	2	3	4	5	6	7	8	9	10
Commitment	1	2	3	4	5	6	7	8	9	10
Performance	1	2	3	4	5	6	7	8	9	10

APPLICATION 8-A
Raising Commitment and Performance

Creating and maintaining a great company ultimately depends on two essential ingredients: the commitment and the performance of the managers and workers. From commitment flows pride, dedication to the mission, and plain old hard work. It comes from the heart. From performance flows expertise, innovation, and working smarter. It comes from the head and hands. If you're looking for competitve advantage, it's hard to beat people who love what they do and are good at doing it. You can start planning now how you're going to instill commitment and performance in yourself, your first few critical hires, and ultimately every employee in the company. What are the most important actions you can take to create or raise employee commitment and performance in your new venture?

Creating High Commitment   **When**

1.

2.

3.

Creating High Performance   **When**

1.

2.

3.

APPLICATION 9
The EPS Troubleshooting Guide

Use the EPS Troubleshooting Guide to raise the commitment and performance of your employees. Review the section, *Creating an Entrepreneurial Performance System* in this chapter before you try it the first time. By carefully going through the following questions, you should discover which of the EPS components needs to be adjusted to change the behavior of the employee or employees. And remember the *power of consequences*. The easiest, cheapest, and surest way to change behavior is to make sure every employee feels the positive and negative consequences from their performance. Based on your analysis, take the appropriate action to implement the necessary change.

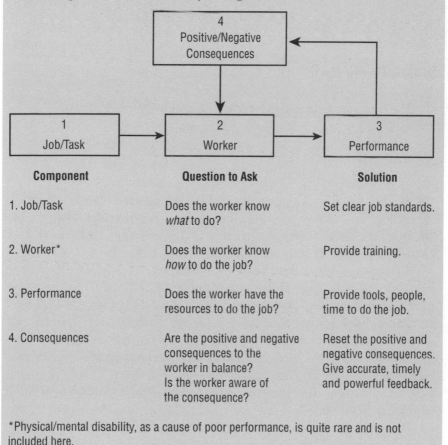

Component	Question to Ask	Solution
1. Job/Task	Does the worker know *what* to do?	Set clear job standards.
2. Worker*	Does the worker know *how* to do the job?	Provide training.
3. Performance	Does the worker have the resources to do the job?	Provide tools, people, time to do the job.
4. Consequences	Are the positive and negative consequences to the worker in balance? Is the worker aware of the consequence?	Reset the positive and negative consequences. Give accurate, timely and powerful feedback.

*Physical/mental disability, as a cause of poor performance, is quite rare and is not included here.

CONCLUSION

What's Really Required for Getting Entrepreneurial

What's Really Required

The most successful businesses don't do anything new, exotic, or dramatic. They do very simple things very well.

— Ron Doggett, Founder,
GoodMark Foods

I've known Ron Doggett since we were at the Harvard Business School in the late seventies. For the last two decades, Doggett has lived the great American entrepreneurial dream. And I must add, he's living proof that sometimes the good guys do finish first.

Twenty-one years ago he led a management buyout of a small, money losing subsidiary at General Mills, the fifth largest food company in the United States. The price on paper was $31 million, but over 99 percent was to be paid out of future revenues. Doggett and his team only had to come up with $200,000 in equity—which they borrowed from a local bank—because General Mills couldn't find anyone else to take the bleeding subsidiary off their hands. Sixteen years later, he sold the company to ConAgra, the biggest food company in the United States, for a whopping $240 million—and he personally owned 34 percent of the company. His entrepreneurial career, sandwiched between two giant bureaucracies, made him a very rich man and gave him a unique perspective on the cultural divide between a *Fortune 500* company and an entrepreneurially driven business.

Here's his story. "When General Mills acquired the Slim Jim company, they transferred me to become the CFO, and we renamed it Good-Mark Foods. At the time, General Mills was also acquiring a lot of other businesses. They were trying to grow a fashion division, a jewelry division, a toy division, all businesses way beyond foods. They even owned some great furniture companies. This was the era of the conglomerate. They were going off into all kinds of different and unique businesses and like usually happens, they lost focus. General Mills was eager to build the Slim Jim product but they couldn't relate to the business and it wasn't a product that fit well with their product lines. That's not being critical of General Mills, it's just how it was. At any rate, they wanted to build this business through supermarkets, and give it to the General Mills salesforce who were busy selling Wheaties, Cheerios, Bisquick, Gold Medal Flour, and O-cello Sponges. So we were the last one on the sales order form, just below O-cello Sponges! General Mills was just a huge company. They were what I called a company that could relate to boxcars. To boxcar loads of products like Wheaties and Cheerios—whereas we shipped parcel post. We shipped Slim Jims a case at a time.

"Then, out of the blue, General Mills decided to sell the business. They had decided to get out of all the 'less than boxcar load' kinds of businesses. We were among the first to go in this big change of strategy. This was at the time that all the conglomerates were turning right around and shedding all the acquisitions they had just made. I think General Mills was having a difficult time managing them. They weren't growing. It was a small business that was taking more time than they wanted to devote to it, and I really think they realized they had lost focus and they wanted to go back to things that were more mainstream if you will—and easier to manage. Ours was not an easy business to manage. It's fairly unpredictable. Meat costs, our primary ingredient, were highly volatile. You could make a lot of money one year and three years later you could lose a lot of money, and General Mills didn't like that

"We just didn't fit into a big company picture for all these reasons. There wasn't time to be responsive, there wasn't time to put a personal touch on it. There wasn't time to have one-on-one relationships with small customers. At GoodMark we dealt with one-man wagon jobbers up to distributors with a thousand trucks. It takes a variety of talent to work with these customers. It isn't like calling on headquarters accounts and covering the nation as a result of your headquarters call.

"In any event, General Mills executives told me although there 'could' be something for me in General Mills, they strongly encouraged me to look elsewhere. That moment was when I became very motivated to try to buy the business. Here was a product, Slim Jim, that I really liked, and which I knew had a great future. So I went to see the President of GoodMark and brought my team in and we announced that we were putting together an offer to acquire the company. It was a big decision and we weren't very sure that we were going to be successful. The President told us that 'us little guys' were not likely to get the company so everybody should relax. Our offer wasn't accepted at first. We were told to hang on, and if nothing better came along they would talk with us. That was the gist of General Mills's response. The fiscal year ended in May and they didn't have a better offer so they agreed to meet with us to talk about our plans. Of course I didn't have any money. We owned a $35,000 home and had only about $7,000 equity in it. That was our biggest asset!"

After long and torturous negotiations, which included looking under every rock for a way to finance the purchase, Doggett and his team became the proud owners of a sausage company hemorrhaging cash. The financing was unique for the time. General Mills reluctantly took back a lot of paper and a 10 year stream of royalty payments. I asked Doggett what he did to turn the company around. His answer covered some pretty obvious things—nothing dramatic, "At that time GoodMark was doing about $40 million in revenues and losing a lot of money so we had to move fast. There were several things we did immediately to get the business moving in the right direction. The first thing we had to do was to restore the quality of the product, which we did. Secondly, we had good people but they didn't have direction, they didn't have focus, and they didn't have respect for the vision of the company. I knew that we had to change this. And we did. So once we straightened out the quality issue, and we straightened out the people issue, we then straightened out some of the things that were lacking, which were marketing and sales support. Beyond these things it was paying a lot more attention to the customers. So we did that also and together with the other things I mentioned, we got GoodMark going."

I wondered why such obvious things weren't handled long before. If these basics were the kind of things that were needed, why didn't General Mills do them long before? Doggett's response was a knock-out punch to bigger-is-better thinking: "Well, they were the simple things. Easy things. Little things. Easy to identify but difficult to do on a consistent basis. General Mills's focus was on the large corporate overview with a large structure. We spent most of our time, at General Mills, on developing reports, analyzing results, building plans. Our long range strategic plan each year was about 70 pages. And then we had a program review session which went on for three months of the year. We had program reviews, budget reviews, that sort of thing. We spent more time on management procedures than we did on creating and leading. So I'm talking about little things that weren't working that we really needed to fix and make them work. But you succeed at the things, I believe, that are important to you, that you are committed to, and that commitment was just not there for this business at General Mills. But as owners I can tell you *we* were committed to it. We had simple plans and implemented them day by day. We lost a lot of sleep and shed a lot of tears too. The result was we started making a profit in nine months with the business.

"So the things we did were very simple things, whether it was customer service related, people related, product related, operationally related, financial, they were all simple things. I'm convinced, and I often told our people this, the most successful businesses don't do anything new, exotic, or dramatic. They do very simple things very well. They're companies that are highly focused on their mission, just as you point out in your seminars, and they consistently do the simple things in their businesses that are most appreciated by their customers. Those are the kinds of things that we did here at GoodMark. They're customer driven kinds of things and very simple: time, relationships, shipping an order, good quality, being responsive to needs, recognizing what stores need for displays or promotions, that sort of thing.

"By 1983, things started to turn for us. The business was going well, we were really getting some enthusiasm going for the business, the people were starting to have fun, they were enjoying what they were doing, the quality was restored, capacities were up, we had installed some higher technology equipment, our packaging was better, and the marketing programs were coming together. It was getting to be fun. And we owned the business! Well, actually General Mills and the banks owned the business because we owed them a lot of money. And that was one of the reasons we decided to go public early on. But the main reason for going public, in my heart at least, was I believed this was going to be very successful, and here's a way to share with the people. I assured them when we took over the business, that if we were successful, we'd share that success with them. I said that as the business grows you're going to grow with it. We'll do this together. And as it turned out, we did do it together.

"We worked hard at these simple things. That's *the* thing that made this business successful. We started with a $40 million business, that was losing money, made it profitable in nine months, and for the next 18 years that I was CEO, had a compound revenue growth rate of 12 percent and a compound earnings growth rate of 19 percent. Today the company is doing about $250 million in sales and is one of ConAgra's most profitable subsidiaries. And, I should add, GoodMark Foods is number one in the world in the meat snacks category! Even our troops in Afghanistan carry them because of their high protein content!"

Ron Doggett, the mild-mannered entrepreneur and all around nice guy from Minnesota, closed our discussion with this advice for would-be entrepreneurs: "I told my wife, we've used the kids' college funds, we've used our insurance, we've used all the equity we have in our home, we've got everything including the lawn mower riding on this thing. Do you still think we should do it? She said, 'If you're excited about it, if you really like it, well then, go for it!' It was the best advice I ever got. I thought it was a great opportunity. I've often said it was an opportunity of a lifetime, and it was. So my message to others is to seize your opportunities. Seize your opportunity and leverage yourself to get it if you have to. Too many people pass their opportunities by in this life."

The Three Requirements

Being an entrepreneur obviously isn't the only way to spend the rest of your life. And for some it may not even be the right way. But if you're among the 70 percent of the population who is at least dreaming about it, there can be no wrong reasons for giving it a try. As Ron Doggett suggests, if nothing else, you owe it to yourself to seize your opportunities—and fully explore your possibilities! Whether you're a Gen Xer looking for your first million, or a middle manager stuck in a Dilbertesque bureaucracy, or someone who just wants to make a few bucks on the side doing something fun, welcome to the new and improved world of getting entrepreneurial!

So, what do you actually have to do to start pursuing your entrepreneurial dream? By now, you should be fully armed with the four practices of the world's great entrepreneurs. They will guide you well once you're up and running. But if getting entrepreneurial is really what you want to do, you should consider one final question. What's really required to get started? Are there any broad, general requirements for success you need to consider just before you hang out your shingle? As matter of fact there are and that's what this concluding section is about. Like all the other areas covered in the book, this final topic has been pared down to its simple, practical basics. In that spirit, there are only three absolutely, essential things you need to have in place as you start down the road to becoming a successful entrepreneur. None of the three should surprise you. As Ron Doggett's story shows, and the stories of millions of other entrepreneurs, you'll need to acquire a bit of money and a bit of knowledge, and create the most entrepreneur-friendly culture you can. Let's start with how you can create an entrepreneur-friendly culture in and around your company.

✔ An Entrepreneur-Friendly Culture.

> *I decided to run the big company the same way I ran the small company.*
>
> — Fraser Morrison, CEO,
> Morrison Construction

By the numbers, it's an amazing story of selling a profitable $3 million family enterprise and regaining it 15 years later as a money-losing $300 million bureaucracy. This is the story of Fraser Morrison in Edinburgh, Scotland. He provides us with an extraordinary road map for creating an entrepreneur-friendly culture in any organization.

To Morrison himself, the human side of the story is more important than the numbers. He was saving his father's entrepreneurial business from the clutches of a giant, faceless conglomerate. Morrison fits in nicely in a long line of legendary Scottish entrepreneurs from Andrew Carnegie to—well, himself. His uniqueness, however, is that he has seen it from all sides: from growing up working in the small family business, to a very long and tough 15 years running the business under the most antientrepreneurial conditions imaginable, and then finally bringing it back to the entrepreneurial fold—with the added twist of having to stop the hemorrhaging losses quickly or lose it all forever. And in the process he has become a guiding light for demonstrating what's really required to instill a high-growth, entrepreneurial culture in your business.

When I interviewed Fraser Morrison, it was clear this had been a gut-wrenching experience for him. In his own words, he tells how it all started. "In 1948, my father started the business from a cold start with absolutely nothing. It was very small, what we called a jobbing contractor. He slowly built up the business, virtually on his own, within a very small radius of his hometown which was a place called Tain, Scotland. I joined him right out of school. In that kind of situation you get the opportunity to get involved in everything that's going on. So I might have been setting roads or houses one day and go home that evening and help prepare the accounts. It was, very much, an all-hands-on-deck situation. Anyway in 1974, we sold the family business to Mining Finance House, a large public conglomerate in London. We were still small, working only in Scotland, and turning over maybe $3 million. My father retired and I became the Managing Director, reporting to people I didn't even know in London."

From these modest beginnings, Fraser Morrison traveled a long, miserable journey until finally regaining his family's business. Along the way, everything that could go wrong in a big conglomerate went wrong. The holding company changed hands four or five times. The construction group, which Morrison Construction was a small part of, began bleeding huge losses in Asia, the United States and even in the U.K. Dozens of corporate managers came and went, each with their own agenda. Meanwhile Morrison Construction was the only profitable piece of its group and was minding its own business in Scotland as best it could. But the losses from the construction group, now being run by finance people, were overwhelming the entire holding company. No one in London seemed to have the foggiest idea of how to fix it. Here's Morrison's description of the environment in which the giant conglomerate in London worked. "We were part of the big holding company, and we watched our parent group just write themselves off. You see it everyday— companies who are having constant changes at the top or companies that are in an endless restructuring process. Again and again you see the focus of attention going away from the operation of the business. The senior people lose touch with what is happening in the real business. They don't understand what the people are thinking. They aren't particularly interested in what they are doing. I had always thought, even when you are in a financially difficult situation, if the day to day operations are working well, you'll get back to a strong position. But the more effort the headquarters people put into corporate politics at the holding company, the worse the situation became down on the sites and the weaker the overall situation became."

Finally the holding company became very disillusioned with the entire construction business and wanted to chuck it all. Morrison tried to buy back Morrison Construction but was flatly rejected. The holding company wasn't about to "sell the only good part and keep all the dogs."

Instead, in a total misjudgment of Morrison's personal ambitions, they promoted him to run the entire construction group. He hesitantly agreed but asked for an option to buy the whole group if it were put on the block. Another rejection, this time because the Board was already testing the market for a spin-off. Not surprisingly there weren't a lot of buyers for a hugely unprofitable construction group. So finally Morrison was told he could buy "the bit in Scotland but only if he took the bad parts of the dog along with it." He decided to go for it as the only way to regain his company. He went deeply into debt, and to avoid financial collapse he would have to turn around the big losing operations practically overnight. Morrison continued, "So we ended up buying back Morrison Construction. I had finally reached my long held ambition to restore family control. But we also had to buy the parent company along with it. So I had a business with overall sales of about $300 million but losing very big. But we owned 100 percent and I thought I knew how to turn it around. Thankfully, my hunch was right. In our first year, we increased sales and actually made a small profit. The next year we pushed sales up a bit again and made a respectable $11 million profit—and have never looked back."

How exactly did Fraser Morrison change years of losses into profits in just 12 months? He simply transformed the total atmosphere in which the company operated. He completely changed the focus and behavior of senior management. He overhauled the daily operating practices at the work sites. And he dramatically altered the performance environment of all employees. He started running the big business the same way he'd always run the small business—in an entrepreneurial environment. "We made an awful lot of changes on day one. We retained only two directors and the rest, 8 or 10, went. We structured the company so that it was operating on similar lines to the business that we had in Scotland. One of the great difficulties we found, when we added up all of the contract delays on the sites, was the sites were cumulatively eight years behind contract schedules. When you think of the overheads on our construction sites, they can be anything from $15,000 to $150,000 a month, and we were eight years behind schedule! So, I focused peoples' attention throughout the business on bringing those eight years delay back to zero within twelve months. Everybody said it couldn't be done. Well, giving people impossible targets sometimes works. In fact, we got it back to plus 30 weeks on the twelfth month."

Morrison changed five key factors in the overall operating environment of the company. These translate into valuable general principles you can apply to create and maintain an entrepreneur-friendly culture in your own business.

1. **Keep It Small.**   "We split the business up into relatively small—I call them family size—units. So a director will have a business between only $7.5 to $30 million turnover. They have a team of between 30 and 60 staff plus the hourly paid employees. That way they can get to know all of their people quite well. It's worked very well for us. A small operation just works better. The people enjoy it more and take a huge amount of satisfaction from it. You can get the team spirit which is very important in construction. The same with commitment. I think it's in the small companies that you tend to find it. As we grow, it's a priority to make sure that we maintain the structure to be able to continue feeling like a small company."

2. **Keep It Personal.**   "I learned a lot of lessons from seeing the people in London try to run our company because they always gave us the feeling that they knew, better than we, what to do. We weren't important. We only just dug holes in the ground. It was a huge lesson to me on how to run a business because you have to let the people feel that they are the key element of the business. Hopefully our structure now is such that people have got a strong personal interest in developing the business. A strong sense of feeling important and that they themselves have a strong input to the business."

3. **Keep It Honest.**   "The main factor that contributed to our success is the enormous commitment that I and the people around me have. When we bought the business back, we sold about 18 percent of it immediately to the key managers. So we have all senior people who have a share holding in the new company. I also have committed to all of the employees that we will run this business in a way that's in their best, long term interests also. Business needs this kind of personal commitment and honesty at the top and I'm sure we have it today."

4. **Keep It Simple.**   "As in life generally, you shouldn't try to make things complicated. You've got to try to make it simple. And the simpler it is the easier it is to understand by everyone. The single most important thing that I've learned throughout this process—and I haven't found a situation yet where it isn't appropriate—is that if you forget about the nuts and bolts of the business, you're lost."

5. **Start Over with the Basics.**   "I'd been telling the parent company I knew what needed to be done to sort this business out for a long

time, but they decided that they knew better, and weren't interested in our philosophy. They were running it as one big company. So when we got it, we split it up and very, very quickly refocused the attention of the people away from looking toward the group in London, back to the sites and the operations of the business. We put new directors in who we knew would put all their attention on the sites. We had to very quickly refocus everyone back to the basics of the business—at the sites—which in the construction business is the only place we make money."

Fraser Morrison's culture problems and solutions were 99 percent internal to the company. However, there are also external factors which can affect entrepreneurial activity. Some of the most common ones are government ideology and policy, the quality of education, access to risk capital, and even the politically incorrect notion of a population's work ethic. So do entrepreneurs have to play with the hand they're dealt in terms of the external environment in which they operate? Well, not entirely. Of course you can't, by yourself, change the macroeconomics of the day or control the political/social fabric of your country. You can try to enlighten the culture you're in, which I would certainly applaud as a noble cause. But the truth is, regardless of your external environment, you can do a lot more good for yourself by designing the right kind of culture inside your own company. Again, as Morrison's story highlights, some companies struggle to survive in depressing, antientrepreneurial environments while others flourish in supportive, entrepreneur-friendly cultures. Learning how to navigate these tricky waters could mean the difference between your own entrepreneurial success and failure.

Even so, it's still interesting to look at, and be aware of, the so-called *entrepreneurial hot spots* around the world and in your own backyard. For your interest, we've drawn together recent lists by country, state, and city to identify those hot spots, plus the key indices that underpin entrepreneur-friendly areas.

Country Entrepreneurial Ranking

As a Kaufman Foundation study found in 2001, there are vast differences in entrepreneurial activity between countries. The study identified the percentage of the country's total workforce who are working in start-up ventures. The range can be astonishing even among the highly industrialized nations. At the high end, 1 in every 12 persons in the United States is involved in a business start-up, while only 1 in every 63 persons is similarly involved in Japan. Is it any surprise that the two countries at the bottom of the list, France and Japan, have become the perennial economic basket cases of the Group of Seven (G7) countries?

Country	Workforce in Start-ups
United States	8.4%
Canada	6.8%
Germany	4.1%
Italy	3.4%
United Kingdom	3.3%
France	1.8%
Japan	1.6%

The only surprises in the listings may be that Germany ranks a bit higher and the United Kingdom ranks a bit lower than their popular images. Bravo for the Germans, and whatever happened to the Thatcher Revolution?

State Entrepreneurial Ranking
Even within the same country, there can also be huge differences. In the United States for example, The Small Business Survival Committee (SBSC) ranks all 50 states and the District of Columbia on entrepreneurship. The SBSC is a public policy advocacy group, whose listings are admittedly heavily weighted by public policy factors such as taxes, quality of education, crime, government regulations, and labor laws. Their current listing ranks South Dakota at the very top and Washington DC dead last. Of course, the cultural differences between the Coyote State and the District, America's ground zero of government bureaucracy, could fill several Ph.D. dissertations. If you're interested in packing up and moving to an entrepreneur-friendly state, the following are the top 15 on the list.

1. South Dakota
2. Wyoming
3. Nevada
4. New Hampshire
5. Texas

6. Washington
7. Florida
8. Alabama
9. Tennessee
10. Mississippi
11. Alaska
12. North Dakota
13. Colorado
14. Pennsylvania
15. Missouri

City Entrepreneurial Ranking
Finally, moving down to the local economic level, business magazines and think tanks love to rank even cities for their entrepreneur-friendly quotients. Last year, *Inc.* magazine ranked U.S. cities by the number of business start-ups per population. The following are the top 25.

1. Las Vegas, NV
2. Boise, ID
3. Anchorage, AK
4. Ann Arbor, MI
5. Austin, TX
6. Boulder, CO
7. Houston, TX
8. Denver, CO
9. Dallas, TX
10. Fort Collins, CO
11. Colorado Springs, CO
12. Albuquerque, NM
13. Kalamazoo, MI
14. Fort Worth, TX
15. Provo, UT
16. Portland, OR
17. Salt Lake City, UT

18. Orlando, FL
19. San Francisco, CA
20. Salem, OR
21. Santa Rosa, CA
22. San Antonio, TX
23. Anaheim, CA
24. Seattle, WA
25. Eugene, OR

Do you notice anything odd about this list of America's most entre-preneurial cities? Twenty-two of the 25 are in the West and about two-thirds of the them are small-to medium-sized cities. Only 4 of these 25 entrepreneurial hot spots are among the top 25 cities in population. Those four are Houston (#8), Dallas (#12), Anaheim (#16), and Seattle (#22). Is there a message in here somewhere?

Key Indices of Entrepreneurial Capacity
From our friend Kris Kimel, the President of Kentucky Science & Technology Corporation, we offer the following list of critical factors his research firm analyzes in rating a region's entrepreneurial capacity—or as we might label it, their entrepreneur-friendly culture. Here are the indices they look for, and just for interest, we've included the top two states for each category, on a per capita basis.

Key Indices	Top Two Ranked States per Capita
• Small Business Innovation Research Grants	Massachusetts, New Mexico
• Patents Issued for Inventions	Colorado, California
• World Wide Web Servers	New Mexico, Massachusetts
• Initial Public Offerings (IPOs), Technology Sector	Colorado, California
• Ph.D. Scientists and Engineers in Workforce	Delaware, Maryland
• Science and Engineering Graduate Students	Massachusetts, Utah
• University Graduates	Maryland, Massachusetts
• Venture Capital Funding	Massachusetts, California

- Inc 500 (High Growth)   New Hampshire, Massachusetts
  Companies
- New Company Formations   Washington, Colorado

You're entitled to ask, what do all these surveys mean? Probably not too much really. While fun and interesting to look at, the practical point is that there may be political, legal, and cultural factors influencing the level of entrepreneurship in a country, a state, or even a community. If you find them negatively affecting your efforts to get started as an entrepreneur, you can try to change them, or as most entrepreneurs do, find creative ways to go around them. You can be sure, however, you won't really have to move to South Dakota or Las Vegas to start your company. Just remember, the most important culture you should be worrying about, by far, is the culture inside your own company. If you have any doubts, reread Ron Doggett's and Fraser Morrison's interviews.

✔ A Bit of Money.

I was operating out of a spare bedroom and making only local calls. There was no capital involved. Zero.
                                        —Fred Gratzon, Founder, Telegroup

There's something about money that seems to bring out the worst anxieties in people. Many would-be entrepreneurs suffer a particularly bad case of this. Some never get beyond the first step because they just can't imagine themselves raising the money necessary to start their own business. Making it even more scary, the media hype about billion dollar IPOs gone bad and Silicon Valley millionaires gone bust has blown public perception of start-up financial requirements out of all proportion. A dose of reality may help.

Our research shows the average cost of starting a business in the United States today is about $14,000. Not a big deal when you consider the relative economic and social cost of some other ways you could spend your time:

Five years of heavy smoking	$15,000
A year on welfare	$17,500
A year at Harvard	$25,000
A year in prison	$30,000

Crazy comparisons aside, the point shouldn't be missed. On average, the cost of starting up your own business is modest. And, of course, everyone knows the smart way is to get everything lined up as much as possible before you give up your current source of incoming cash. This usually means don't quit your day job before you're ready.

I dug up the aforementioned figures after discussing entrepreneurship with Charles Millard, the former President of the Economic Development Corporation (EDC) of New York City. Millard, who served under Mayor Rudy Guiliani, created the first venture capital fund run by a city, and was known as the godfather of Silicon Alley, New York's ambitious project to bring high-tech firms to the Big Apple. Millard's driving mission at the EDC was to foster a more entrepreneurial economy in New York City because he believed it was a terrific investment in taxpayers' dollars. If your local government leaders don't realize that funding entrepreneurship is a bargain compared to funding welfare, you might want to find out what planet they've been on for the past 50 years. You might even convince them to start a venture capital fund in your city, with you as the first customer! Seriously, when government leaders realize that the average cost of starting a business is less than keeping a person in prison or a family on welfare, they get very interested.

In any event, even if you agree it's not a lot of money, you still have to come up with it. Where are you going to get $14,000? According to a survey conducted by *Inc.* magazine, the multiple sources of start-up financing* used by entrepreneurs breaks down as follows:

Personal savings	73%
Credit cards	27%
Loans from friends and relatives	14%
All other cash sources	14%
Loans against personal property	7%
Bank loans	5%
Equity investments	2%

As all entrepreneurs know, you don't have to be on welfare or a convicted felon to have problems getting start-up financing. That's why the

---

*The total adds up to more than 100% because some entrepreneurs use more than one source to finance their start-up.

Small Business Administration (SBA), established in 1953, has become one of the most important economic tools of the American government. With a portfolio of business loans and loan guarantees worth more than $45 billion, the SBA is by far the nation's (and for that matter, the world's) largest financial backer of small businesses. Last year, the SBA also offered management and technical assistance to more than 1 million small business owners. These are big, impressive numbers, and you should not hesitate to contact the SBA and/or any local possibilities for government funding. It's available today and it's no secret why. For politicians this is an ideology free idea, so far. And the notion that it's better to help people start their own small business than give them food stamps, is so compelling it has attracted political leaders from both the right and the left.

One obvious lesson from the listing of financing resources is to not waste too much time talking to bankers or equity investors. They're not generally into first-level, start-up financing. If and when you do talk to them, being forewarned is forearmed. You need to know how to attract venture capital and what kind of risk assessment all venture capital firms will put you through. So for your eyes only, here are the four fundamental risks that John Doerr, the dean of all Silicon Valley venture capitalists, says he always looks at.

1. **People Risk:** Will the founders stay or move on?
2. **Market Risk:** Will the "dogs eat the dog food?"
3. **Technical Risk:** Can the product be made?
4. **Financial Risk:** Can capital be raised again if needed?

On the other hand, in a pinch, most people could come up with $14,000 with a couple of credit cards—so getting entrepreneurial seed money can't be that much of an obstacle. There are in fact, thousands of successful companies started for $10,000 or less.* Here's a diverse list of some boot-strapping start-ups to illustrate the point.

Company	*Started With*
Kodak, 1880	$5,000
Coca Cola, 1891	$2,300

---

*The sampling purposefully excludes very recent start-ups. We try to only use examples with a decade of performance behind them.

UPS, 1907	$ 100
Black & Decker, 1910	$ 1,200
Clorox, 1913	$ 500
Marriott (A&W Root Beer), 1927	$ 3,000
Hewlett Packard, 1938	$ 538
Johnson Publishing, 1946	$ 400
Lillian Vernon, 1951	$ 2,000
Domino's Pizza, 1960	$ 900
The Limited, 1963	$ 5,000
Nike, 1964	$ 1,000
Electronic Data Systems, 1965	$ 1,000
DHL, 1972	$ 0
Body Shop, 1976	$ 6,000
Apple Computer, 1976	$ 1,350
Taylor & Boody, 1977	$ 0
Messer Landscape, 1980	$ 0
PC Connection, 1982	$ 8,000
White Line Trucking, 1983	$ 300
Gateway, 1985	$10,000
Telegroup, 1989	$ 0
Horn Group, 1991	$ 0
Fawcette Publications, 1993	$ 0

Just to counter the notion that every new entrepreneur has to have venture capitalists and investment bankers raising millions of dollars, the final three examples of zero-based start-ups are included. All three founders declare they didn't need a penny of start-up money. You've already read about the Horn Group in Chapter 3 of this book. Sabrina Horn's financing method was to acquire her first paying customer before she quit her job, and before she started the business! Fawcette Publications, founded by Jim Fawcette in California, is an electronic and print publisher with over $25 million in sales. Telegroup, the brain-child of Fred Gratzon in Fairfield, Iowa (about as far away from Silicon Valley as you can get) is generating $300 million in revenues reselling AT&T long distance services. To be sure, starting a company with no money at all is rare and you would be well advised to not count on it.

To really drive the main point home, the current roster of the *Inc 500* shows that an amazing 41 percent of the companies on the list started their businesses with less than $10,000—and an amazing one-third of those spent less than $1,000 on their start-up. So how much will you really need? Apparently not so much. That's why I titled this section A *Bit* of Money!

But, lest we forget, while this list of successful companies didn't need or have a lot money to start, they all did have the one asset that is absolutely essential—a product or service that customers needed and were willing to pay for. This brings us to the third requirement.

✔ A Bit of Knowledge.

General graduates of the university are twice as likely to start their own businesses as the MBA graduates of Wharton.
                    —Professor Ian MacMillan, Wharton
                    School, University of Pennsylvania

The number one reason for new business failure is not a lack of money. It's more basic than that. It is, simply, you haven't come up with a product or service that anyone wants to buy. Or at least not enough people want to buy it to keep the business afloat. So you need to learn how to make something or do something that the world needs. And where are you going to learn that?

Apparently one place you won't learn it is at the leading business schools of the world. Ian MacMillan, the innovative British professor at the Wharton School, developed the first entrepreneurial studies program at a blue-chip business school. And why did Wharton approve his pet project? Because MacMillan's research on how to educate entrepreneurs revealed huge shortcomings in the MBA program, powerfully summarized by his mind-bending quote. Those general graduates who are becoming entrepreneurs, at twice the rate of the MBAs, are knowledgeable in subjects like science, engineering, health care, and social studies. Apparently they're better equipped than the business school graduates to make something or do something that the world needs.

Predictably, the business education establishment hasn't taken this criticism from one of it's own lying down. As an illustration, *Across the Board*, the respected magazine of The Conference Board, recently published opposing views in a provocatively titled article: "Do Universities

Stifle Entrepreneurship?" Arguing yes was, ironically enough, another British professor. Adrian Furnham heads the Business Psychology Unit at University College London. In a wonderful example of the pot calling the kettle black, Furnham claimed that academic universities and their "antibusiness and socialist" professors are killing off the entrepreneurial spirit in young people. His solution? Send everyone over to the business school.

Across the Board invited me to write a rejoinder to Professor Furnham's argument. I pointed out that his case is simply not supported by the evidence. The idea that business schools are in the business of creating entrepreneurs fails both the test of fact and common sense. It certainly failed Ian MacMillan's careful research at Wharton. At best it sounds like more misguided nonsense from B-schools on what entrepreneurs need to know to succeed. If it weren't so important, this kind of intellectual debate on how to educate entrepreneurs would be hilarious. But what knowledge is required to be a successful entrepreneur is an absolutely critical point for the 70 percent of the workforce who are thinking about starting their own business.

Of course, it's always great sport to blame academia for all manner of fuzzy and misguided thinking, but let's be honest. The educational institutions that have done the most damage to the spirit of entrepreneurship over the past 50 years are the business schools, not the broad based universities around them. Universities may be guilty of a lot of things, but one thing they do very well is to impart knowledge that entrepreneurs need. They are the primary source of knowledge on everything from molecular biology and high-tech engineering to the social sciences and even the arts. In case the point is missed, these are all fields of study that teach young people about the technologies needed to respond to some of the greatest economic opportunities facing the world: biogenetics, aerospace design, computer architecture, reduction of crime and poverty, and of course America's number one export, entertainment.

Business schools (and their step-children, corporate training departments) by contrast, have majored for half a century in teaching theory after discarded theory about how to manage. Ask yourself, how many entrepreneurs have ever been created by studying strategic planning, matrix management, sensitivity training, total quality management, reengineering, leadership, or the current raging fad, six sigma? Learning how to be a successful entrepreneur simply does not require a business school degree. In most cases it will just slow the process down. Sure, an evening course in accounting could be useful to you. And you may need technical training from your vendors to learn how to operate your equipment. That's useful knowledge you need. What you don't need is taking two years of your life, and $50,000 of your money, to get an MBA to learn all the latest management theories. As Steve Jobs said, "Managing is the easy part—growing is the hard part and that takes knowing how to make great products and deliver great services."

So bit-of-knowledge tip number one is to remember that there has never been a successful enterprise created out of a management technique. If learning management theories won't help, then what kind of education would be helpful? The bedrock essential of entrepreneurship is being able to come up with a great product or service. That leads us to bit-of-knowledge tip number two; become an expert at something. Become good at designing and making some product or service that answers a real need in the marketplace. It could be simple or complicated, high- or low-tech, but you must become expert at it. And where can you learn this? While not essential for every possibility, a decent university can be a terrific place to get started. Let's look at a few real-life examples.

Take the case of Edward Penhoet, co-founder of Chiron, the hugely successful biotech company that discovered the vaccine for hepatitis B. Where did Penhoet learn his trade? At a business school? Of course not. He learned it by getting a Ph.D. in both biology and chemistry at the University of California. None of this is new. Bill Hewlett and David Packard never studied management either. They, like a thousand other computer entrepreneurs who followed them, were engineering students. A prime example: Andy Grove made Intel the "essential company of the digital age" with an engineering degree from tuition-free City College of New York. Or how about Clark Abt? He founded Abt Associates, the largest social/economic research think tank in the world. With 1100 scholars and researchers on the payroll, Abt knows a thing or two about the value of intellectual capital in building an organization. His academic inspiration? A Ph.D. in Political Science from MIT. And finally, for an even more off-beat example, consider the career of Jodie Foster, one of the most powerful women in filmmaking today. Acting in, then directing, and now producing Hollywood blockbusters is big business by anyone's standard. Yet she's never seen the inside of a business school. She learned her business at the Yale Drama School. On and on it goes— in an ever spiraling coincidence of being highly knowledgeable and skilled at something that people want and need.

There are even less recognized sources of essential entrepreneurial knowledge sitting at the opposite end of the spectrum from academic universities. Ray Kroc, the great entrepreneur behind McDonald's and a high school dropout, had the right idea. He was notorious for giving large gifts to good causes but he drew the line at giving to most schools saying, "They will not get a cent from me unless they put in a trade school." He held the old-fashioned belief that young people ought to come out of school knowing how to do something practical, like grow a tomato, repair a two-stroke engine, or put up a wall that won't fall down. Kroc may have stumbled onto an even bigger socioeconomic idea. In America, a blue-collar education began to lose status in parallel with the mid-century notion that everyone had to have a full university degree to be socially respectable. By the 1960s, if parents couldn't get their children into a decent four-year university, let alone an ivy league school, well, it was just a family disgrace. The thought of having to send your kids off to a technical school to learn a trade was downright embarrassing. It was somehow more honorable to hold a boring, dead-end, middle management job at AT&T than be a prosperous, self-employed electrician, plumber, or farmer.

This was not only a crazy elitist notion but it obscured an important fact: Vocational and technical schools were, and are, a rich breeding ground for entrepreneurs. Today, whether you choose landscaping, computer repair, medical testing, construction, or graphic design, you'll be in a trade with great entrepreneurial promise for the twenty-first century. So don't get hung up on higher education being the only path to entrepreneurial prosperity. Certainly the list of world-class entrepreneurs who were university no-shows is very long, from Walt Disney and Soichiro Honda to Sam Walton and Richard Branson. There are also plenty of famous college dropouts like Bill Gates and Steve Jobs who tasted academia and decided they didn't need it after all.

And speaking of Steve Jobs (once more), he can always be counted on to serve up a powerful summarizing thought. A real showstopper was his famous line, "The managers knew how to manage but they couldn't *do* anything," Of course he was talking about the virtues of making a better computer, not devising a better management system or producing color-coded organization charts. But then Steve Jobs never attended a management seminar. And I doubt he spends much time now boning up on the latest theories from business schools and consultants. Of course he's been pretty busy creating three great companies over the past 30 years. And that's the point, isn't it? Learning about and thinking about *getting entrepreneurial* won't mean a thing unless you also learn how to actually make or do something the world needs. We call it *doing something great*.

The important lesson in all the examples that fill these pages, from self-educated Sarah Walker to Harvard Ph.D. (in sociology) Ben Tregoe, isn't where and how they acquired their knowledge. It is the one mighty thing they *do* have in common when it comes to knowledge, is that they all managed to become very good at *something*. They understood that what's required to create a high-growth enterprise is not becoming great at managing, but becoming great at making and doing something that a lot of people in the world need and will pay good money for. If you can do that, as sure as night follows day, customers and employees and shareholders will scramble to get on board your rising star. You'll be doing something great—and that, indeed, takes a bit of knowledge.

Even *The New York Times* Gets It

It's an odd feeling when something you've been preaching for years shows up as a revolutionary insight on the editorial pages of *The New York Times*. I didn't know whether to feel proud, vindicated, or ticked off. So I settled for putting it in this book as a form of blue-chip endorsement.

A recent op-ed piece by *Times* columnist Flora Lewis was headlined: "For Europe's Jobless, Self-Employment Might Work." Now this is the same *The New York Times* that editorially, has never seen a social welfare program it didn't like. So when even *they* start pushing entrepreneurship as the way to solve chronic unemployment, we have to believe we're on to something anyone could agree with. Lewis was writing about Europe, where the seemingly permanent unemployment rate hovers in the 10 percent to 20 percent range. She hits the nail on the head with the assertion that Europe's answer to unemployment has been generous benefits, followed by a lot of hoping and praying that someday more jobs will be created. She argues, "The assumption has always been that someone must hire you. The new economic revolution reopens the question. Big factories and offices are laying off workers, but the possibilities for self-employment have been little explored." Bravo! Now here's where it gets interesting. The column goes on to suggest there are three requirements to transform Europe's unemployed welfare recipients into self-employed entrepreneurs. These requirements are:

1. **Microcredit:** ". . . the magic breakthrough tool is credit—microcredit—at commercial rates but without the commercial requirements of collateral or existing earnings."
2. **Advice on How to Do Business:** ". . . the provision of advice on how to do business, set prices and so on."
3. **Reform the Regulatory Environment:** ". . . an important reform of the huge jumble of regulations, licenses, permits, and so on that countries impose on new small businesses."

There you have it—*The New York Times* version of a bit of money, a bit of knowledge, and an entrepreneur-friendly culture. They sound rather familiar, don't they? And for all you future entrepreneurs who have stuck with me all the way to the end of this book, I'm sure it will give you an extra shot of inspiration and confidence to now know, that even *The New York Times* is on your side!

Getting Entrepreneurial! One Last Thought

The inclination of my life has been to do things and make things which will give pleasure to people in new and amazing ways. By doing that I please and satisfy myself.

—Walt Disney, Founder,
The Walt Disney Company

We've now come full circle to where we began this book, with Walt Disney's eloquent description of the entrepreneurial basics. Throughout the book we've labeled those basics *sense of mission, customer/product vision, high-speed innovation, and self-inspired behavior.* They are, indeed, the bedrock fundamentals of the entrepreneurial spirit—and they *will* be the best weapons you'll ever have to survive and prosper in a downsized and uncertain world.

I think the most important concluding thought we can leave with you is: For goodness' sake, don't become an entrepreneur just because you think it's your best shot at getting rich! This is not moral indignation over greedy CEOs or backlash against Silicon Valley wanna-be zillionaires. There's a more mundane rationale: For aspiring entrepreneurs, doing it just for the money just doesn't work!

Don't take my word for it. This is a consistent theme of all the entrepreneur's interviewed in this book. Listen one more time to Ed Penhoet, megastar of the biotech industry, "Doing it just for the money is a recipe for disaster." Or how about Ron Doggett, the entrepreneur who made it big with his famous Slim Jim brand? "If you're going after this to become rich, you're facing a very high failure probability. I'm probably like everyone else who considers themselves an entrepreneur. I never thought about getting rich. I never even thought about it." And finally there's Ben Tregoe, co-founder of the firm that has taught 5 million people around the world how to improve their decision making, "If somebody starts a business, they've got to be absolutely nuts about what they're doing, and be totally dedicated to it and work 100 hours a week, or whatever it takes. And in my experience you just don't do that unless there's something more fundamental in it than just saying, well, we're going to make a few bucks at this thing."

I truly hope *Getting Entrepreneurial!* has inspired you, given you great confidence, and will continue to be a valuable and practical guide in your business and in your life.

APPLICATION 10
What's Really Required

This chapter covered the three broad, but essential, requirements for getting your new venture off the drawing board and into the real world. The three general requirements for starting up any business are: operating in as supportive an environment as you can, securing the necessary money for the start-up period, and arming yourself with great product and market knowledge. This exercise will help you think through how you can manage to meet and surpass these requirements.

- Review the ideas discussed in the An Entrepreneur-Friendly Culture section of this chapter.

- How will you ensure that you will be operating in as supportive an environment as possible, both inside the company and in the external environment? Consider the geographic location you choose, the professional networks you can utilize such as entrepreneur incubator facilities, and certainly the level of support you can expect within your own family.

- Review the ideas discussed in the A Bit of Money section of this chapter.

- How will you secure both the start-up capital required and your cash flow needs over the first year? Have you really identified every possible financial resource available to you—from the SBA to borrowing from relatives to taking on partners? Can you start up while maintaining another source of income?

- Review the ideas discussed in the A Bit of Knowledge section of this chapter.

- Are you now an expert in your chosen product and market? If not, how will you acquire that level of product and market knowledge? If you are an expert, how will you stay on top of the latest developments in your field? And how will you ensure that every employee you hire will also be very knowledgeable about your company's products and markets?

APPLICATION 10-A
What's Really Required?

How will you manage the three essential requirements for your start-up business? For each of the following requirements, what are the most important action steps you can take, and when will you take them?

Ensuring an Entrepreneur-Friendly Culture   **When**

1.

2.

3.

Securing the Necessary Bit of Money   **When**

1.

2.

3.

Acquiring the Necessary Bit of Knowledge   **When**

1.

2.

3.

APPLICATION 11
My Getting Entreprenurial! Action Plan

We started off, in Application 1, asking you to imagine the most important things you would have to do to get a new company up and running. Now that you've completed the book, and all the other applications, it's time to ask the same question again—for real! What are the most important actions to take, starting today, to *actually* get your entrepreneurial venture off the ground? And if you've already started your own business, which I suspect many of you have, what are the most important actions you can take now to keep it on a steady course of high growth? In the following spaces, write down the actions you commit to take over the next three to six months, to *really* start getting entrepreneurial!

What Are the Most Important Actions to Take?   **When**

1.

2.

3.

4.

5.

6.

INDEX

Internet, B2B sales, 70
Intrapreneurs, 181–182
Invention:
  Burger King International illustration, 124
  DHL illustration, 120–123, 127–128
  DryWash illustration, 141–146
  Hertz International illustration, 123–124
  necessity of, impact of, 125, 141–146
  3M corporate culture, 119–120
Inventory management strategies, 70
ISO 9000 certification, 92, 186

Japan:
  Disney, 73, 170
  genius of the average worker, 133–134, 178
  innovation strategies, 108–110
  management techniques, 67, 70
  soft running, 177
Jim Pattison Group, The, 125–126
Job description, 48, 164, 183–184
Job description exercise, *see* Entrepreneurial job
  description
Jobs, Steve, 7–8, 11–13, 60, 76, 80, 125,
  215–216
Johnson, Jon, 164, 179
Johnson Publishing, 164, 212
Just-in-time production, 67, 70

Kanban, 67, 69–70
Kaufman Foundation, 205
Kepner-Tregoe, Inc., 21
Kimel, Kris, 208
K-Mart, 85
Kodak, 211
Kozlowski, Dennis, 6
Kristjansson, Thordur Jon, 118
Kroc, Ray, 60, 79, 169, 215–216
Kume, Tadashi, 133

Laggards, defined, 161–162
Lauder, Estée, 79–80
Leadership style, impact of, 10, 44–45, 49–50,
  125, 151, 158, 163, 171, 214
Leprosy business, 29–30
Lever, William Hesketh, 11–12, 14, 25,
  157–159, 179
Lever Brothers, 158
Lever Co-Partnership Trust, 157–158
Levi Strauss, 182
Lewis, Flora, 217
Lillian Vernon, 212
Limited, The, 212
Lincoln Electric, 172–175,
  183–184

Loving the customer, *see* Customer service
  application exercises, 105–107
  importance of, 84
Loving the product:
  application exercises, 105–107
  customer knowledge, 90–91
  high-speed production, 92–93
  importance of, 89–90
  improvement strategies, 91–92
  pride, 91
Low commitment, high/low performance
  behavior, 156
Loyalty, importance of, 159

McDonald's, 124, 140
McDougall, Ron, 138–140, 160–161
Mackenbach, Fred, 172–173
MacMillan, Ian, 213–214
Management practices, impact of, 22–23
Management science, 8, 68
Managerial style, 10–11, 111–112
Market capitalization industry leaders,
  68
Marketing, 76, 86, 89, 95, 111
Market need, 27–29, 31–32, 34–36
Market Need/Competitive Position matrix, 29,
  31–32, 36
Market/product winners matrix, 35–36
Market research, 68
Market researchers, functions of, 61
Market risk, 211
Market selection, 28–32, 34–37
Marriott, 212
Mass production, 61–62
Matrix management, 214
Matsushita, Konosuke, 11–12, 24–25
Matsushita Electric, 24–25
Matsushita Management Philosophy,
  25
Mentzer, Josephine Esther, *see* Lauder, Estée
Mergers, 94, 96
Messer, Buel, 50–55, 94–96
Messer Landscape, 50, 55, 94–96, 212
Microcredit, 218
Micromanagement, 68
Microsoft, 68
Middlemen, elimination of, 70
Millard, Charles, 210
Mind-set:
  customer/product, 75–81
  kanban, 67
Minnesota Mining and Manufacturing
  Company, *see* 3M
Mission, *see* Sense of mission